2004

Critical Acclaim for *Strategic Supply Chain Management*

Cohen and Roussel effectively capture and communicate the critical elements and roadmap of world-class supply chain management. Put into practice, this book will serve as a timeless tool for those looking to transform their organization's supply chain into a sustainable competitive advantage.

Jim Miller
Vice President, Operations, Cisco Systems

The five core principles behind this book are deceptively simple. Yet few supply chain practitioners have the authors' depth and breadth of experience. Cohen and Roussel take the topic far beyond the theoretical, offering numerous examples of how companies have adopted and adapted these principles. Senior executives can use this book to structure a supply chain strategy that will result in immediate top- and bottom-line benefits.

Geoffrey Moore
Author, Crossing the Chasm, Inside the Tornado, Living on the Fault Line

Cohen and Roussel successfully balance the "why" with the "what" of supply chain management. This practical book assembles the components of an effective supply chain in a clear, well-supported way. Those who want to drive supply chain success would be well-served in reading this book and learning from its many examples.

Dick Hunter
Vice President, Dell Americas Operations, Dell, Inc.

It is rare to find a book that covers both the supply chain principles and the organizational and practical aspects so well. Cohen and Roussel have given management and practitioners a most insightful treatment of the secrets to supply chain success.

Hau Lee
Thoma Professor of Operations, Information, and Technology,
Graduate School of Business, Stanford University

The authors successfully describe the many complex trade-offs that companies must consider in developing a winning supply chain strategy. Consequently, their book is as relevant and useful to the company CEO and CFO as it is to the COO, who should use it as the "how-to" guide to develop an operations strategy for the corporation.

Gary McIlraith
Supply Chain Director, British Sky Broadcasting Ltd

Cohen and Roussel provide a valuable overview for any CEO who intends to make supply chain management a competitive advantage. Whether you're the CEO of an established global company or the founder of a start-up, *Strategic Supply Chain Management* can provide you with the guiding principles and a roadmap to get your company moving in the right direction.

Guerrino De Luca
President and CEO, Logitech International

The authors have captured the essential elements of how a company can drive superior performance by positioning supply chain management as a core management discipline. The book creates a template for how you can align an organization to transfer a winning strategy into meaningful results.

Bill Cantwell
Vice President, Supply Chain, Air Products and Chemicals, Inc.

Cohen and Roussel take a rich set of strategies and explain them in a way that a relative newcomer could understand, yet retain the necessary depth to benefit seasoned professionals. Throughout this book, the authors provide powerful methods for organizing and implementing supply chain improvements. Their linkage of these strategies back to elements of the Supply-Chain Council's SCOR model provides the practitioner with a thorough approach to drive tangible results. The real-life examples are invaluable.

Steven G. Miller
Chairman, Supply-Chain Council

The supply chain presents a significant opportunity for cost reduction and customer value creation. This is the underpinning theme of this easy-to-read and practical book. Cohen and Roussel have skillfully drawn from their extensive experience working with organizations in diverse industries to synthesize best practices in supply chain management. Of the many books that discuss supply chain management, this is one of the better ones.

Martin Christopher
Professor, Cranfield University, United Kingdom

Finally, a practical guide that links the latest in supply chain management thinking with relevant examples of how successful practitioners apply these principles in the real world. A must read for all supply chain professionals attempting to take their supply chain performance to the next level.

David J. McGregor
Senior Vice President, NAFTA Logistics, BASF Corporation

Cohen and Roussel provide a disciplined, practical, and insightful approach to achieving a world-class supply chain structure. Their book's concepts are relevant to the many challenges corporations face today, and consistent with our experiences at HP. This book is transformational, and should help any supply chain professional achieve excellence.

Dick Conrad
Senior Vice President, Global Operations, Supply Chain, HP

STRATEGIC SUPPLY CHAIN MANAGEMENT

The Five Disciplines for Top Performance

SHOSHANAH COHEN

JOSEPH ROUSSEL

McGraw-Hill

New York Chicago San Francisco Lisbon London Madrid
Mexico City Milan New Delhi San Juan Seoul
Singapore Sydney Toronto

9 10 11 12 13 14 DOC/DOC 1 5 4 3 2 1 0

ISBN 0-07-143217-5

This publication is designed to provide accurate and authoritative information in regard to the subject matter covered. It is sold with the understanding that the publisher is not engaged in rendering legal, accounting or other professional service. If legal advice or other expert assistance is required, the services of a competent professional person should be sought.
        —*From a Declaration of Principles Jointly Adopted by a Committee of the American Bar Association and a Committee of Publishers and Associations.*

McGraw-Hill books are available at special discounts to use as premiums and sales promotions, or for use in corporate training programs. For more information, please write to the Director of Special Sales, McGraw-Hill Professional, Two Penn Plaza, New York, NY 10011-2298. Or contact your local bookstore.

Library of Congress Cataloging-in-Publication Data

Cohen, Shoshanah. Roussel, Joseph, 1962–
    Strategic supply chain management : the five disciplines for top performance / by Shoshanah Cohen and Joseph Roussel.
        p.   cm.
    Includes index.
    ISBN 0-07-143217-5 (hardcover : alk. paper)
    1. Business logistics.
HD38.5 .C64   2004
658.7—dc22   2004004456

We dedicate this book to our families: to husband Collin and children Meredith and Riley for Shoshanah Cohen and to wife Jana and children Robert and Claire for Joseph Roussel. Thank you for your loving support over the months of labor during 2003. We couldn't have dedicated the time and energy to writing this book without your understanding and teamwork on the home front.

CONTENTS

F O R E W O R D

In many ways this book is overdue. It is the book that we at PRTM wanted to write almost a decade ago, and yet at that time we merely would have been speculating about the future development of supply chain management as a core management discipline. For instance, we very likely would have underestimated the impact of information technology and ignored some emerging best practices. This book is the result of a 15-year history of research, benchmarking, and client results in this discipline at PRTM and an equivalent level of experience by the authors, PRTM partners Shoshanah Cohen (Mountain View, California) and Joseph Roussel (Paris, France).

In this book we set out to offer readers our understanding of the current state of supply chain management theory and practice based on our experience and observations from engagements on supply chain projects at over 600 organizations. We also offer profiles of recent transformative supply chain initiatives at major companies and the U.S. Department of Defense (the largest supply chain in the world). Finally, we offer our perspective on future challenges in the development of competitive, customer-facing supply chains.

This book focuses rightly on the present and the future; it is here in the Foreword that we hope to provide some historic perspective on how supply chain management came to be the dominating management discipline of the late 1990s and how it has become the root of huge investments in enterprise resource planning (ERP) and advanced planning and scheduling (APS) systems implementations in almost every major global corporation.

We can trace the origins of good supply chain management discipline to the late 1800s. The following extract dates from Bremner's *Industries of Scotland* (1869):

> Gartsherrie Ironworks are the largest in Scotland. . . . More than 1,000 tonnes of coal are consumed every 24 hours; and, as showing how well-chosen is the site of the works, it may be mentioned that 19/20ths of the coal required is obtained within a distance of half-a-mile from the furnaces. One coal-pit is situated close to the furnaces. . . . The coal from this pit is conveyed to the furnaces by means of a self-acting incline. Most of the ironstone was at one time obtained from pits in the neighborhood, but

now it has to be brought from a distance of two to twenty miles; and a complete system of railways connects the pits with the works. . . .

The establishment is also connected with the great railway systems of the country, and possess additional facilities for transport in a branch of the Monklands Canal, which has been carried through the centre of the works. . . . A great proportion of the manufactured iron is sent out by the canal.

The furnaces, sixteen in number, stand in two rows, one on each side of the canal. . . . A constant supply of coal and ironstone can be reckoned upon, and therefore only a small stock is kept at the works. The mineral trains are worked with unfailing regularity, and their cargoes are deposited conveniently for immediate use.

From this description of an integrated supply chain infrastructure in Victorian Scotland we learn that integrated inbound and outbound logistics, efficient inventory management, and delivery to point of use are supply chain disciplines that are more than 150 years old. For most readers, Ford Motor Company is a better-known example of the historical development of efficient supply chain and manufacturing practices. The history of Henry Ford's manufacturing innovation is widely known, as are the productivity gains achieved on the Model T assembly line, but what may be less well understood is how the supply chain that supported Model T production was developed.

Ford's "division of labor" approach to Model T production created the need for both industrial engineers and material planners to ensure that the right material was delivered to the manufacturing line in the right quantities at the right time. The efficiencies gained by the division of labor in mass production were enabled by the creation of a new management discipline: the discipline of procuring and delivering parts directly to the assembly line.

As Womack, Jones, and Ross explain in their 1991 book, *The Machine That Changed the World:*

Henry Ford was still very much an assembler when he opened Highland Park. He bought his engines and chassis from the Dodge Brothers, then added a host of items from a host of other firms to make a complete vehicle. By 1915 Ford had taken all these functions in house and was well on the way to achieving vertical integration. . . . Ford wanted to produce the entire car in one place and sell it to the world. But the shipping systems of the day were unable to transport high volumes of finished automobiles economically without damaging them. . . . By 1926 Ford automobiles were assembled in more than 36 cities in the United States and in 19 foreign countries.

The problem of efficiently satisfying global demand for technologically advanced products became a driving force in the story of supply chain management as a core management discipline. During the 50 years of mass production as the main feature of the industrial landscape (1920–1970), the pursuit of quality and materials and labor efficiency dominated management thinking.

It was at this stage of development of the global industrial landscape that PRTM came on the scene in 1976. At our beginnings, we worked primarily with the emerging high-technology sector to address its problems of high-volume production, rapid innovation, and globalization. The challenges faced by our clients forced our consultants to leverage and integrate many of the disciplines of the time in both innovative and practical ways. For example, we realized early on that MRPII, just-in-time (JIT) manufacturing, *kanban,* statistical process control, total quality management, and process management all could be brought together intelligently to yield a superior result. In the mid-1980s, under the topic of "operations strategy" in a series of executive seminars that PRTM conducted on behalf of the then-fledgling American Electronics Association, we talked about a cross-functional set of integrated processes that we called *supply chain management.*

In 1986 we conducted a client-sponsored study of the global manufacturing strategies of almost 100 major high-tech manufacturers. (The study was refreshed in 1989–1990 and was titled, "The Emergence of the Globally Integrated Corporation.") It concluded that we were entering an age of global integration between major economic regions and identified the competitive importance of what are now thought of as core supply chain processes.

In 1988 George Stalk, Jr., published a seminal article entitled, "Time—The Next Source of Competitive Advantage," in *Harvard Business Review.* Stalk's article added the dimension of time to the other process-management dimensions of cost and quality. And by 1989 the empirical and conceptual bases for competitive, customer-focused, cross-functional supply chain management were in place.

These disparate threads of emerging practice came together in one significant client project of PRTM. In 1989–1990, Rick Hoole, a PRTM director, began work with Fred Hewitt of Xerox Corporation to examine the opportunities that might be available to Xerox through globally integrated cross-functional process management. The joint PRTM-Xerox project team concluded that there were four core supply chain processes that Xerox needed to manage—*plan, source, make,* and *deliver.* Xerox then formed a project team to deliver results based on the findings of the study and realized benefits amounting to 2 percent of revenue over the course of the next few years.

Another "early adopter" of supply chain management as a discipline was Digital Equipment Corporation (DEC). It contracted with
PRTM in 1991 to launch the first of what became a series of "integrated
supply chain performance" benchmarking studies sponsored by IBM,
DEC, Xerox, Lotus Development Corporation, and NCR. To ensure that
this study did not simply become a compendium of functional metrics,
PRTM sought to create a new set of truly cross-functional supply chain
metrics. It is remarkable to reflect that it was just 13 years ago that
the activity-based definition of *total supply chain management cost* was
first designed and the now-widespread metric of *cash-to-cash cycle time*
was created.

With a process definition *(plan/source/make/deliver)* and with performance benchmarks available, PRTM was able to introduce a new
approach to managing global operations—an approach that yielded tangible benefits but required much change at companies.

Industry's early adopters, together with sponsors and participants in
the early benchmarking studies by PRTM, came together with us and three
leading academic institutions (MIT, Stanford University, and Pennsylvania
State University) in June 1994 to form the Supply-Chain Consortium. Its
aim was to promote the success of supply chain integration and implementation efforts across industries. The consortium had four objectives for
the first phase of its work:

- To establish a common baseline definition of the supply chain
- To define a common set of critical supply chain performance
  metrics
- To adopt a framework for consideration, presentation, and application of supply chain metrics
- To promote sharing of supply chain best practices and implementation approaches

PRTM's leadership of this body resulted in creation of the metrics
that would define the new Supply-Chain Operations Reference-model
(SCOR) developed two years later and now adopted widely by industry
through the Supply-Chain Council.

While most of this pioneering work was being done in the United
States, January 1992 was the scheduled date for the dismantling of trade
barriers (which included product specifications, mobility of labor, and
border delays) between member states of the European Economic Community. This dateline encouraged many companies to look at the opportunities
to create integrated European manufacturing and distribution operations

to replace the country-based strategies that had been the standard operating model since Ford Motor Company established operations in Europe in the 1920s. Working with the emerging supply chain management frameworks and metrics, PRTM helped many clients to use the cross-functional *plan, source, make,* and *deliver* framework to create a vision of integrated European operations.

One early adopter of the integrated supply chain methodology was Pitney Bowes. At that time, it had a complex manufacturing and customization operation that not only was costly but also resulted in long order fulfillment lead times. Integrated ERP systems functionality was not available in 1992; in fact, most companies had inherited country-based models that led to islands of information about customer orders and in-country inventory levels. To deliver cross-functional (and cross-entity) integration with a focus on time-based competition, Pitney Bowes developed a "technology" solution for a pilot program for postal franking machines destined for the German market. The solution was to install a fax machine on the manufacturing floor in England. This enabled country-specific machine variants to be configured to order, which reduced customer order lead times by weeks and eliminated finished goods inventory and configuration activity in country warehouses.

In 1994, PRTM also worked with ICL Computers and Siemens Nixdorf, Ltd., in the United Kingdom to define future integrated supply chain architectures using the *plan, source, make,* and *deliver* process framework. In both these projects we used a top-down process design approach, applying the four-level process logical data modeling at the core of the Structured Systems Analysis Design Method (SSADM), an early CASE methodology that we applied to integrated process design. This modeling approach became part of PRTM's supply chain project toolkit.

By 1995 it was clear that no standards existed by which our clients could objectively assess the value of the functionality of the new ERP systems that were emerging. In collaboration with AMR and a representative group of companies drawn from our respective client lists, we began to develop a supply chain process reference model. Many of our clients participated in giving design input to and reviewing the output of the working parties engaged in development of the model. In Boston, in November 1996, the SCOR model was presented to an audience of almost 100 major companies. This meeting resulted in formation of the Supply-Chain Council (SCC), formally launched in the spring of 1997 as an independent, not-for-profit organization. The SCOR model was transferred subsequently to the SCC, which is charged with supporting its development through research, use, and education. The SCC now numbers over 800 corporations worldwide.

Since 1997, supply chain management has become one of the major topics and challenges facing all companies, and the past seven years have been years of growth, convergence, and adoption of supply chain best practices. Now that many companies have addressed major supply chain challenges through selection and implementation of ERP and APS tools, they are finding that after implementation they are once again challenged with discovering and managing the core disciplines of supply chain management. Unlike the situation in the early 1990s, today's supply chain managers have many tools to support supply chain management in the form of integrated information systems, in-depth supply chain benchmarks, a mature SCOR process model, and an extensive community of practitioners. The challenge of the next decade is to leverage the founding principles of supply chain management and move this management discipline forward.

This book is about the future, not the past. It structures current emerging best practices into *five core disciplines:*

1. View your supply chain as a strategic asset.
2. Develop an end-to-end process architecture.
3. Design your organization for performance.
4. Build the right collaborative model.
5. Use metrics to drive business success.

In doing so, it points to some of the emerging practices likely to determine future competitiveness. We'll outline briefly some of these practices, handled in more depth at the conclusion of each chapter.

In Chapter 1 the supply chain is viewed as a strategic asset, something that leading companies have already begun to do but which will represent a challenge for many. Most companies do not have a documented and communicated supply chain strategy, and when asked to create one, many practitioners confess that they would not know how to write one or get top-level sanction for it. At the core of the difficulty is choosing your basis of competition: Is it cost, innovation, quality, or service? Where are the mathematical optimization models, the knowledge base, the decision trees, and the decision-making bodies? Without these, what allows a supply chain practitioner to set down clearly the corporation's basis of competition and develop a strategy that supports it? When we have challenged management teams to make a decision on the trade-off between inventory levels and service levels, they have had a hard time doing so. How much more difficult is it, then, to decide on the true basis for competition.

If developing and documenting a strategy represent a challenge, the next tough step is to develop a supply chain strategy that integrates with both the product strategy and the marketing strategy. When these three are aligned, a company can expect to generate additional revenues during the product life cycle, deliver superior customer response, and operate from a lower cost base than competitors. The authors talk about becoming adaptive—a much-needed capability driven not just by changes in the customer base or by competitors but also by the need to integrate strategies internally.

In the second core discipline—developing an end-to-end process architecture—we recognize that many companies (again exemplified by the cases in this book) have made great strides to achieve what the authors have identified in Chapter 2 as "simplicity." This has been especially true in corporations with a long industrial past and with a global footprint as they have simplified their processes in order to be competitive.

As we look at future challenges, we can identify product and service proliferation as a driver of cost and inefficiency in many companies, yet frequently there is no ongoing management process in place to contain this phenomenon. Perhaps the absence of an integrated strategy makes management of proliferation impossible for many companies.

What are the skills that will be needed to manage the supply chain of the future? In Chapter 3 the authors have given us frameworks and examples for the third core discipline—designing your organization for performance. This is an area of great challenge for both supply chain and human resources functions, for it is only in recent years that we have seen companies really tackle this topic seriously. Until recently, supply chain organization design simply was a case of putting previously disparate operational functions under single-point accountability and leadership. Many companies have established at least a baseline supply chain organization and have seen it settle and mature, but there is much more to do to develop the supply chain organization of the future. How will you identify the next generation of skills that will be required to develop and manage the infinitely more complex and more rapidly changing supply chains of the future? What will those skills be? How will they be acquired or developed? How much should you outsource without "thinning the core"? These are some of the critical questions that must be answered.

In Chapter 4, on the fourth core discipline—building the right collaborative model—the authors rightly bring to our attention that the emerging practice of supply chain collaboration has failed in many cases to deliver on its promise. Is this the case because there was more promise than could ever be delivered? Or is it perhaps because there was, again, an incomplete management framework on which to build a management process? Or perhaps collaborative partners never were realistic about the underlying economic assumptions that drove them to collaborate. Perhaps a good starting point would be to ensure that everyone (external as well as internal to your company) who manages or interacts with collaboration partners should read Chapter 4 and then assess honestly the current state of their collaborative relationship.

How well is your supply chain performing? How can you tell? The fifth discipline—use metrics to drive business success—teaches about the power of measurement as a management tool. Far from being simply a collection of numbers, the right set of metrics can provide information about the health of each core supply chain process and identify problem areas on which to focus. As important, the right performance management approach will drive behaviors in accordance with your overall business strategy.

In Chapter 5 the authors show how to choose the metrics that will inspire desired performance and how to establish worthwhile goals. The authors emphasize the importance of balance—the need to look at performance both internally and from your customers' perspectives and the need to develop a portfolio that includes a selection of financial and nonfinancial and functional and cross-functional metrics, as well as metrics designed to assess innovation and ongoing improvements within the supply chain.

When you are engaged in managing supply chains day-to-day amid the operational challenges of quarterly and annual business cycles, industry economic cycles, and shifting management emphasis, it is difficult to lift your eyes up from the printout, the computer screen, or the factory floor and envision your supply chain in the future. We believe that this book will help readers to lift their eyes and dream a little. It will encourage you to know that no matter what you have achieved until now, there remains more opportunity and challenge ahead.

End-to-end supply chain management is not just about logistics; it's about building a core competency that will lead to your future competitiveness and contribute mightily to your top and bottom lines.

Gordon Stewart and Mike Aghajanian, Managing Directors
PRTM

ACKNOWLEDGMENTS

Ever since its founding in 1976, PRTM has shone the spotlight on *operations*—the component of the business world that often goes unheralded. But as one of the executives interviewed for the General Motors profile in these pages notes, it's the operations staff that are the "oaks" of any organization—providing the solid support for manufacturing and supply chain management that makes for progress in the gross national product of every country worldwide.

We hope we've captured some of the esprit de corps of supply chain management in these pages, especially in the seven organizations that agreed to be profiled for this book: Eli Lilly, Autoliv, Avon, Owens Corning, the U.S. Department of Defense (the largest supply chain in the world), General Motors, and Seagate Technology. We'd like to thank all the executives we interviewed at these organizations for their candor, their passion for their work, and their desire to share the state of their art with others. These companies were chosen by us because they understand the strategic role the supply chain plays in their businesses and are engaged today in large-scale transformative initiatives to wring more value from supply-chain investments, create better return on investment from process and technology improvements, and establish an end-to-end supply chain at their enterprises.

These interviews were made all the more lively by the facilitation and expertise of our stellar internal marketing communications staff at PRTM. Victoria Cooper, our director of corporate communications, led this book project from start to finish, establishing an early vision for its structure and content, managing all aspects of the project, and integrating all the strands of the book. She also conducted many of the interviews for the profiles. We also are indebted to Martha Craumer, our Atlantic Region editor, who shared the development role on the book, also leading several interviews, but most important, continually driving us to clarify our thinking. Martha made the book much more readable through her editing and rewriting skills.

We'd like to thank Sherrie Good, our Pacific Region editor, who endured the lengthy process of fact-checking the statements pertaining to client and other company examples in the text with good grace. We also owe thanks to our assistant editor, Bridget Brace, who ensured that our manuscript met the publisher's guidelines for style and format and who kept all the files straight over the many months of discovery and revision. We'd also like to thank Erik Schubert, PRTM's art director, for making the charts for this book.

The following directors made the company profiles possible because of their relationships: Shoshanah Cohen and Jan Paul Zonnenberg for Lilly; Bob Pethick for Autoliv and GM; Brian Gibbs for Avon; Amram Shapiro and Steve Pillsbury for Owens Corning; Jeff Berg and Mike Finley for the U.S. Department of Defense; and Mike Anthony for Seagate Technology. We are also indebted to Jennifer Parkhurst for her contributions to the Lilly profile.

And we thank PRTM business analysts Pranay Agarwal, Paul Ibarra, Amanda Jenkins, Chris Barrett, Neil Kansari, and Andrew Yiu for early research on these and other companies' strength and history in supply chain management. We'd also like to thank the following freelance writers: Michael Cohen and Michael Lecky, for their contributions to the Autoliv and DoD profiles respectively.

This book would not have come into existence without the championship of Craig Divino, a recently retired director of PRTM who worked on many supply chain challenges at companies in Europe and the United States during his 25-year tenure at the firm. We are also indebted to Gordon Stewart, PRTM's Atlantic Region managing director, for his exploration of PRTM's history of leadership in supply chain management in the Foreword.

As for the creation of the five disciplines explored in this book, there are many contributors from the many worldwide offices of PRTM:

- For the strategy chapter, we are grateful to Tom Godward, Bob Moncrieff, Craig Divino, Jim Welch, and Brad Householder.
- For the process chapter, we are grateful to Didier Givert, Jakub Wawszczak, Craig Divino, Torsten Becker, Hans Kuehn, and Brad Householder, who provided significant input for the definition of the five processes *plan, source, make, deliver*, and *return* and how they work together to form an end-to-end supply chain. We also thank Paul Cantrell, who researched some of the examples in the chapter, and Peter Vickers, who provided significant input for the four tests of supply-chain architecture.
- For the organization chapter, we are grateful to Kate Fickle, Gordon Stewart, Bob Moncrieff, and especially Craig Kerr, who provided the framework for the evolution of the supply chain organization.

- For the collaboration chapter, we thank Steve Palagyi, Gordon Stewart, and Tony Paolini.
- For the chapter on performance measurement, we thank Gary Galensky, Robert Chwalik, and Rick Hoole for research on examples given in the chapter.
- For the chapter on the roadmap to change, we are grateful to Didier Givert, Craig Divino, Craig Kerr, Jakub Wawszczak, Harald Geimer, and Brad Householder for their contributions to our thinking.

One of PRTM's great strengths is its benchmarking capability. We have been benchmarking performance in the high-tech sector since the mid-1980s and have expanded into other sectors—such as consumer products—in the last few years. We couldn't have fulfilled on our promise of "results and fact-based consulting" without the ongoing support of our benchmarking subsidiary, the Performance Measurement Group, LLC, led by Michelle Roloff. She paid particular attention to the chapters on process and measurement, contributing significantly to their content. We wouldn't have all the data and analysis in this book either without the expertise of Julie Cesati, PMG's senior analyst for supply chain studies, with early support from PRTM business analyst Neil Kansari.

A book of this scope would not have been possible without the years of cumulative experience available at PRTM. Our over 600 engagements in supply chain work with clients have helped us understand what's state of the art, what's emerging, and what the next generation of supply chain practices is likely to promise in technology and process enablement. We thank all the companies with whom it has been our privilege to work.

Eli Lilly Profile: Supporting Product Lifecycles with Supply Chain Management

Pharmaceutical companies must do two things well: Invent new products, and create and supply demand for them in the marketplace. And when a new product makes it through the complexities of development—an extraordinary long shot—the number one rule is to never run out. This is where the supply chain comes in.

Eli Lilly is one of the world's leading pharmaceutical companies. With $11 billion in revenues, it markets its products in 159 countries and has 43,000 employees. The Indianapolis-based company creates pharmaceutical products that treat a broad range of ailments, including depression, schizophrenia, cancer, and osteoporosis.

Lilly is committed to product innovation, spending about 19 percent of its annual revenue, or $2 billion, on research and development every year. The high risk and enormous expense of inventing, developing, and testing pharmaceutical products mean that companies in the industry often depend on just one or two flagship products for the bulk of their income. When the patent for those products expires, the financial consequences can be profound.

Lilly suffered a potentially devastating setback when a judge unexpectedly ruled in 2000 that the company's patent on Prozac, a classic blockbuster that made up over 20 percent of sales, would expire in 2001—three years earlier than expected. Within six months, generic competitors had siphoned off more than half of Prozac's sales.

> Lilly spends about 19 percent of its annual revenue on R&D.

1

In anticipation of this possibility, Lilly turbocharged its R&D efforts during the late 1990s. Today, the company has what is widely acknowledged as the industry's strongest pipeline, with products in every stage of development—from early-stage molecules through late-stage clinical trials. Lilly's ambitious plans for the future include launching two to four new products per year over the next several years and doubling sales revenue.

To deal with this growth and to accommodate new manufacturing technologies, the pharmaceutical giant will nearly double the number of manufacturing locations in its supply chain. And more third-party manufacturing operations will be incorporated into the mix. Its registration strategy will have multiple manufacturing locations supplying each marketplace to enhance flexibility and reliability and manage capital investment.

> To deal with its growth, Lilly is doubling its production facilities from 20 to 40, largely by using contract manufacturers.

Explains Ken Thomas, director of manufacturing strategy and supply chain projects, "With three times as many products, twice as many manufacturing sites, and far greater sourcing complexity, the real supply chain challenge for us is just managing the unbelievable complexity of the business."

LIFESAVING MEDICINES AND THE HIGH COST OF MISSING A SALE

Pharmaceutical companies take a different approach to supply chain management. *Too much inventory* is not a meaningful term to use when people's lives are at stake. In many industries, the cost of goods sold is high relative to price, so gross margins are relatively low. As a result, companies tend to focus on controlling supply chain costs by minimizing inventory levels and improving efficiency. Missing a few sales can be less important than managing inventory levels overall. In the pharmaceutical industry, it's different: People's lives and health depend on an uninterrupted supply of medicine. Disrupting patients' lives by missing a sale is simply unacceptable. Financially, missing a pharmaceutical sale is bad business. The cost of goods sold is low relative to price, so gross margins can be comparatively large—the income of the few successful research products is the only financial stream feeding the R&D engine. A new blockbuster product can generate millions of dollars in sales in just a few months, and at peak, sales may amount to as much as $10 million of income per month. Thus even short-lived supply problems are considered very seriously. This is why Lilly focuses its supply chain management efforts primarily on never missing a sale and only secondarily on keeping inventory levels low.

This is not to say that inventory levels don't matter. Expired products are costly. So is squandering manufacturing capacity on low-demand, low-margin products. As a result, accurate forecasting and demand management are critical to Lilly's supply chain operations. The company consequently takes a global approach to supply chain management—especially given its aggressive growth plans. Explains Stephan Bancel, executive director of global manufacturing strategy, global supply chain, and U.S. distribution, "If we want to scale this company, we have no choice but to have common, global processes."

> Lilly focuses its supply chain management efforts on never missing a sale—and only secondarily on keeping inventory levels low.

STANDARDIZED GLOBAL PROCESSES

During the 1980s and 1990s, each site planned and scheduled its own operation with a focus on optimizing local results. This approach didn't recognize the additional efficiency and productivity that could be gained from a global supply chain focus—especially as the business grew larger and more complex. Consequently, in 1997, Lilly began developing global supply chain management capabilities with standardized processes, metrics, and terminology throughout the world, capturing this knowledge in its Operational Standards Supply Chain Excellence (OSSCE) program. As a part of OSSCE standards, for example, market affiliates and plants are graded on their adherence to these standards. This standardized approach means that the activities required to convert raw materials into final products that are distributed to customers are planned and scheduled in the same way around the world.

Additionally, Lilly has put in place a series of manufacturing networks—groups of plants with standard equipment and processes geared to specific product types, such as dry products, freeze-dried products, and parenteral products. As a result, development of processes prior to the launch of a new product is consistent from product to product. Each new drug being developed fits within an established "toolkit" environment.

> Each new drug being developed fits within an established "toolkit" environment.

This approach saves millions of dollars each year while boosting productivity and efficiency. It also results in greater security because redundant facilities can back each other up.

Common processes also help demand forecasting—a critical element of Lilly's never-miss-a-sale approach. The company's global demand management center is the link between sales, marketing, and manufacturing around the world. The center owns the forecasting processes and tools and ensures that the 159 marketing affiliates around the world deliver accurate forecasts to manufacturing. All plants use Manugistics' Web-enabled global planning system.

Other companies may predict demand accurately in a particular country or region, but Lilly has established truly global precision. Overall, the company forecasts demand with 76 percent accuracy, and in the United States, that figure soars to 90 percent. What is the key to this capability? Notes Allison Leer, manager of global demand management, "We have extremely good, experienced people working in this area, who stay on the job forever." Well-documented processes, good training materials, and sound practices supplement the group's expertise. Vigilance helps, too. Forecast accuracy is measured monthly. If a market submits an errant or incomplete forecast, someone calls to find out why.

LAUNCHING NEW PRODUCTS

Bancel led an effort over the past few years to look at the full contribution of supply chain management to business success. As he describes it, this meant focusing on supply chain design first and operations second. By designing the supply chain during development, and not afterward, the company could support regulatory requirements. It could balance the risk of clinical failure with speed to market and enable a robust and responsive supply after launch.

Another major concern was supply chain optimization. Lilly determined to maximize the value of manufacturing by selecting the best product mix for its networks. It determined to explore contract manufacturing whenever it could enhance revenue.

Lilly's supply chain management efforts start well before the launch of a new product, about four years before supply chain design is begun, according to Bancel. About one year before Lilly submits a new product to the Food and Drug Administration (FDA) for approval, a global launch leader is assigned to the case. The launch leader's job is to maximize long-term margins during the very critical early days of the launch by determining the global sequence of the release and creating an integrated launch plan for all aspects of the launch—including product flow, label approval, and sales-force training.

During the same period of time, the supply chain management team starts planning for the new product, answering such questions as when and where to make the new product and how to get it to wholesalers and retailers—all with an eye toward the long-term success of the new product while optimizing manufacturing and distribution. The launch leader integrates the manufacturing and supply chain plans and aligns them with plans from the marketing, sales, clinical, and regulatory departments.

Despite these measures, there's always uncertainty around a new product launch. Lilly always prepares to accommodate the "upside forecast," but when a drug is much more popular than expected, finding extra manufacturing capacity or making other arrangements can take some creativity. For instance, when demand in Europe for Cialis—a treatment for erectile dysfunction—exceeded Lilly's upside forecast, the company delayed introducing the drug in some countries to ensure that initial supplies were adequate where launch had already been initiated.

OPTIMIZING CAPACITY

Lilly has a corporate group that provides global supply chain management across the company. The group works with local sites to help optimize global capacity and inventory allocation by determining what product will be made where and for which markets. This often means making short-term sourcing changes within a framework provided by the Strategic Facilities Planning Team, which, in turn, makes long-term sourcing and capacity decisions. Since it takes somewhere between two and five years to bring on new capacity, Lilly must make the best use of the capacity it has at any given time.

Because of its standardized manufacturing processes, Lilly can optimize capacity by shifting work among plants. If the Spanish plant is making a particular product at 90 percent capacity, whereas the Indianapolis and U.K. factories are only at 60 percent, the company can distribute part of that work to other plants in the manufacturing network.

Taking work away from plants can be a concern for plant managers because they are judged in part on their production levels. However, ongoing efforts by the corporate supply chain management group are helping people to realize that such production shifts are for the greater good of the company. "We bring our manufacturing management together monthly to review and approve how some moves can benefit the organization as a whole, even though they may cause a temporary 'adverse variance in a single plant,'" explains Jon Rucker, director of supply chain. "It's a consensus-driven exercise. All the plants are involved in optimizing global capacity in the two- to five-year horizon."

ORGANIZATIONAL CHANGE

The central supply chain management group makes business decisions as well as manufacturing decisions. For example, it may make sense from a manufacturing standpoint to discontinue an old, off-patent drug that takes up valuable capacity that could be better used for a more profitable product. From a business standpoint, though, the legacy drug may be an integral part of a product portfolio for a therapeutic need that patients rely on. Some products are more valuable than the bottom line indicates. Gaining this degree of insight means looking beyond the manufacturing function.

During the late 1990s, Lilly set up an organizational structure of global product teams to enhance speed-to-market capabilities. Product teams are cross-functional teams of development, medical, clinical, marketing, and regulatory staff who focus on a single product. The team creates a global, integrated plan for the product over its entire life cycle, including new indications, line extensions, and marketing programs. A supply chain steward, acting as a liaison between the product team and the supply chain, interprets and translates that plan into supply chain tactics and targets. In this way, widely dispersed manufacturing units around the world are provided with very clear objectives that align precisely with the global marketing strategy for every product.

> A supply chain steward acts as a liaison between the product team and the supply chain.

Lilly is also making the transition to running the manufacturing organization globally instead of regionally or locally. Until recently, the company created short-term materials requirements planning (MRP) plans at each site and attempted to reconcile the plans using supply chain models designed for single products. After experiencing a number of challenges for which this approach was clearly insufficient, Lilly realized that the only way to resolve them was to optimize networks of sites instead of individual sites and to optimize families of products instead of single products. To this end, the company created a global sales and operations planning (GS&OP) process and model that create one long-term plan per manufacturing network. Once approved, the plan provides input to the site GS&OP process.

Each site reconciles the long-term global network view with short-term local demand and supply signals. The goal is to optimize capacity and inventory across the network of plant sites and the supply chains while ensuring an uninterrupted supply of medicine. Lilly believes that the only way to do this is with a GS&OP process.

Of course, managing complex global operations is easier with integrated information systems. In the 1980s and 1990s, Lilly had a wide range of computer systems throughout its local and regional branches. Today, the company is in the midst of a global ERP rollout to all manufacturing sites and most of the major sales offices as well. This will allow managers to see production plans, sales forecasts, inventory levels, and capacity utilization across the enterprise. Until the rollout is complete, however, pulling together the performance data needed for global supply chain management is a major undertaking.

If the past is any indication, Lilly will continue to improve its supply chain management organization and capabilities in response to changing market conditions. The company's supply chain management structure has gone through three different organizational forms in the last four years, a continuous evolution to better align the structure with business needs. The company believes that this ongoing alignment is the key to supply chain management in the pharmaceutical industry.

CHAPTER

Core Discipline 1: View Your Supply Chain as a Strategic Asset

If you're like many companies, you only think about changing your supply chain when something's broken—inventory levels are too high, customers are complaining about poor service, or a supplier is late with a critical shipment. Or maybe a benchmarking analysis shows that your supply chain performance is subpar relative to others in your industry.

If you only think about changing your supply chain when there's a problem, chances are that you don't see it as a valuable asset that can give your company a competitive advantage. And if this is the case, you risk being blindsided by companies that use their supply chain as a strategic weapon. Companies such as Dell, Amazon, Shell Chemical, and Airbus are rewriting the rules of competition in their industries—and forcing the laggards to play catch-up.

Market leaders such as Wal-Mart and Dell understand that the supply chain can be a strategic differentiator. They constantly search for new ways to add value and push the boundaries of performance. And they keep refining their supply chains so they stay one step ahead of the competition. They know that today's competitive edge is tomorrow's price of entry.

Michael Dell is widely viewed as a pioneer in the personal computer (PC) business. He transformed Dell from struggling PC maker to market leader by introducing supply chain innovations such as direct-to-consumer sales and build-to-order manufacturing to the computer industry. In truth, Michael Dell is a visionary in supply chain management. PCs simply were the medium he used to introduce his idea for a competitive supply chain: Sell direct, build to order, and ship direct. Sam Walton was another supply chain visionary. Wal-Mart's legendary partnership with Procter & Gamble to replenish inventory automatically showed the power of integrating with key suppliers. To further reduce inefficiencies and costs, Wal-Mart shifted from buying from distributors to buying directly from manufacturers for a broad range of merchandise. These and other supply chain actions combine to deliver on the promise of "always low prices"—the strategy that has helped Wal-Mart become the world's largest retailer.

FIVE KEY CONFIGURATION COMPONENTS

Strategic supply chain management is more than just innovation for the sake of being innovative. It's creating a unique supply chain configuration that drives your strategic objectives forward. To get the most from your supply chain, you need to consider five critical configuration components:

- ◆ Operations strategy
- ◆ Outsourcing strategy
- ◆ Channel strategy
- ◆ Customer service strategy
- ◆ Asset network

Your decisions around these components and how they play together define your supply chain strategy.

Until now, companies tended to either address these components informally or make decisions about them in isolation—often as part of a functional strategy related to sales, purchasing, or manufacturing. However, companies that view the supply chain as a strategic asset see their components as interdependent—part of an integrated whole. Let's look at each more closely.

Operations Strategy

Your decisions about how you'll produce goods and services form your operations strategy. Will you choose make to stock, make to order, engineer to order, or some combination? Will you outsource manufacturing? Will you pursue a low-cost offshore manufacturing strategy? Will you complete your final configuration outside the manufacturing plant and closer to the customer? These are critical decisions because they influence and shape the whole supply chain and the investments you make. Your operations strategy determines how you staff and run your factories, warehouses, and order desks—as well as how you design your processes and information systems.

> Strategic supply chain management is more than just innovation for the sake of being innovative. It's creating a unique supply chain configuration that drives forward your strategic objectives.

- *Make to stock* is the best strategy for standardized products that sell in high volume. Larger production batches keep manufacturing costs down, and having these products in inventory means that customer demand can be met quickly.

- *Make to order* is the preferred strategy for customized products or products with infrequent demand. Companies following this strategy produce a shippable product only with a customer order in hand. This keeps inventory levels low while allowing for a wide range of product options.

- *Configure to order* is a hybrid strategy in which a product is partially completed to a generic level and then finished when an order is received. This is the preferred strategy when there are many variations of the end product and you want to achieve low finished-goods inventory and shorter customer lead times than make to order can deliver.

- *Engineer to order*, which shares many of the characteristics of make to order, is used in industries where complex products and services are created to unique customer specifications.

Changing your operations strategy can be a key source of performance advantage (see Figures 1-1 and 1-2). Several of our clients in consumer packaged goods, for instance, found that moving from make to stock to configure to order improved service levels while reducing inventory. In the past, these companies manufactured and shipped products directly to the end market. Small pack size, combined with the need for local language variants, meant that products were dedicated to a given market very early in the production process.

FIGURE 1–1

Types of operations strategies.

Strategy	When to Choose This Strategy	Benefits
Make to stock	For standardized products selling in high volume	Low manufacturing costs; meeting customer demands quickly
Configure to order	For products requiring many variations	Customization; reduced inventory; improved service levels
Make to order	For customized products or products with infrequent demand	Low inventory levels; wide range of product options; simplified planning
Engineer to order	For complex products that meet unique customer needs	Enables response to specific customer requirements

FIGURE 1–2

Operations strategies by industry.

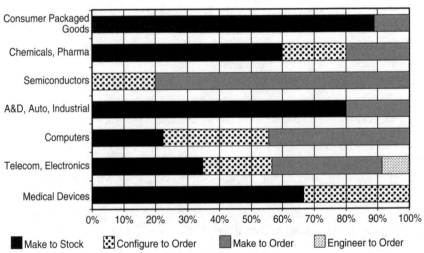

■ Make to Stock   ▨ Configure to Order   ▨ Make to Order   ▨ Engineer to Order

We worked with these companies to combine make-to-stock and configure-to-order strategies. "Vanilla" products were produced and stored in a central distribution center. When orders came in from each market, products were customized and shipped accordingly. Availability shot up and inventory went down in part due to the central inventory but also because the new approach simplified supply chain planning since procurement and manufacturing could focus on generic products instead of hundreds of language variants.

It may be to your advantage to choose different operations strategies for different products or market segments. Automobile makers have long pursued a make-to-stock strategy, but some—especially European manufacturers of high-end vehicles—have aggressively pursued make-to-order and configure-to-order strategies, an approach we call "Dell on Wheels."[1] However, make to order has its limits, as automobile makers are finding. Offering passenger cars on a make-to-order basis while maintaining a competitive lead time is a tremendous challenge given the millions of potential end configurations. Unless suppliers can be fully integrated into the make-to-order supply chain, the inventory risk is very high. In addition, changing the manufacturing process to allow each car to match a unique set of characteristics is a very costly undertaking that few OEMs have been willing to embrace. In 2002, only about 20 percent of passenger cars sold in North America were made to order. The rest were made to stock and sold from dealer lots. In Europe, the percentage of made-to-order vehicles was greater. In the German domestic market, for instance, about 60 percent of the high-end cars made by BMW, Audi, Porsche, and Mercedes were made to order.

Like the other supply chain configuration components, operations strategy is dynamic. A key driver is the product life cycle. As demand for products peaks and then decreases, companies can move from make to stock to make to order to reduce inventory risk while still ensuring availability at a competitive price. Another driver is the number of product variants. It is not unusual to find that 80 percent of volume shipments comes from just 20 percent (yes, Pareto at work again) of your sales item numbers (or possible configurations). In this circumstance, a hybrid make-to-stock and make-to-order strategy may be more appropriate.

Channel Strategy

Your channel strategy has to do with how you'll get your products and services to buyers or end users. These decisions address such issues as whether you'll sell indirectly through distributors or retailers or directly to customers via the Internet or a direct sales force. The market segments and geographies you're targeting will drive your decisions in this area. Since profit margins vary depending on which channels are used, you have to decide on the optimal channel mix—and who gets the goods in times of product shortages or high demand.

Market leaders use effective channel strategies to reap significant gains. Dell, with its direct-sales model, and Wal-Mart, with its superstore model, offer compelling examples of how channel choices can deliver a competitive advantage. Novell's value-added reseller channel, one of the best early examples of a technology-oriented channel, helped prop the company up at a time when it had serious technological problems to overcome. And Microsoft's dealer channels provide a range of services to buyers from leasing to training and help-desk support.

Consider the multi-billion-dollar bottled water industry and its two major markets: spring water and distilled water. While spring water requires on-site bottling, distilled water can be bottled at any municipal water source using any local bottling company. The industry uses three different distribution methods to serve its three major consumer segments: Traditional retail distributors serve the retail customers, vending machines serve the individual consumer market, and service agents install, maintain, and replenish on-site water units for home and office users. Each segment requires different supply chain processes, assets, channels, and supplier relationships and performance levels.

If you were a new player in the bottled water industry, would you sell your product through distributors that already have relationships with key retailers or distribute directly to those retailers? If you chose the distributor channel, would you integrate your order management and inventory management systems with the distributors' systems? If so, to what extent, and who should pay for it? Would you maintain dedicated inventory for all distributors or only those distributors which you consider to be strategic partners? These decisions drive your company's asset and cost performance and must be a part of your overall channel strategy—along with decisions on pricing, vendor financing policies, promotions, and other terms and conditions.

Outsourcing Strategy

Outsourcing decisions begin with an analysis of your company's existing supply chain skills and expertise. What is your company really good at?

What areas of expertise are—or have the potential to become—strategic differentiators? These are the activities you should keep in-house and make even better. Consider outsourcing activities with low strategic importance or that a third party could do better, faster, or more cheaply.

Outsourcing allows companies to ramp up or down quickly, build new products, or reposition themselves in the marketplace—all by leveraging the expertise and capacity of other companies. This added flexibility and agility can make an enormous difference in today's competitive global markets. Most important, though, outsourcing allows companies to focus on their core competencies and enhance their competitive positioning.

> Consider outsourcing activities with low strategic importance or that a third party could do better, faster, or more cheaply.

Before moving forward, however, be sure to carefully consider the risks and strategic ramifications of your outsourcing decisions. Introducing new products, managing inventory levels, and ensuring that the supply chain configuration supports competitive customer lead times—these are strategic activities that cannot be delegated to a third party. Be sure to consider other key questions that will drive your decision. Should outsourced skills also be maintained internally, or are they no longer needed? Which existing skills should be strengthened? Will new tools or skills be needed, such as the ability to manage inventory across the extended supply chain?

Thinking only in terms of "Can it be done more cheaply outside?" is unlikely to provide a strategic solution.

Outside partners can deliver three potential advantages:

- *Scale*—Third-party providers often can offer services more cheaply because of a large customer base that keeps utilization rates high and unit costs low. External partners also can help companies to scale up production quickly without having to invest in new manufacturing capacity.
- *Scope*—For companies that want to expand into new markets or geographies, outsourcing partners can provide access to operations in new locations which would not be economical to replicate internally at current business volumes.

- *Technology expertise*—Outsourcing partners may have mastered a product or process technology that would require a sizable investment to develop internally.

Despite these benefits, outsourcing isn't always the right decision. Before turning to external providers, consider four things: your source of differentiation, your operating scale, your power position, and the uniqueness of your operations.

First, know how your company differentiates itself. What gives you a competitive edge? If your product or process technology is a source of differentiation, don't outsource that aspect of your operations. Consider the case of one of the world's leading brands in watches. The Manufacture des Montres Rolex SA, known around the world for its Rolex brand, not only produces the components for its watches, but also produces machines, tools, and supplies for the manufacture of movements and other products.[2] Manufacturing is an integral part of ensuring the high standards of quality that set Rolex apart as a premium watchmaker.

> If your product or process technology is a source of differentiation, don't outsource that aspect of your operations.

For many companies, however, manufacturing is not strategic. Cisco, Compaq, and IBM outsource most of their production to contract electronics manufacturers such as Flextronics, Solectron, and Celestica. And most industries use third-party logistics providers for transportation, customs, warehousing, and other value-added services, such as final packaging, configuration testing, software loading, and site installation.

Next, compare the scale of your internal operations against your requirements. If your operations are at or near full capacity utilization—with no plans to boost production—you're unlikely to gain any cost benefit from outsourcing. For smaller players that want to expand, however, working with a partner can be the best solution. Outsourcing manufacturing operations to lower fixed and total costs is common practice across many industries. Top performers have set up these practices to yield other benefits as well.

Tellabs, a U.S. manufacturer of communications equipment, provides an example. This company's approach to external manufacturing provides benefits to strategies in procurement, design, repair operations, and market penetration, in addition to reducing manufactured cost. Through external agreements and integration of internal practice disciplines, Tellabs is leveraging manufacturing partners' common parts lists, engaging in collaborative product design reviews, and leveraging partner repair capacity in its own spare-parts and service network. Additionally, Tellabs has established its manufacturing agreements to allow for movement of production and repair operations into countries where a local presence benefits market-share growth goals.

Third, consider the uniqueness of your internal operations. Do you have business processes or unusual product characteristics that would be difficult for an outsider to replicate? If so, you have little to gain by going outside—an outsourcer's scale advantage won't apply to your unusual requirements. Wal-Mart, for example, has developed a highly customized internal logistics operation that manages inbound inventory flows from its central distribution centers to the shelves of its retail locations. As the owner of one of the largest warehousing operations in the world, Wal-Mart has nothing to gain—and everything to lose—by outsourcing this aspect of its operations.

Fourth, consider the balance of power between you and your outsourcing partner. Many providers of manufacturing, distribution, and customer-fulfillment services are already larger than their customers. As these service providers consolidate further, they'll gain even more power. Will you get the services that you need at a competitive price if your volume of business isn't high enough?

To choose the best service provider, go beyond technical criteria and consider the overall business context. Weigh the volume you represent against the service provider's strategy and overall size. You may end up changing your decision about which service providers to use, how to divide the volume among them, and even whether to outsource at all.

Customer Service Strategy

Customer service strategy is another key configuration component. Your customer service strategy should be based on two things: the overall volume and profitability of your customer accounts and an understanding of what your customers really want. Both pieces of knowledge are integral to your supply chain strategy because they help you to prioritize and focus your capabilities.

Should all customers get same-day delivery, or should you aim for different service levels depending on customer importance? Should all products be equally available, or should some customers have quicker, easier access? If your company never examines its service strategy, you may be providing more costly levels of service than your customers need—or you may be missing important market opportunities.

Not all customers warrant the same level of service, but it's critical to know who your high-value customers are. For instance, an Internet service provider (ISP) was planning to raise the level of customer service across the board in response to complaints about slow problem resolution. We suggested a more strategic approach—basing service levels on each customer's value to the company. By analyzing each customer's total revenue potential and strategic relationship value, the company learned that just 5 percent of its clients were high-value customers.

What these high-value customers wanted most was rapid problem resolution. Therefore, for this subset of customers, the company set up a customer care account team with highly trained technical people and a dedicated account manager. For the remaining 95 percent of customers, service problems were routed to a separate, cost-efficient service center, with specific resolution pathways depending on the technical complexity of the problem.

Problem-resolution time for high-value customers was cut dramatically, with the percentage of problems resolved at first contact improving from less than 5 percent to 80 percent. Even for the lowest-priority accounts, service issues typically were resolved on the same day. In addition, the new setup reduced total customer care costs by 30 percent.

More important, the new service levels meant that the company was better able to compete in its chosen market—a market increasingly made up of sophisticated customers with higher service expectations.[3]

The lesson? Tailoring your customer service strategy to deliver the best cost/service trade-off by customer segment can pay big dividends, especially as you design your supply chain for strategic advantage.

Asset Network

The final component of your supply chain configuration includes the decisions you make regarding your company's asset network—the factories, warehouses, production equipment, order desks, and service centers that make up your business. The location, size, and mission of these assets have a major impact on supply chain performance.

Most companies choose one of three network models based on such factors as business size, customer service requirements, tax advantages, supplier base, local content rules, and labor costs:

- *Global model*—Manufacturing of a given product line is done in one location for the global market. The choice of this model is driven by factors such as the need to colocate manufacturing with research and development (R&D), the need to control unit manufacturing costs for very capital-intensive products, or the need for highly specialized manufacturing skills.

- *Regional model*—Manufacturing is done primarily in the region where the products are sold, although some cross-regional flows may exist based on production-center specialization. The regional model is often chosen based on a mix of factors, including customer service levels, import duty levels, and the need to adapt products to specific regional requirements.

- *Country model*—Manufacturing is done primarily in the country where the market is. This is the model of choice for goods that are prohibitively expensive to transport. Other factors include duties and tariffs and market access that is conditional on in-country manufacturing.

Due to price competition, many companies are manufacturing in low-cost countries to lower unit production costs. When choosing such a location, key considerations include manufacturing costs, corporate tax rate, export incentives, the presence of key suppliers or duty-free imports, infrastructure, and skilled labor. While unit costs are important, supply chain leaders know that supply chain flexibility and total supply chain cost are also critical considerations when designing an asset network, particularly for products with highly variable demand and short product life cycles.

China has emerged as a favored lost-cost manufacturing spot among electronics companies because of the presence of component suppliers and contract electronics manufacturers, as well as the quality of its infrastructure (roads, electricity, etc.). Although electronics assembly may take only one to two days, transporting goods by ship between China and Europe takes three weeks. Add to this the time needed to reach the regional or country distribution centers, and the total fulfillment cycle can be six weeks. In a highly volatile market, these long fulfillment times can result in inventory that is out of sync with market demand—the problem that Michael Dell designed *out* of his supply chain.

Companies can reduce this risk with several different options. One approach is to increase manufacturing flexibility to ensure that the supply chain plan is refreshed weekly instead of monthly to better meet changing market demand. Another approach—in-market postponement—creates standard products in the low-cost production center but does final configuration and packaging at a distribution point closer to the customer. Yet another option is to move to a low-cost manufacturing base closer to the target market. For example, many companies serving the European market have moved production from Asia to central European locations such as Romania and Hungary. This approach lowers both production costs and in-transit inventory levels.

The product life cycle drives many asset network decisions. In rapidly evolving industries such as consumer electronics, companies may start with a global model during new product ramp-up to test the manufacturing process or to benefit from colocation with R&D and then transition to a regional model to improve customer service. At the end of the product life cycle, the global model once again may be a better choice as a way to fulfill demand at the lowest product cost and inventory investment.

FOUR CRITERIA OF A GOOD SUPPLY CHAIN STRATEGY

The configuration components—operations strategy, channel strategy, outsourcing strategy, customer service strategy, and asset network—are the fundamental building blocks of your supply chain strategy. However, to drive forward your strategic business objectives and really gain a competitive edge, these components and the choices you make about each one must be

- ◆ Aligned with your business strategy
- ◆ Aligned with your customers' needs
- ◆ Aligned with your power position (your influence)
- ◆ Adaptive, because competitive advantage is temporary and market conditions change

These four criteria may sound elementary, but few companies actually follow them. In fact, the practice of developing and managing a supply chain strategy is not widespread. Many of our clients over the years have had only the most rudimentary supply chain strategy process in place, indicating that these concepts are either not well understood or difficult to implement. Let's examine them one by one.

Align with Your Business Strategy

Your supply chain strategy should directly support and drive forward your business strategy. We believe that an effective business strategy begins with a *core strategic vision* (see Figure 1-3) that lays down the boundary conditions for your business: what you are, what you'll do, and—just as important—what you are *not* and what you *won't* do.

F I G U R E 1–3

Boundary conditions of the core strategic vision.

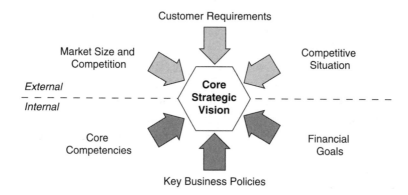

The core strategic vision clarifies the answers to key business strategy questions such as: What are your overall strategic objectives? What value do you deliver to your customers? How does your company differentiate itself in the marketplace? Unless the answers to these key questions drive your supply chain strategy and configuration, your supply chain will be operating in a vacuum.

Here's one example of many. We worked with an electronics company that had spent millions to improve production and order-fulfillment times. The company's on-time delivery performance was excellent. There was only one problem—delivery performance was no longer the key to profitable growth. Increased competition meant that customers were demanding, and getting, lower prices. What's more, a slowdown in several of the company's primary markets was cutting into revenues and sharply reducing return on assets. The company's president recognized the need to move to a much lower breakeven point, but supply chain operations were focusing on yesterday's priority—customer delivery excellence.

Where does this type of disconnect come from? Simply put, the new business vision of the company's president had not been translated into new objectives for the supply chain. Although the overall business plan clearly showed the volume and price declines and their impact on margins, the implications for supply chain operations had not been considered. It was only when the company began to lose money that a major supply chain reorganization occurred, which led to factory closures, facility consolidation, and outsourcing of manufacturing.

Translating your business strategy into an effective plan of action requires communication and discipline. The matrix in Figure 1-4 offers a framework for thinking broadly about four typical ways that companies compete—on innovation, cost, service, and quality—otherwise known as the *basis of competition.* The matrix shows the key supply chain contribution for each strategy.

Some aspect of innovation, cost, service, and quality is a part of almost every company's strategy. But leading companies focus on just one of these as a primary strategy—their basis of competition for winning in a chosen market. From a supply chain perspective, each basis of competition requires distinct structure, processes, information systems, and skills.

Competing on Cost

Companies that compete on cost offer low prices to attract cost-sensitive buyers or to maintain share in a commodity market. This strategy demands highly efficient, integrated operations, and the supply chain plays a critical role in keeping both product and supply chain costs down. The low-cost supply chain focuses on efficiency-based metrics such as asset utilization, inventory days of supply, product costs, and total supply chain costs. Product standardization and process standardization are critical, as are supplier and production quality and inventory control.

FIGURE 1-4

Supply chain contribution to business strategy.

Primary Strategy	Source of Advantage	Basis of Competition	Key Supply Chain Contributor
Innovation	Brand and unique technology	Desirable and innovative products	Time to market and time to volume
Cost	Cost-efficient operations	Lowest prices in the product-category	Efficient, low-cost infrastructure
Service	Superb service	Tailored to meet customer-specific needs	Designed "from the customer in"
Quality	Safest, most reliable products	Product you can count on	Supply chain excellence and quality control

Hewlett-Packard (HP) traditionally pursued an innovation-based strategy—until an upstart competitor changed the industry dynamics. In 1997, HP and other printer manufacturers were taken by surprise by Lexmark's launch of a below-$100 printer. When Lexmark had doubled its market share by mid-1999, HP embarked on an ambitious program called "Big Bang" to sharply reduce product costs through new design and supply chain changes. The goal? To compete directly with Lexmark on price. "Big Bang" was a big success. By 2002, HP had won back its market share.[4]

Efficiency and low cost are good things—but not at the expense of service, innovation, or quality if one of those is a key element of your business strategy. Consider the low-cost offshore manufacturing that we discussed earlier. Most apparel manufacturers outsource their production to Southeast Asia, where contract manufacturers insist on fixed production schedules to minimize costs. This low-cost approach also results in low flexibility and can hurt margins at the retail level. If one style lags while another takes off, the retailers are limited in their ability to change volumes and mix. With too many of the wrong garments, the stores end up with marked-down inventory and eroded margins. Too often the missed revenue and reduced margins associated with a poorly aligned supply chain strategy are not included when assessing the total impact of supply chain strategic choices.

Zara, the retailer owned by Spanish textile giant Inditex, chose a very different model. Zara positioned itself as the designer-boutique alternative for the price-conscious but trendy consumer. To deliver its strategy, it manufactures almost 50 percent of its garments in-house—an industry exception. Although its manufacturing costs are 15 to 20 percent higher than the competition, Zara more than makes up for the cost differential by using its supply chain to ensure that merchandise in the stores matches what customers want.[5]

Competing on Innovation

Companies whose primary strategy is innovation focus on developing category killers—"must have" products that benefit from significant consumer pull. And because their products are category killers, these companies can command a price premium,

> Companies whose primary strategy is innovation focus on developing category killers—"must have" products that benefit from significant consumer pull.

the innovator's advantage. Companies such as Sony, Nike, and L'Oréal seem to have a finger on the pulse of the consumer and are fast to market with new products that buyers want. The underlying source of power for such companies is unparalleled marketing and product development.

How does the supply chain support a company that competes on innovation? For new products and services, the window of opportunity—before the fast followers start taking market share—can be small. Innovative companies are acutely aware of the benefits of getting into a market early and gaining first-mover advantage, so new product introduction (NPI) is key. By getting new products to market faster, the supply chain can boost revenues and profits. This is why it's important for a company with innovation as a primary strategy to integrate the supply chain with the *design chain,* which we define as all the parties—both inside and outside the enterprise—that participate in defining and designing a new product or service.

The challenge isn't just time to market, however. Time to volume is critical too. The faster a company can pump up production to meet demand, the greater are the profits, and the less likely imitators are to catch up. Creating strong demand for a new product and then being unable to meet that demand is one of the worst things that can happen to an innovation-driven company. Achieving that time-to-volume advantage is a major competitive weapon.

Design chain/supply chain integration[6] is critical to innovation-driven companies, ensuring the fast and sustainable launch of new products. Moving from product development to volume production at the target level of quality requires management of processes, assets, products, and information. Design chain/supply chain integration also ensures that when demand cranks up, the whole supply chain is ready—that suppliers can handle your needs, that order-management systems support the new product information, and that sales channels and service people are trained.

Consider again the example of clothing retailer Zara. While most of the industry focuses the supply chain on delivering the lowest purchase price, Zara's supply chain supports its primary innovation strategy. Designers and planners use point-of-sale information to adjust production plans and designs to focus on bestsellers. This translates into a much shorter time to market, higher revenues, and fewer markdowns.[7] Between 2001 and 2002, when many fashion retailers were struggling to break even, Zara's performance translated into steady double-digit growth and healthy EBIT (earnings before income taxes) margins, growing from 18.1 to 18.5 percent.[8] By combining innovation and cost performance, Zara created an NPI-focused supply chain that delivers spectacular results for the company and its investors.

Competing on Quality

Companies that compete on quality are known for the premium nature of their products and services, as well as consistent and reliable performance. Quality products include well-known names such as Lexus automobiles, Maytag appliances, and Tropicana juices. Product development is obviously critical to quality, but so are key supply chain processes such as manufacturing, sourcing, quality assurance, and return. And if a product is perishable or fragile, transportation and storage play an integral role.

One key supply chain attribute relative to quality is *traceability*—the ability to trace a product back to its point of origin—a growing requirement in a number of industries. Concerns about food safety and the booming market for organic and "ethical" products mean that consumers want to be able to trace a product from "farm to plate." In the U.S. tire market, for example, traceability back to the point of manufacture is a legal requirement. Moreover, counterfeiting has emerged in a growing number of sectors, such as luxury goods, entertainment, and pharmaceuticals. To offset this risk, manufacturers increasingly use special tags, such as RFID (radio frequency identification), that identify merchandise as genuine and closely control product flows to consumers.

The example of Barlean's Organic Oils shows how a supply chain strategy can deliver quality as a basis of competition. Barlean's is a $22 million family-owned company that sells health supplements. The company's flagship product, flaxseed oil, outsells the competition 20 to 1. Freshness makes the difference. Barlean's oil carries a four-month expiration date, compared with other oils that can be up to five months old before they even hit store shelves. Barlean's manufacturing and distribution processes give the company its edge. Conventional manufacturing techniques expose flax seeds to heat, light, air, and overpressing, all of which compromise quality. Barlean's designed a manufacturing process that protects its seeds from the

> One key supply chain attribute relative to quality is *traceability*—the ability to trace a product back to its point of origin—a growing requirement in a number of industries.

elements. The company doesn't even press the seeds until an order comes in—a "press-to-order" production method. Barlean's also uses Express Mail to ship orders so that they arrive faster and fresher—a more expensive choice, but one that further supports the company's commitment to quality. In the crowded health supplements market, Barlean's uses the supply chain to deliver on its commitment to quality, profitably growing sales every year by 40 percent since 1999.[9]

Competing on Service

Companies that compete on service tailor their offerings to their customers' specific needs and are known for exceptional customer service. These companies customize their products and services to build customer loyalty and lock in repeat sales. To excel at service, all of a company's customer-touching processes and information systems such as order capture, order fulfillment, and invoicing must be fast, consistent, and trouble-free. The ability to integrate internal processes and systems with those of key customers is a core skill.

Our research shows that best-in-class deliver companies—those with exceptional order-fulfillment processes overall—are more than 20 percent more profitable than average companies and are growing their top-line sales 25 percent faster.[10] Why does better service lead to such striking financial gains? On a basic level, companies with superior customer service processes avoid the costs related to expediting and the short-term churn that other, less adept companies face.

On a more strategic level, companies that excel at customer service develop the ability to segment their customers. They understand the relationship between cost to serve and profitability and can assess the cost of offering customized services. As a result, they avoid offering customized services to customers who don't meet hard business criteria. They also tend to focus on the higher-value segments of an industry and on developing relationships with their priority customers, resulting in lower account turnover and a decrease in customer retention costs—all of which add to the bottom line.

A case in point is Shell Chemical. It offers its manufacturing customers an inventory-management solution called *SIMON* (supplier inventory management order network) that simplifies their purchasing process and cuts costs from the supply chain at the same time. With Shell's automated replenishment system, customers no longer place orders, run out of inventory, or build "safety cushions" of stock. Instead, they've integrated their information technology (IT) systems with Shell's so that they can share information. Every night, data on consumption, inventory levels, and usage forecasts are recorded at the customer's site and forwarded to Shell. At predetermined inventory trigger points, Shell places a refill order for the customer, schedules order transport, and tracks the shipment until it arrives. The system is invoiceless. Each month, based on consumption figures that both parties share, the customer sends payment electronically.

Shell's solution makes life easier for everyone. By cutting administrative costs for customers and the safety cushions of stock that result from forecast uncertainty, the solution reduces the total amount of inventory in the supply chain and vastly simplifies inventory management. Shell gains an added bonus. In exchange for using the company's service, and because the solution couldn't work if inventory from different suppliers were mixed in the same tanks, customers agree to use Shell as their exclusive vendor for products managed under SIMON. By offering a value-added service and integrating with its customers' IT systems, Shell is able to forge extremely tight relationships with its customers—a powerful supply chain-driven, strategic advantage.[11]

The best companies understand that they can't be all things to all people. They identify how they will differentiate themselves and drive their supply chain to best-in-class performance for that basis of competition. This sharp focus sets them apart from the competition and helps them gain a competitive edge.

The supply chain supports every business strategy, so make alignment a top priority. Remember, though, that strategy is a balancing act. No cost leader can afford to ignore customer service. Nor can an innovator ignore the price ceiling of a market. Supply chain performance leaders understand the trade-offs among service levels, lead times, assets, and costs and make decisions that best fit their overall strategic mission. By choosing where to focus and achieving best-in-class supply chain performance in those key areas, companies can set themselves apart from the competition.

Align with Your Customers' Needs

Barlean's Organic Oils identified freshness as a key differentiator. Shell Chemical realized the advantage of providing a new service concept to its customers. Zara understood the market for high fashion at attractive price points. Each of these companies identified solutions that would create a competitive advantage and aligned their supply chains accordingly.

Do you really know what your customers want? Are there opportunities that you're not exploiting simply because you can't envision them?

Answering these questions can be a challenge. Often our assumptions about what customers want are wrong. Just as often customers are unaware of or can't fully articulate their needs. *Voice of the customer* (VoC) is a methodology we use that helps our clients really listen to their customers and understand their environment. VoC can help uncover and translate customer needs into requirements for new products and services that leverage your existing supply chain capabilities or pinpoint changes you can make to exploit new business opportunities.[12]

Aligning with customer needs also means identifying the particular requirements of different market segments. As we shall see, Michelin's passenger-car tire business has two different market segments—automobile makers and the after-market customers. The automobile makers are far more demanding, requiring that tires be delivered directly to the assembly lines right on time because any delay can back up production schedules. Besides being more demanding, the automobile makers deliver only razor-thin margins, compared with healthier margins for the less-demanding replacement market. Thus, you'd think that the after-market segment would be a priority, right? Wrong. Tire manufacturers such as Michelin always put the automobile makers first because being on a new car creates a pull for replacement sales and because supply contracts contain severe penalties.

If you're a tire manufacturer, you have to play according to the automobile makers' rules. If reliability and timeliness are key customer requirements, as they are for manufacturers such as Michelin, then you'll make it a priority to continually improve all the supply chain activities that support those performance goals—or pay the price with high levels of finished-goods inventory.

If customers don't get what they need, you'll lose market share. If you don't know what your customers want, then, ask them. Or use VoC to find out. And check back periodically to understand how their needs are changing.

Multiple Segments, Multiple Supply Chains?

For some companies, one supply chain with a single set of physical assets, processes, and information systems makes the most sense, even with different products, suppliers, and customers. A company with very flexible operations can "design anywhere, build anywhere," so product assignments are made based on available capacity, product costs, and target markets.

Some companies, however, find that they can serve their markets better with separate supply chains. Why? Different products, market segments, or regions may call for very different approaches. Or separate business units may want their own supply chains so that they can have the business control needed to achieve their specific business objectives.

There are inherent risks in trying to manage disparate requirements such as increased complexity, increased costs, or unmanageable processes, organizations, and information systems in one total supply chain. When managed correctly, however, these risks can be mitigated while achieving significant benefits through tailoring key supply chain steps to enhance specific business unit (or product line) performance.

One positive example of this approach is Seiko Epson Corporation's (Epson's) European Group company. Epson is a global leader in printer and imaging products for both home and business based on its strong technology, brand recognition, and reputation for quality. Behind Epson's overall leadership on imaging products there is a wide range of diversity of technology within its product portfolio. Products include inkjet printers, scanners, laser products, ink and toner cartridges, point-of-sale printers, and liquid-crystal display (LCD) projectors, to name a few.

The back-end supply chain for these various product lines and businesses is often made up of separate global supply chains, each with its own suppliers, factories, and logistics routings. But the front end of the supply chain—encompassing the processes that touch the customer, such as order management and distribution—is common. This derivative approach allows Epson to optimize its back-end supply chain and gain substantial efficiencies in the production processes of its varied products. It also ensures that its customers interact with "one Epson" at the front end and can easily do business with Epson regardless of the mix of products they wish to purchase. According to Ramon Ollé, Epson Europe chairman and chief executive officer (CEO), this combination allows Epson to achieve an overall efficiency in its end-to-end supply chain while increasing customer satisfaction.

Another example is Michelin. A capital-intensive manufacturer, Michelin uses the same factories for customers in both its automobile makers' segment and the after-market segment to increase capacity utilization, along with a single production planning process. Once the tires leave the factory, however, everything else—from demand planning, order entry, and shipping to invoicing and warehousing—is different. The company uses two separate supply chains to meet the needs of two different markets. For automobile makers, the company delivers tires to mounting centers, which move them directly to the assembly line, because timeliness and reliability are critical. By contrast, tires for the after-market are shipped to distributors and a variety of retailers, such as auto repair shops, car dealerships, and other retail outlets, where on-time delivery is less critical because most hold some level of inventory.

Companies with both new product sales and after-sales support businesses often have different supply chains. Besides managing different activities, such as returns, repairs, and refurbishment, the after-sales support supply chain must meet very different customer service expectations. Although new product sales and after-sales support are usually structured as two distinct business units, both typically use the same production centers to gain economies of scale. Yet customer-facing processes, including demand planning, order entry, and invoicing, are tailored to the two different markets.

If your company has multiple business units, identify your greatest point of shared leverage and use that as a starting point. For Michelin's passenger car business, the answer was raw materials and manufacturing assets, so the company structured its supply chains accordingly. If you can standardize within a single supply chain and avoid additional fixed assets and unnecessary variations in processes and information systems, do so.

If different processes or multiple locations performing similar activities are the result of acquisitions or historically independent geographic or business units, check to see if these duplications are still needed. In many industries, converging customer requirements and the emergence of regional and global logistics service providers have opened the door to more streamlined and standardized supply chains. Leverage any synergies that you can.

Here's a general rule of thumb: If you can meet the needs of your most profitable customer segments at an acceptable service level and at a reasonable cost with a single supply chain, then do so. If supply chain performance targets such as cost, lead time, and delivery for different products or market segments are truly at odds with each other, or if business control is an issue, then consider partially or completely separate supply chains.

> A good supply chain strategy is grounded in an understanding of your power and influence relative to customers and suppliers.

Align with Your Power Position

A good supply chain strategy is grounded in an understanding of your power and influence relative to customers and suppliers. Why is this so important? Your relative power determines what can be achieved realistically in terms of reconfiguring the supply chain to meet your overall strategic objectives.

The reality is that many of the supply chain innovators you read about are in an enviable position: They're big, with enormous market clout. But not every company is a Wal-Mart, able to strong-arm its suppliers to eliminate inefficiencies. When it comes to making fundamental changes in your extended supply chain, you need to understand how much power and influence you really have.

Scale matters. Big companies can leverage their volume of output to buy inputs more cheaply, boost asset utilization, and reduce the cost of everything from information systems to transportation. Just as important, they can impose their own processes and rules on suppliers and customers. In the automobile industry, any supplier who shuts down the production line by not delivering on time can be subject to a penalty up to the equivalent of the revenue lost while the line is down. It's written into the supply contract. Of course, not every company can do this. It requires power—the power of scale.

Companies with scale can exercise a high degree of control over the supply chain and structure it in a way that supports their own strategic objectives. When a company is bigger than its suppliers or its customers and they need it more than it needs them, the company calls the shots. But scale is relative. Companies often underestimate their own power because they're thinking in broad, global terms instead of narrowing their scope to a country or market segment. Even relatively small companies can find ways to work strategically with select suppliers or customers to gain a competitive edge. The key is to segment, focus, and consolidate.

If you're not a priority for your suppliers and aren't getting adequate collaboration and service, rethink your supplier relationships. Consider shifting the power equation by focusing on a few, smaller suppliers and giving them an opportunity to grow their business in exchange for working with you more collaboratively over time to cut costs, boost efficiency, and improve overall performance.

Brand also can be a major source of supply chain power, especially in the consumer markets. If your products are highly desired by consumers, you'll have more clout with retailers and other channel partners. Think of Louis Vuitton bags or Rolex watches. Lack of availability only heightens the brand's prestige. Customer service, fast delivery, or squeezing out supply chain costs and inefficiency can seem irrelevant to companies with the hottest brands or products. Buyers of highly desirable products have learned to wait—and to pay a premium.

Make sure that you understand your relative position before trying to exercise your supply chain power. Even consumer packaged-goods brand leaders, those whose product dominates a product category, are modifying their physical logistics to satisfy the demands of key retail accounts. Manufacturers that occupy the less desirable second position on the retailer's shelf typically have to go even further to contribute to the logistics efficiency of their key accounts by, for example, modifying product packaging and providing very high supply flexibility. The hard reality is that second-tier branded-goods suppliers just don't have the supply chain power of category leaders. Changes to their supply chain must accommodate the retailer requirements, even to the detriment of manufacturer supply chain cost and inventory performance.

When you're developing your supply chain strategy, take some time to assess the situation. Is your supply chain brand-led, channel-led, or supplier-led? Do you need your channels more than they need you? How about your suppliers? Who has the power? If you're a supplier in an industry that's fragmented on the sell side but concentrated on the buy side, like the automobile industry, your power may be limited. The same is true if you're one buyer among many in an industry with just a few suppliers—such as an electronics buyer of specialty components.

As we've seen from these examples, supply chain control is a possibility. For most companies, though, collaboration is the best bet. Therefore, analyze your position in the supply chain. Explore how you can rethink your interactions to cut costs, eliminate inefficiencies, boost satisfaction, or add value. And since collaboration is tough to do well, pick your targets carefully. Focus on key customers or suppliers, and look for opportunities where collaboration will have a real strategic impact (see Chapter 4 on the Fourth Discipline).

Become Adaptive

Change is a given. Market conditions shift, business strategies evolve, and new technologies emerge. If you're not paying attention, your supply chain can get out of sync. Your supply chain strategy, just like your business strategy, has to adapt.

Your supply chain strategy, just like your business strategy, has to adapt.

Although change is constant, the frequency of significant change will differ by industry. In the PC industry, companies make fundamental changes to their supply chains about every three to five years, driven by the constant pursuit of lower costs and the need for rapid new product introductions. Companies have adopted new operating strategies such as make to order, white-box packaging, and resale from low-cost producers and are opening their own stores, selling directly through the Internet, and exploring other new channels.

In other industries, such as aerospace, fundamental supply chain changes can occur less often—every 10 years or so—and have major consequences. Consider the supply chain strategies of Boeing and Airbus. Airbus's network of partners delivers finished subassemblies direct to the company's assembly line in Toulouse, France, where fewer than 500 workers do final assembly.[13] Airbus's production model requires lower capital spending, spreads development risks, and leverages the know-how of many partners.

Boeing today is in a state of continual change. The company is achieving marked improvements in efficiency by reducing its supply base and is working within the company and with suppliers to implement techniques of lean manufacturing. At the same time, the company is involving more risk-sharing supplier partners in its business and making great progress toward large-scale systems integration.

Given the major changes experienced by the airline industry in the late 1990s and early 2000s, including bankruptcies, mergers, and acquisitions, and the impressive growth of low-cost carriers, it is likely that the supply chain strategies of major commercial aircraft manufacturers will evolve further to meet the airline industry's demand for cost-efficient solutions and to deliver profitable growth.

Both internal and external factors determine your supply chain's shelf life and can trigger a need for a change in configuration. These factors include

- *A new technology that transforms the dynamics of your industry.* The Internet, for instance, created a direct link to customers so that companies such as Amazon could sell direct and cut out the middleman.

- *A change in the scope of your business.* If your company is offering new products or services, targeting new markets, or expanding geographically, you may need to expand your manufacturing capacity, add new distribution capabilities, develop new channels, find new suppliers, and rethink your supply chain strategy overall.

- *A change in your basis of competition.* Perhaps a new competitor has emerged with a stronger value proposition, or you need to change the type of service you offer to increase market share, or you want to compete in a new market that requires faster delivery, greater flexibility, or higher quality. Any major change to your company's basis of competition should drive a reexamination of your supply chain strategy and components.

◆ *The need to assimilate a new acquisition.* Mergers and acquisitions can create a need to reconfigure the supply chain. You'll have to see where it makes sense to eliminate redundancies, where to keep operations separate, and where to integrate.

A company's growth trajectory can have major implications, too. Is your sales volume increasing or decreasing? Is your industry expanding or contracting? An organization and processes designed to manage and support a growing company may no longer be appropriate during retrenchment, when the focus is on cost control. In either case, your company may need to adjust supplier requirements and resize fixed assets.

As an example, consider Nokia. Nokia Mobile Phones was facing a crisis in 1995–1996. After ending 1995 with a massive shortfall in profits versus plan, the business was operating at a loss in early 1996, with costs spiraling out of control. Business conditions weren't good either, with a sales slowdown and continuing handset price erosion. Pekka Ala-Pietala, Nokia's president, announced the need to move the company's focus from market share to profitability. Specifically, the company had to review its product portfolio with a critical eye and take actions on a number of supply chain issues, including product quality, forecasting, and manufacturing productivity. As Nokia discovered, producing 100,000 mobile phones a month is not the same as producing 100,000 phones a day. Explained Pertti Korhonen, vice president of global logistics at the time, "We weren't ready for the transition to a high-volume business and rapidly found ourselves with excess inventory and quality problems with key suppliers."

Nokia turned the situation around by implementing new supply chain disciplines in Europe, Asia, and the United States that included improvements in manufacturing productivity and quality, supplier development, supply chain planning, and integration. The results were impressive. For example, on-hand inventory was reduced from 154 to 68 days in nine months, releasing €450 million in cash. Taken together, these actions put the company back on track for profitable growth. Supply chain expertise was developed and maintained to build a foundation for future growth. Today, Nokia's supply chain is recognized by the rest of the industry as a true source of competitive advantage.[14]

Cisco is another interesting example. In May 2001, Cisco shocked the markets by announcing a $2.2 billion provision for inventory write-offs.[15] As the star player of the fast-growing networking equipment sector, Cisco had developed a reputation as one of the most savvy supply chain managers in the world. Outsourcing partners provide Cisco with manufacturing, materials management, warehousing, and transportation services, allowing the company to focus on its core strategy of rapid innovation and rapid growth—without increasing fixed assets. In 2001, when the whole networking equipment sector experienced an unprecedented collapse in demand, few expected that Cisco would suffer as much as other industry players. But the company had built a complex global supply chain without robust supply chain planning between itself and its partners. This led to duplication of planning based on "second guess" estimates and an inability to see and respond quickly to changes in market demand, which resulted in excess inventory across the supply chain.

To minimize the impact of future boom-bust scenarios, Cisco turned to a private Internet-based network called eHub. The result was an innovative, shared environment with top-tier suppliers, distributors, and contract manufacturers.[16] In so doing, Cisco hopes to build one of the most effective supply chain networks in industry.

Given the dynamic nature of industries, businesses, and product life cycles, creating and putting in place a supply chain strategy are not an annual or biannual exercise but an ongoing orchestration of decisions and actions. New opportunities and threats emerge every day. If you can't keep up with these new realities, you risk becoming a footnote in some dusty management text. It's also a fact of life that major supply chain innovations can be copied. Even if you're first out of the gate, your edge will dissipate with time. So stay vigilant, and keep looking for ways to improve and differentiate your supply chain performance.

As shown in Figure 1-1, a supply chain strategy involves many interlocking facets and hundreds of decisions, large and small. Michael Porter, strategy guru and author of *Competitive Advantage*, discusses the notion of *fit*—when a group of activities all support a chosen competitive strategy. Any single activity can be copied, but taken together they form a *system* that is virtually impossible to duplicate.[17] The same concept holds true for your supply chain strategy. Taken together, the choices you make create a supply chain that is uniquely yours—and tough for others to replicate. And that's a source of competitive advantage.

NEXT-GENERATION STRATEGY

Today's supply chain architectures are designed predominately for excellence in cost reduction through a focus on back-end processes, such as purchasing, manufacturing, and physical distribution. This can translate into efficient supply chains that often don't truly support overall business strategy.

Next-generation supply chain strategies will support continuing improvements in productivity but also will drive the achievement of business-level outcomes—with a strong focus on the customer. It will be important in the future to identify these objectives, which will include new revenue-generating services and time-to-market, time-to-volume, and customer-segment-specific capabilities.

In the future, supply chain strategy also naturally will consider the supply chain as part of an extended business architecture and consider key targeted outcomes with suppliers, customers, and partners as core elements. We expect to see the changes shown in Figure 1-5.

FIGURE 1–5

Next-generation characteristics of supply chain strategy.

Theme	Current Dominant Practice	Next Generation Dominant Practice
Supply Chain Strategy Scope	Focus is on the internal organization	Focus is extended to key customers and suppliers
Supply Chain Strategy Content	Focus is on functional excellence, with corresponding emphasis on functional metrics such as unit manufacturing costs and purchasing price variance	Functional strategies are integrated as part of the overall supply chain strategy to achieve enterprise-level performance improvements in areas such as supply chain management costs, order fulfillment lead time, on-time delivery, and inventory days of supply
Supply Chain Support of Overall Business Strategy	Supply chain strategy is focused on core (*plan, source, make, deliver,* and *return*) capabilities and performance objectives	Supply chain capabilities and performance objectives are aligned with marketing and sales, technology, service, and product development strategies
Supply Chain Segmentation	One supply chain model (a set of supply chain capabilities and performance objectives) is dominant, with alternative approaches managed on an exception basis	Multiple supply chain models are developed and optimized based on customer and supplier segmentation
Cross-Enterprise Extension	External relationships with customers and suppliers are managed using existing roles, processes, and metrics	Effective external relationship management is nurtured as a core competency and enabled by new roles, processes, and metrics

Autoliv

Autoliv Profile: Applying Rocket Science to the Supply Chain

Through rapid growth and acquisitions, Autoliv captured a third of the global airbag market. But constant price pressure from the automakers and the economic slowdown of the late 1990s stretched the company's supply chain to the breaking point.

Stockholm-based Autoliv is the world's largest manufacturer of auto safety systems. The company operates in 30 countries, developing and producing airbags, seatbelts, safety electronics, antiwhiplash seats, and related safety systems and components for all the major automotive makers worldwide. Autoliv employs 35,000 people and posts annual sales in excess of $4 billion.

Autoliv's current global operation was created in 1997 by the merger of Autoliv AB of Sweden, then Europe's leading automotive safety company, and U.S.-based Morton ASP, the largest airbag manufacturer in North America and Asia. Innovation is Autoliv's hallmark. From its pioneering work in seatbelts in the 1950s to the first antisliding airbags launched in 2002—to keep drivers from slipping down under the dashboard in a head-on crash—Autoliv is responsible for nearly every major innovation in automotive safety systems.

During the 1990s, the business units that now make up Autoliv prospered as safety became a strong selling feature in the minds of car buyers. Led by the marketing strategies of Volvo and Chrysler and then driven by government regulations, airbags evolved from a luxury item in high-end vehicles to standard equipment for nearly every car on the road. Autoliv grew with that trend, but it was growth that came with significant price erosion in its core products as airbags moved from a specialty item that could command a premium to near-commodity status.

By 1998 it was clear that Autoliv was under stress. It faced annual price reductions for its products, mandated by the clout of the big automotive makers. Autoliv's supply chain, which ran through numerous independently operating business units with disparate systems and processes, was having trouble meeting customer requirements for production and delivery. Then the economic slowdown at the end of the decade hit the automotive industry, and demand for Autoliv's products softened.

With price and demand trending down, Autoliv needed to find major cost savings to remain profitable and generate enough margin to fund innovation and maintain shareholder value. Most important, it had to cut costs without eroding the quality of its products.

Mindful of the magnitude of the challenge, the company saw its supply chain as the key strategic asset that it could use to achieve its business objectives. "One of the major drivers in our business, and really the thing that differentiates us, is our high standard for quality and performance," says Norm Markert, president of Autoliv North America. "We're not making a cosmetic element of the vehicle. This is about life and death. So we need to have an extremely high level of performance, and we understand that the robustness of our supply chain is vital to that performance."

> By 1998, Autoliv realized that it had to cut costs without eroding the quality of its products.

Beginning in 1998, Autoliv embarked on a strategic supply chain initiative that would change the way the company does business. The change began at Autoliv's operations in Utah. The results were so stunning that the new operating paradigm, dubbed the *Autoliv Production System* (APS), is now being rolled out around the globe. "The way we are building equipment today is different [from] the way we built it a year ago, and that change is giving us competitive advantage," Markert says.

ACTUALLY, IT *IS* ROCKET SCIENCE

Autoliv's largest airbag assembly plant is in Ogden, Utah. The plant produces more than 13 million airbag modules a year, supplying automotive makers in North America and Asia. The Ogden plant sits at the end of a

50-mile supply chain linking operations that handle bulk chemicals, textiles, and sophisticated electronic components. The Utah facilities were Morton plants prior to the merger, and they trace their roots to the rocket fuel industry. Morton ASP spun off from Morton Thiokol, which built solid rocket boosters for NASA. Looking to expand into new markets, engineers at Morton Thiokol began exploring airbag technology as a new use for the company's rocket fuel.

An airbag works by the split-second inflation of a textile cushion that, in turn, softens the blow of passenger impact during a crash. The technology required to inflate that cushion precisely when needed, at the right internal pressure, in time to protect the occupants of a car in a crash is the core element of an airbag system. Morton used its chemical expertise to develop an inflator that was, essentially, a small rocket engine mounted within the steering wheel. During an accident, electronic sensors signal the airbag to deploy, starting a pyrotechnic chain reaction. The gas generant pellets inside the inflator burn, generating a rush of exhaust gas that inflates the airbag.

In Utah, Autoliv runs a chemical plant that produces combustible fuel for the airbag systems. The fuel is trucked to a facility where Autoliv manufactures the inflators. Then the inflators are shipped to Autoliv's assembly plant in Ogden, where they are integrated with textile cushions and numerous electronic components to create complete airbag modules for installation in vehicles. This supply chain worked well for years, but in the mid-1990s Autoliv's Utah operation reached the limits of its ability to improve. Autoliv was no longer seeing progress in its key operational metrics, such as defect rate, inventory turns, labor minutes per part, lead time, and the like. With annual price reductions built into its customer contracts, the company could not afford to plateau.

Realizing the dilemma, Autoliv embarked on several internal projects in the mid-1990s to boost efficiency and reduce costs at its Utah operations, but none yielded the desired results. In 1998, the company looked outside for help. It turned to one of its most successful customers, Toyota, which was well established as a pioneer in efficient manufacturing.

Autoliv had a long-standing relationship with Toyota and by 1998 was supplying the automobile maker with nearly 70 percent of its airbag requirements, even though Autoliv faced growing difficulties in getting Toyota exactly what it needed, when it needed it. When Autoliv asked for assistance, Toyota was quick to agree. The automobile maker sent one of its top manufacturing experts, Takashi Harada, to Utah for two years to work with Autoliv managers and teach them the fundamentals of the Toyota Production System.

Toyota paid Harada's salary while on assignment at Autoliv because the automobile maker believed that helping a key supplier adopt and adapt best practices for manufacturing ultimately would be to its benefit. Within three years of Harada's arrival in Utah, Autoliv's manufacturing process would be completely transformed. The changes began on the shop floor in Ogden and rippled back to reshape the company's internal and extended supply chains.

CHOPPING UP THE ASSEMBLY LINES

The Ogden plant was designed originally with 200-foot-long assembly lines. Conveyor systems moved components through the long, linear production process. The lines built airbag modules in large batches. Automated storage and retrieval systems moved 500-pound containers of parts, delivering them from stock areas to stations along the production lines, where they sat until needed. The assembly lines were grouped by customer and tooled up for the needs of that particular automobile maker.

No two cars use the exact same airbag system—not even very similar cars such as the Chevrolet Camaro and the Pontiac Firebird. And subtle variations in design create different crash profiles, requiring different airbag system configurations for every car model. As a result, the production process at the Ogden plant uses hundreds of parts and is subject to frequent changeover, depending on customer demand.

Modeling itself after the Toyota system, Autoliv chopped up those assembly lines and converted the plant to clusters of 20-foot, U-shaped manufacturing cells. Each cell contains all the connected processes that produce a particular airbag module. A typical cell is staffed by four or five workers, all cross-trained to handle each job in the cell. The cells are grouped by product and customer, with significant cross-training among workers on related cells, so shop-floor managers can shift resources to cells where customer demand is the highest.

Gone is some $15 million worth of automated equipment Autoliv had installed to supply the old assembly lines. Now the manufacturing cells are supplied by tuggers delivering small-quantity totes, with each tote containing everything needed for the processes in the cell. When a tote is opened and its contents removed for assembly, an electronic signal is sent back to the supply area so that another tote can be sent to replenish the cell. Based on the *kanban* system developed in Japan, the whole idea is to pull one product through the plant at a time, driven by actual customer demand. It's build to order, not build to stock.

The cell system carries several important advantages. Moving from large-batch production to the very small batches built in cells dramatically increases the plant's flexibility to change from one product mix to another. The bigger the batch run, the more materials are involved, and the longer it takes to change. It's comparable to the difference between turning a cruise ship around and turning a racing car around. "The ability to change over to a new product quickly drives up our asset utilization, drives down lead time, and improves space utilization in our plants," Markert says.

The visual cues inherent in small-cell production have a tremendous impact on efficiency. On a long assembly line designed to build product in large batches, it is impossible actually to "see" the totality of the production process in one glance. This lack of visibility of materials and connected processes made it difficult for Autoliv managers to know how much material was on the floor at any one time and how much needed to be ordered to fulfill customer demand. The plant's legacy enterprise resource planning (ERP) system was running daily, batch-oriented reports, so real-time production data were not available continuously to help managers spot anomalies. As a result, often there were times of excess inventory both of materials and of finished goods, and there were frequent unexpected shortages that forced Autoliv to scramble and ship parts by special freight to avoid shutting down a customer's assembly line.

In contrast, small-cell configurations allow workers and production managers to see the entire manufacturing process at a glance. They can see problems arise and act immediately to address them. The new system makes it much easier for Autoliv to set and monitor precise standards for time and materials in each cell. "Having standards and visual cues is important, so you can tell normal from abnormal," says Tim Ambrey, production control manager for the module facility in Ogden. "The big principle here is having a system in place whereby I can see, just by walking around and looking, if there is an abnormality that needs to be addressed. If I have a criterion for shipment five times a day, with 100 parts in each, and I walk by the loading dock and can see more than 100 parts in a lot, I know there's an abnormality."

Autoliv also has invested in new software that builds on its ERP backbone and provides a continuous flow of production data, monitoring materials as they move through the plant, in order to help manage inventory in near real time instead of by daily reporting. The production data are integrated with advanced forecasting and planning modules, which Autoliv is now implementing globally.

The sequencing of production cells and the design of the components that are assembled in those cells are also vital to the flow of Autoliv's new system. "Our goal is to minimize what's special and increase what's standardized," Markert says. "When you standardize something, you take down cost and reduce cycle time. For each piece we use, we work to build in standard interfaces to enable quick changeovers."

"Our goal is to minimize what's special and increase what's standardized," says Norm Markert, president of Autoliv North America.

Essential to this approach is collaboration between the people who build the products and the engineers who design the products (both internal and from the supply base). Cross-functional teams are set up to make sure that new products are designed with standards that increase modularity and fit well into the APS. In that process, Autoliv includes early input from people who actually will build the airbags. "Before we bring a new product to the floor, we have cell design workshops where the product design engineers, the process engineers, the machine people, and the production people get together as a team and design the production line," says David B. Johnson, forecasting and planning manager for Autoliv's Airbag Module Facility. "Who better than the operators to tell you what works well and what doesn't? They know what motion is hard to do or what process produces a lot of scrap. We're getting user input, and some of the better improvements we've seen on the floor have come from those line operators who are doing the work day in, day out."

After the new production system was fully operational at the Ogden plant, the results were dramatic. Defect rate for parts shipped to the customer dropped 67 percent over two years. Inventory turns increased by 79 percent. Productivity improved 45 percent by reducing labor minutes per part. Total cost per unit dropped 30 percent over four years. Tonnage shipped to landfills was reduced by 41 percent.

The early success in Ogden prompted Autoliv to implement the new production system at its Utah inflator plants, with similar results. The combined accomplishments of the inflator and airbag assembly plants earned Autoliv the 2002 Shingo Prize for Excellence in Manufacturing.

THE UPSTREAM IMPACT ON SUPPLY

Seeing its supply chain as a strategic asset is nothing new for Autoliv. The company has a history of long-term productive relationships with its suppliers. "Our supply base represents over 60 percent of the total manufacturing costs for our products," says Markert. "So we recognize [that] our extended supply chain is vital both from a day-to-day operations sense and for our future process and product development."

For years, Autoliv used all the traditional approaches to manage its extended supply chain. Commodity teams aggregated demand across business units and monitored the global supply markets. Prospective suppliers were qualified carefully, and once engaged, their performance was monitored closely. To support Autoliv's transformation to the new production system modeled after Toyota's, however, the company's supply chain strategy had to evolve.

> ## Autoliv's supply base represents over 60 percent of the total manufacturing costs for its products.

Beyond just tracking cost and performance of each component of the supply chain, Autoliv had to expand its focus and look at the bigger picture—the total cost of ownership of its products and the flow of goods and information from one end of the supply chain to the other. "What we are finding, in many cases, is that there is not a lot of money to be saved in individual parts. The real money to be saved is in the interfaces along the supply chain," Markert says. "There are trade-offs that can be made to realize substantial savings in a system that aren't readily apparent when you are looking at a component level. So that has led us to increased collaboration, both within the company and with our supply base, to identify these interface costs and take them out of the supply chain."

For example, Autoliv's inflator business and its airbag design and assembly business had always operated separately. The inflator unit "sold" products to the airbag unit, and that was the essence of their relationship. The units each worked to cut costs and maximize efficiency, but their individual strategies did not align for the overall benefit of the company. Design changes were made in the inflator technology that saved pennies but forced the airbag designers to make changes that ultimately increased the finished product's cost.

As a result, in the summer of 2002 Autoliv consolidated the manufacturing units into one structure, with all the design teams and assembly units "incentivized" to reduce the total cost of production. "By bringing the systems together, we can make the trade-offs that make sense for the entire enterprise. Now we design the inflator in a way that costs pennies more but captures savings down the line as we integrate it in the airbag,"

Markert explains. "We see many opportunities like that, and we're already capturing substantial savings."

Internal changes, however, would not be sufficient to make Autoliv's new production system work effectively. To meet its objectives, the company had to convince its suppliers to change the way they did business with it. It invested significant resources in supplier development initiatives, precisely as Toyota had done with it. "Because our supply base accounts for 60 percent of the cost of our product, the way they engineer their products, the way they launch their products, the way they assess demand and execute to that demand represents 60 percent of our potential for improvement," says Brett Skinner, director of supplier integration and process development for Autoliv inflators.

At a fundamental level, the suppliers had to agree to make smaller, more frequent deliveries, typically through a cross-dock facility. "Delivery is the key step for the suppliers," Skinner says. "Once we get them to understand why small, frequent deliveries are needed and why it's better for them, then we increase the likelihood for success. If we can get quality and delivery, then we'll work on the systems, and price will follow. And we tell our suppliers straight upfront, we're looking for savings, we're coming after money year in and year out, and we'll help you get there."

As Autoliv executives often say, "Variability costs money." Large-batch production and large shipments are, by definition, subject to larger costs and more waste when demand shifts. This is true for the Ogden plant, as well as for the companies that supply that plant. So Skinner has used the example of the major gains in performance of the Utah operation to develop training programs that will help suppliers make similar improvements. "Our whole approach is to eliminate waste. We focus on quality and delivery, and we take it back upstream to our suppliers—and to our suppliers' suppliers—until we solve the problem that caused the waste," Skinner says. "And when we solve the problem, we have a formal process in place to share the savings with our suppliers."

FROM ONE TIER TO ANOTHER

The case of Greening Donald exemplifies Autoliv's collaborative approach with its suppliers. Based in Ontario, Canada, Greening Donald makes wire-mesh filters for airbag inflators, a key component for Autoliv's products. Autoliv is Greening Donald's biggest customer, but Skinner's team did not use its market clout to dictate the terms of a new relationship with this supplier. Instead, it proposed a collaborative effort that has paid off handsomely for both companies.

"When I first heard that my big customer was going to send a supply-development group to help me run my shop, it wasn't something that I was really looking forward to," says John Rosbottom, production director at Greening Donald. "But now I have nothing but good things to say about it."

Skinner's team helped Greening Donald move from a large-batch production model to a small-batch model and establish standards for every connected process in the production line. A system using cards, or *kanbans,* to pull product through the process was instituted. Within just 14 months of accepting Autoliv's offer to help optimize its production process, Greening Donald cut its scrap volume in half and reduced its inventory of finished goods by 30 percent. "Of all the companies I have ever visited that claimed to be running a lean manufacturing system, Autoliv is by far and away the most impressive," Rosbottom says. "The way that they came to us, understood our processes, and helped us improve the flow of products throughout our facility has really paid off."

The Greening Donald example has been replicated, in varying degrees, with many of Autoliv's biggest suppliers. To further support and enhance collaborative efforts with the supply base and to smooth the interfaces along the supply chain, Autoliv rolled out a new Web-based tool in 2002 called the *Autoliv Partner Portal.* The portal gives its suppliers visibility to all Autoliv's purchasing requirements, standards, production forecasts, terms and conditions, and the status of materials flowing along the supply chain.

IT WORKS, BUT IT'S NOT EASY

From start to finish, including the modest efforts at reform before it turned to Toyota for help, it took Autoliv nearly ten years to fully transform its manufacturing and supply systems. Because of the organizational learning it internalized from that experience, it is helping its suppliers improve at a faster rate. But senior management at Autoliv is quick to point out that change of this magnitude is very hard to achieve and requires complete and active support from the entire organization. "It can't just be an edict," Markert says. "A company has to be willing to invest in a comprehensive

It took Autoliv nearly ten years to fully transform its manufacturing and supply systems.

plan that's local at each site to develop and train the people and put the systems in place."

Autoliv invested millions of dollars and thousands of staff hours in training and organizational development to support its movement to the APS. Furthermore, the initiative is never really over, Markert says. Autoliv is always pushing its people and systems to improve. The company encourages employees to suggest changes and pays a cash bonus for suggestions that improve a process. "We have a lot of open-ended programs where folks come together and work on improvement opportunities. One of our key metrics in human resources is the number of suggestions for improvements that employees put in," Markert says. "Then the trick is to have a structured process to identify what the best practices are and programs to spread those best practices throughout the organization."

2

CHAPTER

Core Discipline 2: Develop an End-to-End Process Architecture

Like any major construction project, your supply chain improvement efforts need a blueprint to succeed. Without a blueprint, you won't be able to envision how the many pieces fit together within the existing infrastructure to form an integrated whole—and you'll encounter delays, rework, and escalating costs. In supply chain management, that blueprint is your supply chain architecture. (See Chapter 6 for an understanding of the essential features of an all-encompassing roadmap to change.)

Your supply chain architecture details the process, applications, and information needed to improve and evolve your supply chain. It integrates rules about the process relationships between business entities and ensures alignment between process and supply chain infrastructure (information technology and physical assets, such as warehouses, factories, etc.).

Companies with supply chain architectures in sync with their business goals have better overall business performance. Their supply chains are "fit for purpose." They're easier to implement and operate. And perhaps most important, they can be reconfigured quickly as business needs change—a valuable source of competitive advantage (see Figure 2-1).

Let's now focus on the process architecture, which includes four primary components:

FIGURE 2–1

Components of the supply chain architecture.

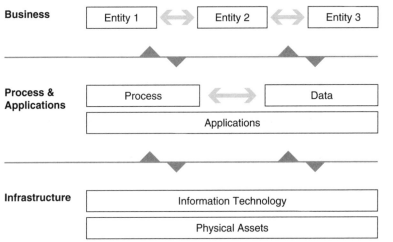

- A description of all supply chain processes (*plan, source, make, deliver,* and *return*) and how they relate to each other
- A view of the interactions between the supply chain processes and other core enterprise processes
- A description of the applications required to support supply chain processes, including the data and performance indicators needed for process execution and control
- A description of how the applications will be integrated, including specific data and frequency of communications

FOUR TESTS OF SUPPLY CHAIN ARCHITECTURE

We find that an effective supply chain process architecture satisfies four tests:

1. *The test of strategic fit.* Your company's overall supply chain strategy must drive the choices you make in your supply chain architecture. Although state-of-the-art practices in supply chain management may be important, your priority should be practices that truly support your basis of competition.

2. *The test of end-to-end focus.* Your supply chain processes must ensure end-to-end management. This requires having an architecture that provides an end-to-end vision of the supply chain and a set of shared objectives that orchestrates the work of each player in your supply chain.

3. *The simplicity test.* A good supply chain architecture is made up of simple, streamlined processes that minimize the complexity that adds cost and reduces manageability. Processes should be clear and easily understood by those who use them.

4. *The integrity test.* Your architecture must be highly reliable, ensuring coherent and robust links among processes, data, and information systems.

Let's look at each of these tests more closely.

Strategic Fit

Some highly touted supply chain practices have been proven to support effective, efficient performance—practices such as only entering customer order data once, considering the total cost of ownership when selecting suppliers, and using a cross-functional scorecard to measure supply chain performance. While these "best practices" may be highly correlated with superior performance, they won't necessarily deliver on your company's supply chain strategy. It's important before deciding *how* you want to operate to think critically about *why* you need to operate a certain way. Market leaders are set apart by their deep understanding of the critical supply chain practices at which they must excel—those which truly support competitive and brand differentiation.

Figure 2-2 shows examples of the critical supply chain practices that enable each of the primary supply chain strategies that we identified in Chapter 1. Although any organization may adopt these practices, their relative importance is determined by a company's specific supply chain strategy.

> It's important before deciding *how* you want to operate to think critically about *why* you need to operate a certain way.

As you think of what practices and processes to make part of your supply chain, consider to what extent they'll drive forward your supply chain strategy. Just as not all supply chain strategies make sense given the overall business strategy, not all practices are equally important given your supply chain strategy.

Amazon, billed as having the "Earth's Biggest Selection," provides a good example of how to select business practices that align with supply chain strategy. The company, which sells millions of different products, stocks only those items designated as top sellers; the vast majority of

FIGURE 2–2

Aligning supply chain practices with the basis of competition.

Primary Strategy	Critical Supply Chain Practices
Innovation	• Design chain / supply chain integration • Collaborative innovation with suppliers • Dedicated NPI supply chain
Cost	• Integrated factory planning and scheduling • Raw materials and manufacturing process standardization • Design for manufacturing, procurement, order management
Service	• Customer collaborative planning • Customer segmentation • Postponement
Quality	• Product and lot-level traceability • Life cycle tracking of sold products

products are offered through partner companies or purchased from distributors when needed to satisfy a customer order. Since this business model means that Amazon does not have direct control over the delivery schedule for most products, it is not possible to conform to the best practice of giving customers an exact delivery date when they place their orders. Providing a shipment date is easy when the product is in stock: The customer is informed that the product "usually ships within 24 hours." Commitments for other products, however, are based on recent actual lead times and are quoted as "usually ships in x days," where x is consistent with recent activity.

Given this failure on the part of Amazon to perform in a "best practice" way, how does the company maintain extremely high customer satisfaction ratings? For one thing, Amazon allows the customer to check order status at any time after an order has been placed and proactively notifies the customer when each product has been shipped. Amazon also provides a link to the carrier's Web site that allows the customer to track order status and the scheduled delivery date after the product has been shipped. The result? Customers benefit from an unparalleled array of products, and Amazon optimizes its inventory investment and keeps supply chain costs low.

The relevance of specific supply chain practices will change as your supply chain strategy changes. When Amazon was founded, developing a core competency in order-fulfillment management was not a key element of the company's strategy. Amazon's original business model was to own no inventory and simply order products directly from manufacturers or distributors as customers placed orders. The supply chain and associated processes were designed to take advantage of the fact that warehousing of the primary product—books—was done already by book distribution companies. Amazon planned simply to place orders to these warehouses and not worry about managing inventory.

However, the company found that this model did not provide adequate control over the supply chain, the customer's experience, and the associated transactions. So it made the decision to build and operate its own warehouses. The company has invested in some costly physical assets but also has become an expert at warehousing. Between 1999 and 2003, through automation and a persistent focus on productivity-enhancing practices, Amazon was able to triple warehouse output productivity. Operating costs fell from nearly 20 percent of total revenues to less than 10 percent. Warehousing performance became so good that Amazon started a side business of running the e-commerce back end of other retailers, including Toys "R" Us and Target.[1]

Allan Lyall, Amazon's vice president of European operations, notes that keeping Amazon's supply chain strategy in line with the company's business strategy is a constant challenge. "It's not like we make fundamental changes to our strategy all the time," he says, "but we do make tweaks. That means we need to tweak the associated supply chain processes. For example, we started experimenting with next-day delivery in certain locations. Everything we had done until that time was based on a model where trucks leave our distribution facilities at 8:00 P.M. With the new strategy, suddenly we had to rethink some of our most basic processes—one pickup per day was not good enough."[2]

Mark Mastandrea, director of fulfillment, explains how constant process improvements are managed: "We place an emphasis on understanding each element of the end-to-end process. So even though we have warehouses that were built at different times and therefore have different levels of automation, we break the process into small enough increments that we can get to the point where we have common denominators that apply across all facilities. Then we do internal benchmarking to understand the best way to perform that particular process, and put those practices in place in the other facilities."

Amazon calls this a *structured methodology* and uses teams consisting of industrial engineers, Six Sigma experts, and representatives from all major functions continuously to "cut" the overall process into increments that can be shared across the company. Mastandrea notes that this approach is effective, even though the warehouse infrastructures can vary significantly. "One warehouse might use processes A and B, and another might use processes A and C. We want to focus on optimizing how we do A [and] then do it the same way in each location."

Today, Amazon has moved to a mixed approach consisting of stocking high-volume products and using partners to inventory lower-volume items, as well as large or irregularly shaped items that use warehouse space inefficiently. The disadvantage of this strategy is maintaining single-shipment orders when items originate in multiple locations. Customers can choose to consolidate all items into a single shipment or have the products ship as each becomes available. If the second option is selected, products are shipped directly from the locations in which they are stocked. In some cases, Amazon may not allow the customer to consolidate all items and will ship certain purchases directly from a partner.

With the consolidation option, customers pay only for a single shipment, but the cost to Amazon actually may be higher than sending multiple shipments. Each nonstocked item is shipped to one distribution center, held until all items are received, and then repackaged and shipped to the customer. Amazon uses highly sophisticated algorithms to plan stocking levels and locations to minimize these split shipments; these algorithms are reviewed and enhanced continuously.

Allowing the customer to choose the delivery mode clearly enhances the customer's experience and also has a significant impact on supply chain processes. Amazon's process design emphasizes the importance of demand planning to predict sales and to determine the appropriate inventory levels to stock at each location. This focus has allowed the company to become highly efficient at organizing warehouses to stock items close together that tend to be purchased at the same time. One indication of the success of tailoring processes to the strategy has been a reduction in order-fulfillment costs to 9.6 percent of sales in the first quarter of 2003 from 10.6 percent in first quarter 2002.[3]

> We caution you to avoid the trap of choosing costly leading-edge practices that provide only marginal support.

While numerous practices can support your chosen strategy effectively, we caution you to avoid the trap of choosing costly leading-edge practices that provide only marginal support. Analyze the contribution that new business practices actually will make, letting your supply chain strategy determine best-practice priorities. These are the practices that you should focus on optimizing.

You know that your architecture has met the test of strategic fit when

+ The value of new practices is quantified before they are integrated into the supply chain architecture.

+ New business practices are prioritized based on their ability to drive forward the supply chain strategy.

+ The supply chain architecture is reviewed regularly to ensure alignment with current strategic direction.

End-to-End Focus

A supply chain architecture with an end-to-end focus identifies where integration—both internal and external—can create value for the company as a whole. By *integration,* we mean shared goals and alignment of the processes, systems, and organizations needed to achieve those goals.

One of our clients, a global manufacturer of computer peripherals, had poor delivery performance relative to its competitors despite maintaining high levels of inventory. The management team did not understand this dichotomy. The company had invested in a costly, worldwide enterprise resource planning (ERP) system to better manage orders, manufacturing, procurement, and accounting and had completed a number of supply chain improvement projects. Despite all this, it still had poor performance and wondered what was accounting for it.

A close look at operating practices revealed that areas such as purchasing, manufacturing, logistics, and sales were focused on achieving their functional objectives—at the expense of enterprise-level outcomes. For example, manufacturing had redesigned its production facilities, set up just-in-time (JIT) supplier deliveries, and boosted production quality with impressive results. Total production time, for instance, had been cut to less than four hours, best in class for the industry. Similarly, the company's logistics department had achieved industry-leading transportation costs by putting in place such practices as allowing only full truckloads to move product from manufacturing facilities to distribution centers.

Because the company didn't have an end-to-end view of the supply chain, however, these "good" practices actually were hurting its delivery performance. The company's order-management system assumed that product was shipped shortly after production and confirmed customer delivery dates based on the end-production date plus a fixed transportation lead time. As a result, customer orders were being confirmed with delivery dates that couldn't be met. Without a focus on end-to-end supply chain processes, overall results suffered: Despite having more than 80 days of finished-goods inventory, on-time delivery performance to customer commit date was only 75 percent, compared with 85 percent for the industry leader.

To fix the problem, the company put in place new supply chain processes with a focus on overall business performance. One of the first steps was to define company-level cross-functional objectives—what we call *end-to-end targets*. To set the targets, the project team created a supply chain scorecard (which we discuss in more detail in Chapter 5). The critical need to improve customer service and working capital led to targets based on four metrics:

- *On-time delivery (to commit date)*. The percentage of orders fulfilled on or before the internal commit date. Delivery measurements are based on the date a complete order is shipped.
- *Order fulfillment lead time*. Average, consistently achieved lead time (in calendar days) from customer order origination to customer order receipt.
- *Cash-to-cash cycle time*. The time it takes for cash to flow back into the company after it has been spent on external purchases. Cash-to-cash cycle time is calculated as total inventory days of supply plus days of sales outstanding minus average payment period for materials.
- *Total supply chain management cost*. Total cost to manage orders, acquire materials, manage and hold inventory, and manage supply chain finance, planning, and information technology costs, represented as a percent of revenue.

Targets for each of these metrics were based on industry benchmarks, and goals for each function were then aligned to these business-level objectives (see Figure 2-3).

Within each region, finished-goods inventory was held at both the regional distribution center and the country warehouses. Each country managed its own supply chain operations. This practice led to different work practices and dedicated inventory in each country. As a result, there

Collaborative planning within the enterprise.

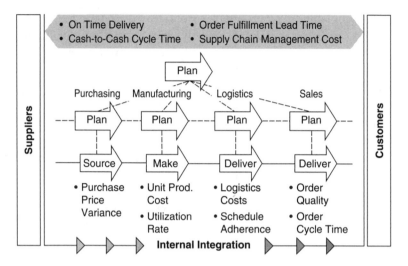

was no inventory visibility at the regional level, and there could be a short-age in one country and excess inventory in another for the same product. In addition, although each region was up and running on the worldwide ERP implementation, different countries used their own stand-alone information systems to manage warehousing and transportation.

To put in place an end-to-end management capability, the company had to redesign its supply chain processes and embrace many new practices. One of the first goals was to make better use of the ERP system by consolidating country-level inventory data into a single database to provide inventory visibility at the regional level. Given the promotion-driven nature and short product life cycles of consumer electronics, the company also focused on shortening order-fulfillment times. By consolidating product-customization activities—previously done in each country—into one regional center and shipping directly to customers, the company was able to shorten lead times and eliminate the need for country-based inventories.

The company reduced the supply chain planning cycle dramatically by redefining the sales forecasting and supply planning processes. The previous processes were based on monthly cycles and provided limited visibility into actual customer demand patterns. The project team set up a weekly cross-functional supply chain planning process using the existing

ERP platform and put in place a new advanced planning system (APS). The APS-enabled demand planning led by sales and supply planning managed by logistics, manufacturing, and purchasing. Using the new planning process, the planning group analyzed current sales data and promotion information each week to decide on adjustments to the supply chain plan.

Although these actions improved overall performance, it became clear that the company would need to improve the flexibility of its external suppliers if its delivery performance targets were to be met. Supplier lead times were long, and the ability to make changes to existing orders was limited. Greater supplier flexibility was needed to avoid costly inventory buildup of products that no longer matched market demand. The company identified the need to integrate business processes with internal key-component suppliers as a priority. Vendor-managed inventory (VMI) was implemented, replenishing component inventories at final assembly factories. High-value items from Asia were replenished weekly by air. This new collaborative planning process cut supplier lead time by 50 percent for some key components and greatly increased supply flexibility (see Figure 2-4).

As this company's experience shows, putting in place an end-to-end process is a major undertaking. Defining and deploying new shared objectives is at the heart of the end-to-end supply chain and can be even more

FIGURE 2-4

Collaborative planning in the extended enterprise.

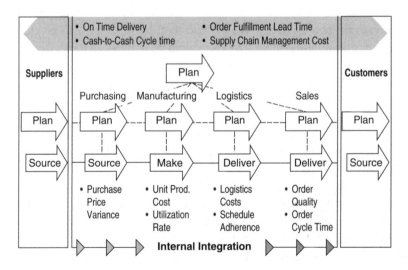

challenging than defining and implementing new practices and information systems. It's critical that companies take the time to define those shared objectives, whether for internal integration among functions or for external integration with customers and suppliers. Without shared objectives, it doesn't make sense to invest in end-to-end processes.

When a supply chain architecture meets the test of end-to-end focus

* Processes and supporting information systems are integrated within and beyond the enterprise—reaching key suppliers and customers.

> Without shared objectives, it doesn't make sense to invest in end-to-end processes.

* Supply chain resources such as capacity and inventory are optimized across the organization and with key suppliers and customers.
* Standard metrics and quantitative objectives are shared across the organization and with key suppliers and customers.
* Performance visibility and management are shared across the organization and with key suppliers and customers.

Simplicity

Complex supply chains are hard to understand, improve, and manage because complexity obstructs the "line of sight" needed to identify what is and what is not working. The costs and risks of complexity are highest when companies integrate their processes and systems with those of their customers and suppliers. When effective supply chain management is dependent on managing beyond your company's borders, each process, data element, and system must be clearly defined and agreed to. And if your internal processes, data, and systems are complex or convoluted, the likelihood of your being able to reach consensus with your supply chain partners is greatly reduced. Simplicity is the solution. But before we see how this complexity can be simplified, let's examine the different drivers of complexity. We see four:

* Supply chain configuration
* Product and service proliferation
* Process and information systems inconsistency
* Overautomation

Supply Chain Configuration

The first source of complexity is your supply chain configuration—how you've structured your network of physical assets and distributed activities within that network. The decisions you make to support your channel strategy, operations strategy, and other components of your supply chain strategy can lead to complex supply chain configurations. And complex configurations drive process complexity. Do you have a large number of order-entry desks, warehouses, factories, engineering centers, and other physical locations? Are you trying to manage too many customer and supplier relationships directly? Each location and relationship is another node in the supply chain that must be designed and managed.

Consider how Alcatel Enterprise, Europe's largest provider of business voice and data Internet Protocol (IP) servers, simplified its supply chain configuration for business advantage. In the late 1990s, Alcatel management realized that the market for its products—business handsets and PBXs—was maturing. The company had to find a way to improve customer service without increasing costs. Alcatel wanted to provide faster transactions with better traceability while reducing inventory levels and eliminating the need for multiple suppliers across different geographic regions.[4]

For Alcatel, the answer was to adopt a cost-based supply chain strategy with a much simpler supply chain configuration; in its case, this meant outsourcing supply chain operations not considered core competencies.

Many of these activities were part of the *deliver* process—getting equipment to customers, having it installed, and then initiating service. The company decided to move most sales, installation, and service activities to its channel partners, resulting in the percentage of indirect sales growing from 25 percent in 2001 to 95 percent in 2002. In addition, Alcatel worked on simplifying the interactions with channel partners, creating an extranet, the Alcatel Business Partner Web site, that sharply reduced order-management costs by replacing electronic data interchange (EDI), fax, and mail orders with self-service processes.

Alcatel used the move to indirect sales as an opportunity to streamline physical distribution of its products around the world. The company managed a huge number of logistics service providers—more than 30 in Europe alone. This complexity made it difficult to measure and improve supply chain performance, so it decided to move all final packaging and distribution from internal operations to a fourth-party logistics provider (4PL). Alcatel chose UPS Logistics, and UPS now manages relationships with logistics specialists covering such operations as kitting, storage, inspection, final tests, picking and packing, and customer delivery.[5]

Alcatel Enterprise created four standard processes to guide UPS and to ensure integration with its manufacturing, sourcing, and sales departments. Instead of producing to stock based on forecasts, Alcatel used demand frequency, volume, and item value to design differentiated processes that minimized inventory risks while meeting service requirements:

* *Configure to order* applies to telephones with documentation, cables, accessories, etc.

* *Build to customer order* applies to complete systems (chassis and boards) built and integrated per customer order and requirements.

* *Pick to order* applies to high-volume printed circuit boards (PCBs).

* *Purchase to consumer order* applies to high-value peripherals procured from external suppliers.

As a result of these changes, customer delivery-to-commit-date performance improved from 65 percent in 1999 to 95 percent in 2001, whereas total supply chain costs declined from 5.8 to 5.1 percent of revenue.[6]

Product and Service Proliferation

Another key driver of supply chain complexity is product and service proliferation. There are two primary causes. The first is a failure to phase out or retire certain products as they are replaced by newly introduced alternatives. The other cause is related to the availability of technologies that allow organizations to "mass customize" their product offerings. These systems, combined with increasingly high customer expectations for products tailored to specific requirements, can lead to an enormous number of product and service offerings. Most companies, therefore, find that they tend to carry an ever-increasing number of products and services. This means more items to *plan, source, make,* and *deliver*—all of which drive supply chain costs and inventory.

Motorola's mobile phone division wrestled with product proliferation. Mobile phones have hundreds of components—aerials, battery connectors, PCBs, connectors, integrated circuits, keyboards, liquid-crystal display (LCD) screens, lenses, microphones, phone housings, screws, speakers, and more. Planning for and procuring these components is a challenge in this fast-moving market. Because of this complexity and the growing cost of high inventory levels, Motorola analyzed its component mix, seeking ways to cut back. As it turned out, the company was using far too many nonstandard and product-specific components, many of which could not be justified. By standardizing components to a greater degree, Motorola was able to greatly improve flexibility and sharply reduce inventory obsolescence and rework costs.[7]

Process and Systems Inconsistency

A third driver of complexity is inconsistent processes and information systems throughout the supply chain. We often find that different locations within the same company have different, incompatible processes. Even when the same software package is installed, it's often configured differently, in keeping with each location's process. Inconsistency can result from acquisitions, but more typically it arises because companies are simply not aware of the benefits of a standard process architecture—or haven't invested the resources needed to create one.

> Inconsistency can result from acquisitions, but more typically it arises because companies are simply not aware of the benefits of a standard process architecture.

When different locations have different processes and systems, the company loses speed and efficiency and is less able to leverage knowledge across the organization. And each location means added investment and maintenance costs. Inconsistency also creates inflexibility. Work can't be transferred among locations as demand shifts because each site works differently. Moreover, cross-site leverage in terms of shared back-office activities, such as strategic sourcing, is harder to achieve. Finally, process and information inconsistency makes it difficult to integrate with customers, suppliers, and other business partners.

Overautomation

The emergence of decision-making applications for supply chain planning and performance management has led to a new driver of supply chain complexity: overautomation. Overautomated processes are difficult to manage because the people who use them don't completely understand how they work. Without this understanding, users can't judge the quality of their output or improve their performance.

Supply chain planning tools offer powerful functionality, but rules and algorithms need to be selected carefully, for these systems contain far more features than are needed by most organizations, with some functionality better adapted to some industries than to others. And trying to build models that represent very complex operating environments can itself be a cause of failure. One leading company in the semiconductor industry simply turned off its system after a two-year effort at building a model that represented its multitier global manufacturing network.

No matter how you focus your improvement efforts, address supply chain complexity as a priority. Complexity is the single greatest cause of poor investment returns in supply chain management. Even without major changes to business practices, companies can improve performance greatly just by making their operations more manageable and creating the visibility that comes with simplification. In addition, simplifying the existing supply chain is a necessary first step toward more advanced supply chain practices, especially in supplier and customer collaboration.

You'll know that your supply chain architecture meets the simplicity test if

Complexity is the single greatest cause of poor investment returns in supply chain management.

+ Supply chain process architecture standardization rules are defined and enforced.
+ Product and service complexity and related costs are measured and tightly managed.
+ Standards for components and materials are defined and adhered to.
+ The physical supply chain configuration (warehouses, order desks, factories, supplier locations, distribution centers) is reviewed regularly and simplified where possible.

Integrity

Your improvement efforts will encounter major delays and budget overruns if your supply chain architecture doesn't have integrity in the form of integrated applications, accurate data, and documented processes. You can't introduce new supply chain practices without a solid foundation.

During the IT investment boom of the late 1990s, many companies added new best-in-breed applications such as advanced planning and scheduling, customer relationship management (CRM), and supplier relationship management (SRM) to their portfolios of systems. These applications often were added without fully reworking the underlying business processes and data. Despite the advent of enterprise application integration tools, the skills needed to create bulletproof integration were not available, and software vendors were slow to provide off-the-shelf integration for common ERP packages. Advances such as portal technology, which can connect multiple locations with multiple applications, are helping to resolve these integration challenges, but many companies still have "applications islands" (see Figure 2-5)— stand-alone applications that support only one piece of the end-to-end process.

The best supply chains have an integrated flow of information. Unfortunately, too many companies use nonintegrated applications that require manual data reentry, changes in data formats, and multiple quality checks. Missing links between processes and information systems result in fragile supply chains that depend on specific individuals, manual handoffs, and work-arounds. The result is a high risk of error, longer cycle times, and added costs.

FIGURE 2–5

Application islands do not support process integration.

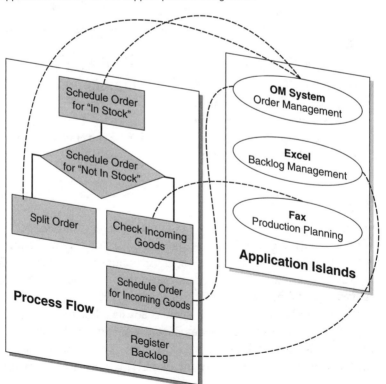

For example, one of our clients was implementing new demand/supply planning processes, supported by a supply chain planning application. As part of the new process, the company wanted to track forecast consumption over time to ensure that demand and supply were balanced on an ongoing basis. This required gathering data from two separate sources—an existing CRM application, which held data related to customer orders, and the new supply chain planning application, which contained information about incoming supply. Unfortunately, the ordering information described products one way, whereas the planning application used different data to describe products for the purpose of planning. The chief information officer was concerned that resolving this disconnect would require restructuring the entire data model, a major undertaking. In the end, an answer was found that integrated the flow of information between the two applications. A translation table was developed that took the elements of a customer's order and translated them into planning items.

Data quality and availability are as important as integration between applications. The typical company orchestrates hundreds, if not thousands, of supply chain activities and decisions every day, each depending on a wide range of data: master data (supplier lead times, material masters, prices, terms and conditions), transaction data (sales orders, inventory data, purchase orders, etc.), and analytics (which compare actual performance with target performance to ensure process management). Despite the importance of accurate data, one study estimates that between 15 and 20 percent of a typical organization's data are wrong or unusable.[8]

Inaccurate or missing data lead to errors and ineffective execution. Consider the example of a procurement system that captures quantities ordered and confirmed by suppliers but doesn't capture backorders—quantities ordered but not confirmed. Backorder management must be done either manually, at the risk of error, or not at all, which could easily lead to overordering and excess inventory.

Inaccurate or unusable data also create manual work, reducing speed and efficiency and adding costs to the supply chain. In the worst case, inaccurate data can drive poor performance. As an example, we had a client that felt the repercussions of inaccurate data for almost a year after it first implemented a supply chain planning solution. When preparing for the cutover to the new system, it had entered standard defaults for supply lead times, with every intention of updating the data before the "go live" date. Unfortunately, day-to-day tasks took precedence, and no one got around to updating the supplier lead-time data—resulting in an increase in materials inventory (lead times too short) for some materials and inventory shortages (lead times too long) for others.

As cleaning and structuring data become top priorities for a growing number of companies, applications that support data quality control are becoming more popular. At many companies, data maintenance is a part of ongoing management processes; data administration positions even have been created specifically to maintain data quality.

A key driver behind this push for data quality is a growing awareness of the costs associated with poor data in transactions such as ordering and invoicing. A study of the electronics industry by the U.S.-based National Electrical Manufacturers Association (NEMA) revealed that product and pricing inaccuracies were costing manufacturers and distributors 1 and 0.75 percent of sales, respectively.[9] These percentages may not sound particularly alarming, but for a $200 million manufacturing company, that's an added cost of $2 million.

New industry initiatives to address data quality continue to emerge. In the retail industry, for instance, the Uniform Code Council started an organization called UCCnet to provide item data synchronization, standards validation, and a global item registry for retailers and their suppliers. By creating a single set of data usable by all, UCCnet plans to drive out the costs associated with invoice and order errors and the time spent on data quality. NEMA has created the Industry Data Exchange Association (IDEA) to do the same for its industry.

When a supply chain architecture meets the test for integrity

+ Required integration between applications is defined in the supply chain process architecture, and the impact of application integration issues on business performance is measured.

+ Processes are documented at each level of the supply chain architecture, with clear descriptions of the data required to execute each process.

+ Data quality is measured and managed, with clear ownership for data creation and maintenance.

ARCHITECTURAL TOOLKITS

Just as a blueprint describes the construct of a building and how each element fits together, your supply chain architecture should describe the construct of your processes and how they interact. In order to be effective, this needs to be done using clear, unambiguous terms. Just agreeing on a definition of what "the supply chain is," though, can be a major challenge. This task has been complicated by the use of many similar-sounding and interrelated terms—*supply chain, demand chain, supply network, demand/supply network, value chain*—many of which sound as though they could mean the same thing but in fact do not.

It is difficult to say exactly when the term *supply chain* came into vogue and even more difficult to find a universally acceptable definition for exactly what a supply chain is. In our work with client companies in the past, we found that many were unable to reach agreement on a supply chain definition. And even when there was agreement inside the enterprise, customers and suppliers might have a very different interpretation. This lack of common understanding led to inconsistencies in how processes were executed and frequent miscommunication about what was expected by one organization of another.

> Your supply chain architecture should describe the construct of your processes and how they interact.

This problem clearly was evident in the 1990s, as issues associated with operational planning and execution beyond the boundaries of a specific organization became a major focus for executive management teams. In the past, most operational process-improvement efforts had focused primarily on improving the performance of internal processes. But new technologies, outsourcing, and the increasing customization of supply chains to meet the needs of key customers meant that supply chain development increasingly looked outside the "four walls."

It became clear that a set of standard definitions for each supply chain planning, execution, and enabling activity was needed. In the mid-1990s, PRTM developed a framework, or process reference model, that included descriptions of supply chain processes and key performance indicators to help our clients benefit from the emerging "science" of supply chain management.[10] We were well aware of the value of process reference models, having earlier created PACE® (Product And Cycle-time Excellence®), which has been adopted widely by companies worldwide to get better products to market faster.[11]

In our supply chain framework, we defined the supply chain as consisting of four processes: *plan, source, make,* and *deliver*. For target setting and performance management, we defined metrics for each of these processes and for overall supply chain performance. We defined the scope of the supply chain as all interactions "from the supplier's supplier to the customer's customer"—a network of organizations linked together by physical, informational, and financial flows designed to satisfy end-customer requirements. Our goal was to ensure that supply chains could be described unambiguously, communicated consistently, redesigned to achieve competitive advantage, and measured, managed, controlled, and refined to meet a specific purpose.

Recognizing the need for a true cross-industry standard, in 1995 PRTM joined forces with AMR Research, an independent research firm committed to providing unbiased analysis of the enterprise software sector. Together, PRTM and AMR founded the Supply-Chain Council (SCC), which initially included 69 member companies. Over the course of a year, the three organizations further developed and refined this standard, called the Supply-Chain Operations Reference-model (SCOR) that defined best practices, performance metrics, and software functionality requirements for each core supply chain process, subprocess, and activity.[12] The SCOR model provides a framework and standardized terminology to help organizations integrate a number of management tools, such as business process reengineering, benchmarking, and best-practice analysis. The SCOR toolbox enables organizations to develop and manage effective supply chain architectures.

Using the SCOR model's top-down design method, an organization can quickly gain an understanding of its current supply chain performance and architecture. It also can compare its own architecture with that of other organizations, identify improvements based on best practices, and design its future supply chain architecture. Since its release in 1996, more than 700 companies have adopted the SCOR model.

In 1996, the Supply Chain Council became an independent, not-for-profit professional association, and the SCOR model was entrusted to it. Since launch of the SCC, the council has grown, establishing international chapters in Europe, Japan, Australia/New Zealand, Southeast Asia, and southern Africa, in addition to North America. Members have continued to advance the SCOR model, adding the *return* process in 2001 and periodically updating recommended practices and metrics. We expect that the model will continue to evolve as the "science" of supply chain management advances (see Figure 2-6 for the top two levels of the SCOR model and Appendix C for a complete listing of metrics in levels 2 and 3).

While the SCOR model is the only framework of its kind for developing a supply chain architecture, other complementary initiatives have emerged that focus on industry-specific practices and implementation-level detail, such as data standards. Two such initiatives that have been adopted widely in recent years are Collaborative Planning, Forecasting, and Replenishment (CPFR) and RosettaNet.

FIGURE 2–6

SCOR version 6.0 level 2 toolbox.

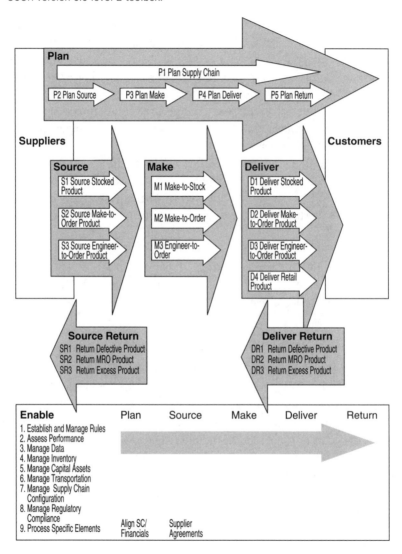

CPFR focuses on the packaged goods and retail sectors. It was created in 1997 through a collaborative effort involving over 30 companies and is managed by the Collaborative Commerce Standards Institute. The CPFR standard is made up of detailed process definitions, required data elements, and metrics for the customer-supplier interface. CPFR's objective is to improve the partnership between retailers and vendor merchants through shared information.[13]

Formed in 1998, the RosettaNet consortium is composed mainly of companies in the electronics and telecommunications industries and is managed by the Uniform Code Council, a leading commerce standards organization. RosettaNet develops Internet-based business standards to align processes through standard data definitions called *partner-interface processes* (PIPs). Widely adopted by the technology sector, PIPs support automated real-time information exchange between companies and cover a broad range of transactions, including inventory management, order management, and ship from stock.[14]

We will be focusing on the SCOR model in this chapter because, to our knowledge, it is the most widely accepted supply chain reference model in use. In fact, it is being adopted by the largest supply chain organization in the world, the U.S. Department of Defense (see Department of Defense profile).

Through its structure and method, the SCOR model makes what might be a monumental undertaking—creating a supply chain architecture—a manageable task. As in a construction project, the SCOR model provides a set of tools to be used in developing the supply chain blueprint.

THE TOP THREE LEVELS OF THE SCOR MODEL

The SCOR model has four levels of detail, the first three of which— processes, subprocesses, and activities—are described in the model. Operable processes, or level 4, are detailed workflow-level tasks and are always customized to an organization's specific strategy and requirements. As such, they are not included in the published version of the model.

Starting with level 1 and ending with level 3, the content of the SCOR model can be used to translate business strategy into a supply chain architecture designed to achieve your specific business objectives. The exact order in which you use the different levels of the SCOR model will depend on your specific business needs and starting point. We will be describing the operational and business benefits that result from configuring supply chains using the SCOR model in this chapter.

SCOR Level 1

At level 1, you confirm how business processes will align with your high-level business structure (business units, regions, etc.) and supply chain partners and refine your supply chain's strategic objectives—the business priorities that your supply chain must support. Level 1 focuses on the five major supply chain processes (*plan, source, make, deliver,* and *return*). Using these processes, the alignment between process and organizational domains can be established to describe where processes must be standardized across entities. Choices at level 1 drive information systems costs because different processes across business units typically involve multiple applications and the associated implementation and maintenance costs. In addition, level 1 decisions also will determine whether an organization will be able to implement certain business practices. For example, does the *source* process need to be standardized between two business units or are differences justified? If the goal is to consolidate volume across multiple business units to gain leverage with suppliers, standardization of a good part of the *source* process will be needed.

Once business processes and organizational domains are aligned, setting performance targets for these key process areas is an important next step. The SCOR model provides a supply chain scorecard for setting and managing supply chain performance targets across the organization. The specific metrics are described in Chapter 5. This step is one of the most critical—and difficult—activities in supply chain design because of the need to gain internal consensus on targets and priorities. It is driven by your supply chain strategy, as discussed in Chapter 1.

As an example, one of our clients, a leader in the consumer electronics industry, was losing market share to competitors with a strong focus on specific market segments. The company had long been organized as a single, centralized business structure and recognized the need to transform to multiple, market-facing business units in order to compete effectively.

> The SCOR model provides a supply chain scorecard for setting and managing supply chain performance targets across the organization.

Once the new business units had been established, executive management reviewed both the strategic vision and the related supply chain requirements for each. Prior to the reorganization, all supply chain processes (*plan, source, make, deliver,* and *return*), supporting information systems, and assets had been shared. The company also had outsourcing policies that limited contract manufacturing to end-of-life products, as well as other rules that limited product customization to control unit costs and maximize inventory flexibility. Deciding which of these policies to keep and which to change was critical to establishing the new strategic boundaries for supply chain design.

In order to establish these boundaries, each business unit developed its own business strategy and performance objectives and then summarized the resulting implications for its supply chain. Given the critical importance of materials costs (up to 85 percent of product cost), product quality, and time to market, it was decided to maintain the shared *plan*, *source*, *make*, *deliver*, and *return* processes and assets while changes were made to inventory policies for each business unit to meet the specific service requirements of the different end markets.

SCOR Level 2

At level 2, you refine your choice of supply chain processes and confirm how supply chain processes align with your infrastructure (physical locations and information technology). Also called the *configuration level,* level 2 involves developing and evaluating high-level options for the supply chain process architecture by choosing the "flavors" of *plan, source, make, deliver, and return*. This is done by selecting the relevant subprocesses— or *process categories*—based on your supply chain strategy, The selection of process categories will drive level 3 design because each category requires very different detailed activities.

For example, manufacturing companies have a number of options for how they will produce their products. They can build in anticipation of customer orders (make to stock), build only after a firm customer order is in hand (make to order), build to a semifinished level and complete the build after an order is received (configure to order), or build the product based on specifications that are unique to the customer and therefore require detailed engagement in advance of starting any work (engineer to order).

Once the process categories are chosen, they are used to describe existing supply chain configurations. This typically takes the form of a geographic map showing where your customers, suppliers, warehouses, factories, and order desks are and using the process categories to describe the major physical and informational flows. In essence, this is like taking an inventory of the processes in use today and where they occur.

Once you understand the current configurations, you can develop and test "to be" options. Be aware, however, that the SCOR level 2 analysis may show you that you cannot optimize what you want because of existing limitations, such as excessive transportation costs. In other words, you may not be able to execute all your "to be" requirements in the near term and will need to develop a roadmap to move progressively toward your target configuration (see Chapter 6).

One of our clients, an international aerospace company, was struggling to manage a complex web of relationships among its own sales, logistics, and manufacturing operations; several key subcontractors; and a major customer, an aircraft manufacturer. The company was a prime contractor in a commercial aircraft program. Ensuring on-time delivery of its subsystem to the customer's final assembly and testing facility required coordinating material, information, and financial flows with subcontractors located on three continents.

Supplier deliveries for the commercial jet program were increasingly late. And when the aircraft manufacturer asked to reschedule orders, the company had to contact its suppliers before providing a confirmation date—a process that took several weeks. Because of these problems, the company was struggling to maintain its credibility with a key account. It used the SCOR model to gain a greater understanding of the underlying problems.

The project team used the SCOR model to map order management, procurement, physical distribution, supply chain planning, and financial flows at the company, as well as all key interfaces with subcontractors. Each activity was associated with a SCOR level 2 process category. For the first time, the company had clear visibility of the subsystem's supply chain as a whole and was able to see which activities were performed by the company, the customer, and subcontractors. In addition, the use of standard process category definitions meant that each constituent was using the same definition for the processes for the first time.

Opportunities to simplify the supply chain were quickly apparent. For example, major subassemblies moved through multiple internal warehouses before being made available for final assembly. This caused significant delay yet added no additional value to the product. The level 2 process map showed the reason for this. All products were routed to a regional consolidation platform. Once they entered the platform, there was an official transfer of ownership from internal manufacturing to the aircraft program. The team realized that a change in process and supporting information systems would allow some product to be shipped directly to the final preparation point near the customer's assembly line, eliminating several weeks in the delivery cycle.

Interestingly, the visibility created by the SCOR process map also forced the company to rethink some long-held beliefs about what was causing customer service to be below desired levels. It had long thought that the order-management process—where orders were transferred automatically from the customer into one system and then manually rekeyed into another system for financial management before communication to suppliers—was the cause of order delays. The analysis showed that although rekeying added costs and introduced potential errors, the management of subcontractors was a much larger problem. The existing process included communication of planned requirements to key subcontractors as part of a formal ordering process, where the suppliers also confirmed quantities and delivery dates. But supplier updates regarding schedule slippages, as well as communication of changes in order volume from the prime contractor, were managed in a less formal manner. Some of the major changes defined by the team included new roles for procurement, monthly subcontractor planning reviews, a process to adjust previously agreed-on plans, and business rules to guide manufacturing schedule changes at the subcontractor. The company's multimonth effort delivered dramatic results: Supplier on-time deliveries improved by more than 20 percent, and order confirmation times were cut sharply. Today, the company can confirm customer orders in two to three days rather than two to three weeks, and customer confidence has been restored.

SCOR Level 3

SCOR level 3 is also called the *process-element level;* this is where you can complete your supply chain architecture by adding operational detail to your SCOR level 2 design. Within SCOR level 3 you will find specific business practices, associated metrics, and guidance about the information systems needed to support the process—in terms of both functionality and supporting data. The tools you'll need to do this work have been assembled for you already. You will develop "as is" maps illustrating the alignment between processes, locations, and organizations. These maps typically will show where inventory is located, the lead times between process elements, and the alignment between process elements and supply chain information systems.

By applying basic lean principles, the level 3 "as is" analysis can reveal a number of improvement opportunities driven by the configuration, including reducing process and information systems complexity, creating better linkages between end-customer demand and end production, eliminating similar activities conducted in multiple locations, and reducing wait time and the associated inventory and customer lead times.

In addition to analyzing the overall configuration, you also will consider best practices, applications, metrics, and organizational models as part of your level 3 "to be" design. By analyzing your current capabilities versus your "to be" design, you'll understand the implications for the existing processes and information systems. Typical information systems implications include system gaps, missing data, and insufficient integration between information systems. Then you can evaluate each "to be" option based on the business criteria set at SCOR level 1 and choose which to develop at the operable level (level 4) of detail needed for a real working solution.

Case in point: We worked with a large retailer that needed to reduce inventory levels without sacrificing service. The company has hundreds of retail locations, ranging from megastores to neighborhood grocery outlets. It had grown through acquisition, and as new acquisitions were made, the acquired businesses were established as independent business units. Some functions were shared, including purchasing, warehouse management, and accounting. For the most part, however, each business unit was allowed to operate independently, maintaining its own processes and information systems. This practice led to very high information-systems costs due to different applications, each requiring dedicated, ongoing support.

The company had been frustrated by several failed efforts to improve its overall performance; it had spent months mapping its key processes and analyzing the resulting improvement opportunities. Still, the project team was not able to reach agreement on the "to be" supply chain. The major roadblock was the lack of an overall architecture. Team members were not even able to agree on which processes were part of the supply chain and which were not! Moreover, processes within specific functions were well defined, but those which cut across functions, such as supply chain planning, were not.

To break the deadlock, the team used SCOR level 3 to map its current processes. An analysis of the *deliver* process elements showed that the physical supply chain was highly optimized in terms of warehousing operations and that highly developed processes were in place to ensure the best handling of its products from suppliers to retail locations. Examination of warehouse practices revealed the adoption of many leading-edge warehouse management practices, such as picking and order preparation using voice-recognition technology.

An analysis of the *plan* and *source* process elements revealed that the supply chain had been optimized to move high volumes of consumer favorites that were purchased every day in predictable volumes. The team closely examined how demand was calculated at each level of the supply chain, starting with the retail store, moving back to the warehouse, and finally moving on to the supplier.

Using *plan source* process elements (see Figure 2-7), the team realized that information on actual sell-through at the store was not used in planning requirements for suppliers and that each store placed orders on the warehouses based on its best view of demand. Using the P 2.1 process element—identify, prioritize, and aggregate product requirements—the team saw that distribution warehouses that supplied the retail outlets were pulling inventory from suppliers based on historical demand patterns for all products—which was fine as long as demand was consistent with historical levels.

In actuality, of course, demand patterns for many products were highly variable, particularly in the cases of new products, store-level promotions, and the periodic introduction of seasonal merchandise. These events distorted demand patterns, creating a baseline demand that was appropriate only for a specific time period. This meant undersupply at the

FIGURE 2-7

Using *plan source* for better performance.

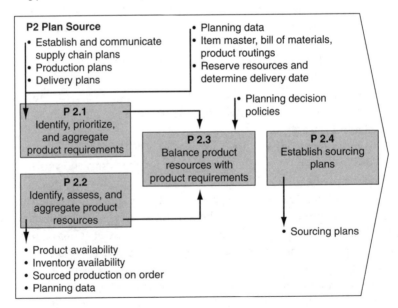

beginning of a promotion and oversupply at the end. The team realized that major changes would be required to planning, including the introduction of collaborative planning with suppliers during promotions and new product introductions.

Making the change to the plan process would have a major impact on existing information systems. And gaining full acceptance of the new process architecture would require involvement of a broader team. Following its initial work using SCOR level 3, the company initiated an enterprise project involving both business managers and information systems managers to further develop the new process and information systems architecture.

As can be seen by these examples, SCOR provides a structured approach to developing a supply chain architecture. SCOR's top-down approach, which moves progressively into more detail, allows you to see the big picture before moving into greater levels of detail. And the model's hierarchical structure, which breaks down processes into subprocesses and activities, means that companies can see how changes will affect the existing supply chain operations. This helps to clarify risks, needed resources, and implementation timelines. For typical benefits of using SCOR, see Figure 2-8.

FIGURE 2–8

Benefits of using each level of SCOR.

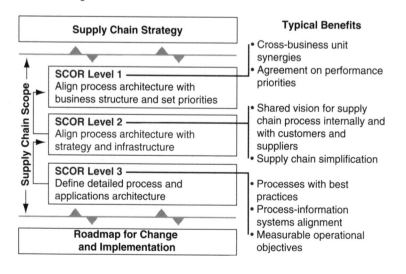

FIVE PROCESSES FOR END-TO-END SUPPLY CHAIN MANAGEMENT

As you develop your own supply chain process architecture, you will need to ensure that each process is integrated not only with the other supply chain processes but also with other enterprise processes such as technology, product and service development, marketing and sales, customer support, and finance. We'll be discussing a number of principles specific to each process design that will help you to drive best-in-class performance.

Plan

Every supply chain process has inputs and outputs. *Plan*'s input is information on demand, supply, and supply chain resources. This information enables better decision making and guides all supply chain activities related to the execution processes—*source, make, deliver*, and *return*. Each of the execution processes has a planning element. For example, *plan source* and *plan make* outline the raw materials needed, the source of those materials, and the quantities of inventory to be produced. *Plan deliver* provides the information needed to commit to customer orders. And *plan return* provides the information needed to schedule returns and replacement orders.

Planning-process excellence contributes to superior business performance by ensuring that decisions are timely and well prepared and that their implications are understood, agreed on, and feasible. Planning excellence has five key principles:

- ♦ *Use timely, accurate information.* From a demand standpoint, this means information on real-time customer and market demand based on such factors as end-user consumption, downstream inventory levels, economic conditions, and market intelligence. Use data from key customers when possible. From a supply standpoint, it means understanding the critical internal and external resources needed to satisfy demand, such as labor, inventory, manufacturing capacity, suppliers, and warehouses. To develop a full view of needed resources, it is necessary to get information from each of the execution processes—*source, make, deliver*, and *return*. Since both demand and supply are dynamic, what's accurate today probably won't be tomorrow. This is why timely information is so critical.

- *Focus resources on business priorities. Plan* is the supply chain process that balances internal objectives (inventory, cost, and asset utilization) with external objectives (service levels, volume flexibility, etc.) while ensuring that decisions support customer- and market-segment priorities.
- *Aim for simplicity.* Make your *plan* processes as simple as possible. Realistic and executable outputs typically require taking into account different views of demand (country, market segment, product, brand, etc.). In addition, different resources (materials, capacity, labor, etc.) across multiple locations (multiple internal plants, partner locations, etc.) need to be considered. Realize that it may become unmanageable, however, to optimize all resources across the supply chain. A focus on critical or "bottleneck" resources is required.
- *Integrate all supply chain requirements. Source, make, deliver,* and *return* are all interdependent processes, so be sure to create an integrated plan for their individual resource and execution requirements, a plan that extends from "the customer's customer to the supplier's supplier." Otherwise, imbalances will occur, adding costs and tying up inventory in the supply chain. For example, if you purchase (*source*) more materials than production (*make*) needs, you'll end up with excess raw materials.
- *Create explicit actions and accountabilities.* The *plan* process must create courses of action that are agreed to internally—by operations, sales, marketing, and all other internal stakeholders— and externally by key suppliers and customers. Performance against these action plans should be visible to all involved and measured as part of an ongoing effort to improve planning quality.

To achieve your company's business objectives, be sure to integrate planning with other enterprise business processes. For instance, integrate with marketing and sales processes for the best view of customer demand, to get input on customer and market priorities, and to evaluate the need for and impact of promotional activities. Integrate with the technology, product, and service development processes to ensure that key programs have the needed resources. This also will improve time to market and time to volume of new products and services. Integrate *plan* with the finance process to ensure the quality of financial information. Revenue projections must be based on the most credible information possible, and all supply chain liabilities—both internal and external—

must be recognized and reported in line with company and regulatory requirements.

Figure 2-9 shows the metrics of top performance in the *plan* process.

Source

Using the plan generated by *plan source*, the supply chain *source* process procures all needed materials and services, performing the operational activities of purchasing, scheduling, receiving, inspecting, and authorizing supplier payment. The *source* activity also involves supplier selection and relationship management.

Process excellence in *source* is built on four key principles:

+ *Aim for the lowest total cost of ownership (TCO).* Getting the lowest purchase price on a service or asset is less important than achieving the lowest total cost of ownership. A cheap vehicle, for instance, isn't a bargain if it breaks down more often or has a shorter useful life. Be sure to consider both direct and indirect costs when determining the value of a purchase or contract. Many supply chain costs—such as supplier ordering, inspection, payment, and inventory holding—are driven by supplier practices, quality, and capability. To reduce TCO, set cost-improvement objectives not just for the product or service but also for total supply chain costs as well. Work with your suppliers to redefine processes with a goal of reducing or eliminating activities that drive up costs. For instance, "ready for use" products

FIGURE 2–9

Metrics of top performance in *plan*.

Plan		Best Performer Advantage Over Median/Average
Forecast Accuracy	Discrete	25% more accurate
	Process	19% more accurate
Customer Service (on time delivery to commit)	Discrete	9% more accurate
	Process	7% more accurate
Total Inventory Days of Supply	Discrete	1/3 the inventory
	Process	1/2 the inventory

© Copyright 2004 The Performance Measurement Group, LLC

eliminate the need for inspection or preparation. Another way to lower costs is to automate manual, paper-based transactions such as purchase orders or to replace them with a more efficient practice, such as setting up automatic replenishment to do away with purchase orders entirely.

+ *Set procurement strategies according to category.* Procurement strategies set the boundaries for supplier agreements, competitive contracts, and global sourcing agreements based on the need for robustness in the supply network. Different categories have different supply-market complexities and business impacts. In addition, sourcing activities, organization, and tools should be differentiated based on these specific strategies. For example, for standard products where cost is the primary selection criterion, focus on global supply-base management and techniques such as online bidding, whereas for more strategic products, partnership management and collaborative workspaces will be needed.

+ *Maintain an enterprisewide focus.* This means choosing suppliers that can service the organization across its different locations and consolidating purchase volume across the enterprise, where possible, for greater leverage with suppliers. It also requires managing the supply base at the enterprise level using standard specifications, common tools (profiles, ratings, and evaluation criteria), and appropriate organizational structures, such as global commodity managers and teams. Managing the global supply base ensures that suppliers use best practices—those which drive lower costs and greater flexibility—whenever possible and that processes are standardized for a more efficient and robust supply chain. Spend management is also a critical part of source excellence, ensuring that your company tracks spending, uses only approved suppliers and standards (approved vendors lists, catalogs, etc.), and has delegation-of-authority processes in place for approving purchases.

+ *Measure and manage performance.* You won't know if you're achieving the objectives of your category strategies unless you track sourcing performance. For example, visibility on spend across all locations (on volumes purchased by suppliers and terms and conditions applied) is needed for contract enforcement. In addition, explicit performance review points should be built into supplier contracts and be based on standard supplier scorecards. Supplier scorecards should include the key performance indicators

needed to support the achievement of mutually agreed TCO
objectives. In addition to reviews, two-way visibility of performance to the scorecard metrics should support day-to-day performance management.

For the supply chain to operate effectively, be sure to integrate
source with the *plan, deliver, make,* and *return* processes both within the
organization and with suppliers. The integration points with suppliers are
multiple because a company's *source* process integrates with a supplier's
deliver processes for many activities (ordering, goods receipt, and payment). Working with suppliers to design a seamless, integrated flow of
these inputs and outputs can lower total cost of ownership significantly.

To achieve your company's business objectives, also integrate sourcing with other core business processes. For instance, by integrating with
technology, product, and service development processes, you can ensure
that suppliers apply design for manufacturing and design for supply chain
practices. These practices improve quality; optimize production, testing,
and packaging; and get new products to market faster.

Figure 2-10 shows the metrics of top performance in the *source*
process.

Make

The supply chain *make* process transforms the resources procured by
source into goods and services according to agreed-on specifications and
any regulatory requirements. To increase flexibility, minimize costs, or

FIGURE 2–10

Metrics of top performance in *source.*

Source		Best Performer Advantage Over Median/Average
Materials Availability (days to increase by 20%)	Discrete	6 times faster
	Process	18 times faster
Raw Materials Inventory Days of Supply	Discrete	1/5 the inventory
	Process	1/4 the inventory
Materials Acquisition Costs	Discrete	Spend 50% less
	Process	Spend 20% less

boost asset utilization, more and more companies are using external partners to execute some or all of their *make* activities, such as production, testing, certification, and packaging. This requires sharing performance objectives and processes across this extended network.

There are four principles for process excellence in *make*:

* *Focus on business priorities.* All *make* scheduling decisions should integrate customer and market priorities. Your company's business managers should provide these priorities as formally defined business rules. Give priority to key accounts and higher-margin products when resources and production capacity are limited.

* *Aim for speed and flexibility, not just low costs.* Reduce cycle times and inventory levels with demand-pull and other lean manufacturing techniques. For example, when time or cost prohibits making customized products, finish products to a generic level and only finalize them on receipt of a customer order. Speed and flexibility require almost real-time visibility. Timely and accurate information on key areas, such as order status, production output, line stoppages, quality performance, and inventory levels, is needed to support rapid adjustments to the production schedule.

* *Set and monitor quality standards.* Capture and review quality information at each step of the production process based on preset standards. Timely data on quality must be accessible to everyone involved in manufacturing activities and then analyzed using a structured approach such as Six Sigma. This focus on quality should cover the whole product life cycle. Products should be traceable at the lot and unit levels to ensure that the source of quality problems can be identified and corrected.

* *Synchronize all manufacturing activities.* Provide information on production schedules, consumption, and inventory levels to suppliers so that they can better monitor and respond to demand. Define and agree on rules to guide supplier decision making for replenishment. To ensure that production schedules are both feasible and accurate, production rules, information, and performance data need to be managed; this requires defining and maintaining formalized processes and accountabilities both internally and with supply partners.

For the supply chain to operate effectively, *make* must be integrated with the *plan*, *source*, *deliver*, and *return* processes. For example, *plan* provides *make* with a production plan stating the amount of product to be manufactured. *Source* provides information on what and when materials will be received from suppliers and what inventory is available for production. *Make* provides *source* with information on materials consumption, which determines how much to order from suppliers. For companies using available to promise as a strategy, *make* provides information on scheduled production to *deliver* for use in order promising.

Integrate *make* with other enterprise business processes. Integrating with technology, product, and service development speeds time to market by inputting engineering changes more quickly. Integrating *make* with the marketing and sales process ensures that customer, market, and product priorities drive production scheduling.

Some of the results such best practices can achieve are shown in Figure 2-11.

Deliver

The *deliver* process starts with the receipt of a customer order and includes all the activities needed to complete that order, from providing a price quote to collecting payment from the customer. *Deliver* makes the order visible to *source* and *make* for execution, ensuring that customer requirements are communicated clearly. *Deliver* also includes all warehousing, transportation, and distribution activities.

Here are the four principles we recommend for *deliver* process excellence:

- ◆ *Balance service with the cost to serve.* Some customers are more profitable—and more desirable—than others. These are the customers you want to take especially good care of. Begin by

FIGURE 2–11

Metrics of top performance in *make.*

Make		Best Performer Advantage Over Median/Average
Direct Labor Availability (Days to increase by 20%)	Discrete	4 times faster
	Process	3 times faster
Work in Progress Inventory Days of Supply	Discrete	36 times less inventory
	Process	14 times less inventory

© Copyright 2004 The Performance Measurement Group, LLC

clearly defining customer segments, and then differentiate your *deliver* processes, business rules, and services accordingly. For instance, you may offer high-value customers several order-management options while limiting other customers to self-service and other lower-cost order channels. You also may give priority to your best customers when allocating inventory in times of product shortages.

♦ *Cut costs and time with straight-through processing.* Send order information to all relevant functions—credit approval, manufacturing (for make to order), warehousing, transportation, and invoicing—so that, where possible, execution activities can be done simultaneously instead of sequentially, and all aspects of *deliver* can be organized for smoother, faster processing. As with information flows, design *deliver* physical flows for *straight-through processing* to minimize non-value-added wait time. Choose your physical network—production, warehousing, and transportation—with an eye toward total costs and delivery time.

♦ *Set up end-to-end tracking and traceability.* The status of all customer orders and shipments, from order signal to cash collection, should be visible throughout the *deliver* process. For example, customers should be able to see where their orders are, and key account managers should have access to full order information for each of their accounts. Moreover, managing supply chain risks such as terrorism, counterfeiting, theft, and spoilage requires being able to seal and track shipments from point of production to point of delivery.

♦ *Manage data for ongoing accuracy and timeliness.* Good delivery performance depends on excellent data management. Customer order creation and management require a broad range of information, including product attributes, technical configurations, prices, and customer addresses. All this information must be kept current to avoid errors. Otherwise, orders and invoices will be rejected and reworked, adding time and cost and tying up cash in the supply chain. In most companies, data creation and maintenance are a challenge involving many departments. The challenge, though, is even greater beyond the enterprise, requiring data and process standards among customers, suppliers, and partners—each of which may have different data structures, definitions, and repositories.

You won't be able to follow all these principles without integrating delivery with other core business processes. For example, data management requires getting product-related data from the technology, product, and service development processes. Customizing supply chain processes as part of customer collaboration will require adjustments to the marketing and sales process so that customer contracts systematically take logistical aspects into account. Moreover, the marketing and sales process must provide *deliver* with information on pricing, customer-specific terms and conditions, and the clear guidelines on customer priorities needed to balance service and the cost to serve.

To meet your customer delivery commitments consistently, you'll also have to integrate delivery with your company's other supply chain processes. *Plan* depends on the *deliver* process for information on demand—based on order backlog and customer shipments—for both resource and revenue planning. In addition, creating collaborative business models and tailoring *deliver* processes can have significant implications on *plan, source,* and *make.* For instance, the *make* and the *plan* processes provide *deliver* with the inventory and production scheduling data needed for customer order promising. Depending on the collaborative model chosen, the type of information needed and transaction frequency can change significantly. See Figure 2-12 for the metrics of top performance in *deliver.*

Return

The *return* process ensures that previously sold products are supported, collected, and dispositioned according to business policies and customer

FIGURE 2–12

Metrics of top performance in *deliver.*

Deliver		Best Performer Advantage Over Median/Average
Order Fulfillment Lead Time for Make to Stock Products	Discrete	4 times faster
	Process	4 times faster
Order Management Costs	Discrete	Spend 42% less
	Process	Spend 31% less
Days Sales Outstanding	Discrete	43% less days
	Process	36% less days

agreements and covers all activities from return authorization to financial settlement. The primary drivers behind *return* differ by industry but typically include the return of defective, wrong, or unsatisfactory products; maintenance, repair, and overhaul (MRO) based on service agreements; excess channel inventory returns; and recycling/refurbishment/reuse. Different activities may be associated with each of these *return* "types."

Return is a *reverse* supply chain process and has specific requirements and characteristics that differ from the *forward* supply chain. For example, *return* involves capturing item-level data from the point of return, tracking a product until disposition, and managing warranties for the complete product life cycle. It also requires capturing a range of analytics, including the causes of returns, originating locations, costs, and credits.

In addition, the *return* physical network entails specific challenges. For example, returns typically feature small volumes of many different items with irregular frequency. Companies must find a way to collect, sort, and distribute this array of items as efficiently and economically as possible. Often, central collection points provide a way to aggregate volume in a cost-effective manner.

For *return* process excellence, follow these four key principles:

- *Create a distinct supply chain for return,* such as deciding whether a product can be returned, how it will be disposed of, and how to manage supplier or customer credits and other financial transactions. *Return* requires a separate supply chain, with its own end-to-end processes, information systems, performance scorecard, and organizational responsibilities.

- *Feed back return information quickly.* Provide timely information on returns to guide both disposal and preventive actions. For example, procurement will deal with suppliers appropriately, based on *return* information. Production, engineering, and logistics will learn from *return* information and use it to take corrective action in their respective areas. *Return* managers will use data on costs, credits, and revenues to manage reverse supply chain operations.

- *Base return policies on total cost of returns.* Set up an explicit return policy for each item sold, whether manufactured internally or purchased for resale. Consider using an external returns specialist depending on the nature of the return, the total costs of the return—including assessment, collection, sorting, and disposal— and your company's existing *return* capability.

♦ *Maximize revenue opportunities.* Define your company's *return* processes and policies with an eye toward revenue enhancement. Identify multiple revenue-generating disposal paths, including resale, supplier return for credit, recycling, auction, and so forth. For purchased items, disposal policies should integrate business rules that are preset with suppliers.

To be effective, your company's *return* process must be integrated with other supply chain processes. For example, by integrating with the *plan* process, *return* makes sure that the resources it needs are available. By integrating with the *source* and *make* processes, *return* can provide information on defects and faults to ensure the quality of purchases and manufacturing. *Return* also provides information to *deliver* on products to be picked up from customers and brought into the reverse supply chain. For MRO items, *return* provides information to *source, make,* and *deliver* for execution of the activities needed to process returns according to customer agreements.

An effective *return* process also requires integration with other core business processes. For instance, integrating *return* with the technology, product, and service development process ensures that information on product defects and poorly understood product features is used to improve existing products and develop better new products. Integration with the marketing and sales process ensures that returns policies are consistent with customer terms and conditions.

Top performers in the *return* process achieve the superior performance of the metrics shown in Figure 2-13.

NEXT-GENERATION PROCESSES

As market conditions and competition evolve, the supply chain needs to adapt. Today's supply chain process architectures are often incomplete

FIGURE 2–13

Metrics of top performance in *return*.

Return		Best Performer Advantage Over Median/Average
Return Lead Time	Discrete	79% faster
	Process	60% faster
Return Costs	Discrete	Spend 71% less
	Process	Spend 75% less

© Copyright 2004 The Performance Measurement Group, LLC

and defined in terms that are not widely understood. This means that the overall impact of new strategies on existing operations is very difficult to assess. Deployment of new strategies is impaired, and potential competitive advantage is lost.

In the next generation of process architecture, companies will be able to rapidly translate strategies into new supply chains. These architectures will seamlessly integrate business processes and information systems. And they'll include the key performance indicators needed to ensure value creation and ongoing management.

Besides providing a unified view of the internal supply chain, the next generation of process architecture will define the integration points among suppliers, customers, and partners. Changes will include the practices described in Figure 2-14.

In the next generation of process architecture, companies will be able to rapidly translate strategies into new supply chains.

FIGURE 2–14

Next-generation practices in process architecture.

Theme	Current Dominant Practice	Next-Generation Dominant Practice
Process Architecture Content	Detailed processes (plan, source, make, deliver, return) are described, but the integration between the processes, and between processes and applications, is missing or incomplete.	The process architecture integrates all supply chain process activities (plan, source, make, deliver and return), data, metrics, and applications.
Decision Support	The process architecture content focuses on execution within the organization of the subprocesses, with limited integration of analytics (performance monitoring, reporting, resolution).	The processes create visibility of a defined set of events and of actual performance versus plan, using standard metrics, in order to support proactive management, extending as required to suppliers, partners, and customers.
Process Automation	Manual intervention is used to resolve even routine exceptions (e.g., late supplier delivery, stockouts, etc.) and each exception typically requires days or weeks to identify and resolve.	For a defined set of critical business events, automated business rules, and problem-solving propose solutions for approval by business owners in real-time environments.
Enterprise Scope	Process architecture content (activities, data, metrics, and applications) may differ by country or region, based on history or organizational control.	Such content (activities, data, metrics, and applications) is standardized to support the work of geographically dispersed virtual teams and to enable the sharing and transfer of work between locations.
Cross-Enterprise Scope	The focus is the organization, and process architecture structure, vocabulary, and content are unique to each organization.	The process architecture integrates standards such as SCOR® (Supply-Chain Operations Reference-model®) and ensures the existence of common processes, data, and metrics with suppliers, partners, and customers. Standards support the management of liabilities, critical resources (inventories, capacities, etc.), and events in the extended supply chain.
SCPA (Supply Chain Process Architecture) Ownership	The development and maintenance of the process architecture are led and conducted by IT; seen as an "IT issue."	The process architecture is seen as "an asset" and is co-managed by business leaders (P&L responsibility) and IT in order to balance business requirements and the advantages of shared process and IT standards.

A V O N

Avon Profile:
Calling on Customers
Cost-Effectively

What do you do when you have an enormous growth opportunity but can't capitalize on it with your existing supply chain? If you're Avon, you embark on a radical transformation—a high-risk venture with no guaranteed returns.

Avon is the world's leading direct seller of beauty and related products, with $6.2 billion in annual revenue. In addition to its cosmetics, skin care products, fragrances, and personal care products, the company offers a wide range of gift items, including jewelry, lingerie, and fashion accessories. Avon sells to customers in 145 countries through 3.9 million independent sales representatives, providing an earnings opportunity to women throughout the world. Its Europe region (spanning Europe, the Middle East, and Africa) accounts for more than $1.2 billion of Avon's sales, with operations in 32 countries and more than 1 million sales representatives.

With a primary focus on marketing and sales, Avon had neglected its supply chain for a number of years, never viewing it as a strategic lever. This presented acute problems for Avon Europe because the region's strong growth threatened to overwhelm the supply chain organization.

Back in the 1980s, Avon Europe had branches in only six countries, each with a separate factory and warehouse supplying the local market. These branches operated independently, with separate information systems, no overall planning, and no shared manufacturing, marketing, or distribution. On a small scale this worked quite well. Each entity could be very responsive to local needs. In the early 1990s, the company began globalizing its key brands and embarked on a strategy to modernize its image through the launch of new products, packaging, and ad campaigns— a strategy aimed at more and younger consumers.

Avon planned to double sales revenue from $500 million in 1996 to $1 billion in 2001 for the European region as a whole—growth fueled in large part by dramatic inroads in central and eastern Europe. But the company realized that replicating its supply chain model in every new market would be expensive and unwieldy. The bottom line: Avon couldn't achieve its aggressive growth target with its existing supply chain. Explains Bob Toth, executive vice president, "Ten years ago we operated country to country, with a very decentralized financial-holding-company model. You just can't compete that way now, especially if you're a fast-moving consumer-goods company."

A GROWING BUSINESS—AND GROWING PROBLEMS

The first problem was a fundamental mismatch between the company's selling cycle and its supply chain cycle. In most European markets Avon begins a new sales campaign—complete with a new brochure, fresh product offerings, and promotions—every three weeks. This short selling cycle is a cornerstone of Avon's direct-sales model. By regularly offering new products and promotions, the company gives its sales representatives a reason to call on their customers more often, strengthening those relationships and driving sales.

In most European markets, Avon begins a new sales campaign every three weeks.

A short selling cycle demands a flexible, responsive supply chain. Here, Avon fell short, especially as the company's European operations grew larger. Avon's factories manufactured everything to forecast and then shipped inventory to the country warehouses before the start of each three-week selling campaign. Inevitably, certain products would be big hits, and the branches would send rush orders back to the factories to make more inventory. However, it took an average of 12 weeks for products to cycle through Avon's supply chain from sourcing to manufacturing to distribution out to the branches—far too long for the short selling cycle.

This timing mismatch led to on-the-fly solutions and enormous inefficiencies during the course of each sales campaign. Avon relied on the heroics of its people to meet customer needs—regardless of cost. This was viable when Avon Europe was relatively small. But as the business grew, keeping up with the needs of the different markets and accurately forecasting demand for individual products became increasingly difficult, especially since Avon was entering new markets at a rate of two or three per year.

The rush orders destroyed manufacturing efficiency too. Since 40 to 50 percent of the items offered in any campaign sold more than expected, the factories were constantly interrupting their manufacturing schedules to switch from one product to another. Changeover costs were high—especially since the factories were set up for high-volume production.

Slow-selling products also were costly. In every selling cycle a number of products would sell less than forecast, so Avon had a growing amount of unsold merchandise. Avon's inventory levels were high—as much as 150 days' worth was typical—far too high for a three-week selling cycle. And most of this inventory consisted of unsold items. The capital tied up in inventory would only increase as Avon's business expanded in Europe.

Language variants presented another growth-related problem. Avon bought preprinted containers from its suppliers. With new markets came new languages and a growing number of print variants. Given its manufacture-to-forecast approach and the suppliers' lead times, Avon had to order a wide range of preprinted containers well before it knew what its sales volumes actually would be in the different markets. This was becoming increasingly complex—and wasteful. Avon often would have demand in one country that couldn't be filled because the only containers on hand were printed in another language.

Fixing these problems and transforming the supply chain would be an enormous undertaking, one that needed support and a big financial commitment from corporate management.

MAKING THE BUSINESS CASE AND MOVING FORWARD

It required a lengthy, detailed analysis to prove that Avon's supply chain wouldn't be able to handle the projected growth of the business. Even then, it took 18 months to build the business case and get executive buy-in to move forward with the far-reaching changes needed. Convincing the organization to invest money that wouldn't be recouped until the later years of the transformation was a tough sell. In fact, the first two years would result in a net loss. "This delayed payback was an uncomfortable notion, especially given that Avon had never invested much in the supply chain before and wanted quicker results," explains Michael Watson, director of Avon's supply chain transformation. "It was very difficult getting that initial momentum going."

By the time Avon started the project, however, corporate buy-in was absolute, and management had committed an extraordinary level of resources. Notes Watson, "We took 45 of our best people in Europe out of their existing positions and put them into the project full time for 18 months." Removing these people from day-to-day operations was extremely painful, costly, and risky from a business perspective, but it was absolutely critical to success. Explains Watson, "If we had tried to do this on the side with a small project team, it would never have worked—and we'd never be seeing the benefits we are now."

RETHINKING THE SUPPLY CHAIN

Avon began by creating a centralized planning function—a critical priority. Explains John Kitchener, head of the supply chain in Europe, "There was no way Avon would achieve its growth targets without a centralized planning group that could see demand and inventory levels across the region and react very, very quickly."

First, Avon had to create a common database. The team spent many months putting in place standardized product codes, descriptions, and other information so that each country was speaking the same language. The database gave Avon visibility into sales trends and inventory so that managers could look across the region and see what was happening from both demand and supply perspectives. The company also installed Manugistics' supply chain planning and scheduling system to support integrated planning and coordination across the whole European region.

To leverage this new capability and manage the growing complexity of the business, Avon put in place a regional planning group empowered to make decisions about service levels, inventory, and costs based on a bird's-eye view of the whole supply chain. Other decisions regarding the new organization, roles, and responsibilities were put on hold until later.

> Avon put in place a regional planning group empowered to make decisions about service levels, inventory, and costs.

The next critical step was to redesign the entire supply chain in a way that made sense operationally. Using the Supply-Chain Operations Reference-model (SCOR), the team identified the key changes to *plan, source, make,* and *deliver*—the supply chain processes that were most integral to Avon's business. Avon kept a manufacturing plant in Germany but consolidated other production into its plant in Poland. This helped in two ways. First, it expanded manufacturing capability in the heart of Avon's emerging markets. And second, it delivered major cost efficiencies, mainly due to the lower cost of labor. Avon also created a centralized inventory hub in Poland—near the production facility—to service the company's branches throughout Europe.

With end-to-end visibility in place and a newly streamlined supply chain, Avon was able to make truly dramatic changes to its business.

END-TO-END VISIBILITY

Once Avon was able to see the supply chain as a whole, decisions that didn't seem to make sense from a purely functional stand-point suddenly were shown to deliver sub-stantial—and often unexpected—benefits.

> Avon created a centralized inventory hub in Poland to service the company's branches throughout Europe.

For instance, Avon had considered the idea of labeling bottles itself instead of having suppliers preprint them, a postponement strategy that would delay the final decision about what language to put on a product until sales trends were clearer. For years, marketing had resisted this idea, convinced that the look of the products would suffer. Manufacturing wasn't interested in adding to its overhead cost structure either because the function was run as a cost center. From a financial standpoint, the postpone-ment strategy didn't seem to make sense. The added equipment and labor costs involved in making labels and affixing them to bottles likely would offset any savings. "All the accountants were telling us it was the wrong thing to do," says Watson.

It was only when Avon stepped back and looked at the supply chain as an end-to-end process that the true benefits of the postponement strat-egy became clear. From a sourcing standpoint, Avon would only have to buy one plain bottle for shampoo or lotion instead of five or six language variations. Avon's manufacturing plants could make one long production run instead of repeatedly switching bottle stock. And customer service would improve sharply because the branches could be more responsive. Now, when inventory runs out in a given market, the warehouse can respond quickly by labeling products with the right language and loading up a truck.

The postponement strategy delivered improvements in cost, effi-ciency, and service all along the supply chain. Yet the strategy seemed counterintuitive until Avon assessed the trade-offs in cost, flexibility, and cycle time across the total supply chain.

Very closely linked to the postponement strategy is a new inventory-hub strategy. Explains Kitchener, "The postponement strategy works well, but only in conjunction with a distribution hub that lets us quickly push products out to the markets." Avon's two manufacturing plants supply the one centralized warehouse in Poland which labels the products and puts loads together for distribution to the different branches. In the old world, Avon pushed products out to country warehouses in the different markets before knowing what demand actually was. Now it holds products back in the centralized hub and diverts them to the markets that need them once sales trends become clear.

Avon is also working to standardize its containers to cut costs and increase efficiency. Once convinced that every product should have a distinct bottle and shape, the company now realizes that cap, color, and labeling can be sources of differentiation too. As a result, Avon has cut back sharply on the number of bottle styles and sizes it uses. This delivers a wide range of benefits. Manufacturing can be far more flexible because changeover time is often zero from product to product. Suppliers can now run Avon's containers down the more efficient, high-speed lines in their factories. And product costs are lower because of standardization. Avon has been able to reinvest savings in improved product formulations and leading-edge package design and marketing activities.

> Avon is also working to standardize its containers and postpone labeling them to cut costs and increase efficiency.

For years, Avon was unable to cost-justify these types of changes. Now, with an end-to-end view of the trade-offs among different actions, the company can see the full effect of pulling one or more levers—and make decisions that improve the supply chain as a whole.

COLLABORATING WITH SUPPLIERS

This end-to-end view also changed how the company works with its suppliers. Avon used to seek out the least expensive materials and buy in large volumes to keep costs low. But the company began to see that the lowest price doesn't necessarily equal the lowest total cost. For instance, Avon found a supplier of inexpensive glass bottles in Mexico, but the delivery lead time from Mexico to Europe was long—8 to 12 weeks on a boat. When product demand was high and bottles were needed, Avon would fly them in, a costly solution. Even though the bottles themselves were inexpensive, the lack of flexibility and high expediting costs more than offset those savings.

Based on these insights, Avon completely changed its sourcing strategy. The company reduced its supplier base by more than half, embraced the concept of supplier partnerships, and focused on lowest total cost instead of lowest price. Today, Avon buys most of its inventory from suppliers that are close to its factories in Poland and Germany. Although the company may pay a slightly higher price on a per-unit basis, the benefits of managing far fewer relationships with more flexible, responsive suppliers result in a lower total cost overall.

Dealing with a smaller number of suppliers delivered other dividends as well. Explains Watson, "Because we have longer-term relationships, we can invest together in new, better ways of working." For example, Avon worked with its suppliers and a London-based design firm to create a better product design. In the process of standardizing the bottles for its different products, Avon asked its suppliers for help in designing new bottles in the most cost-effective way. The suppliers were able to explain why certain approaches were more costly than others—how a lighter-weight bottle saves on materials, for instance, or how a bottle with a specific geometry comes off the production line almost twice as quickly.

Avon also sat down with its suppliers and mapped out the whole manufacturing process, looking for ways to take out time and money. Together they identified where there were inefficiencies and why. In many cases Avon had to change its own approach so that suppliers could manufacture its products more cost-effectively. For instance, Avon agreed to change its order patterns to reduce the suppliers' manufacturing setup costs.

> **Avon had to change its own approach so that suppliers could manufacture its products more cost-effectively.**

Avon has stopped placing orders entirely with some suppliers, instead giving them access to production information via a Web-based system designed on the back of its own avon.com Web site. The suppliers just look at the factories' production schedules and deliver accordingly.

BUILDING ON SUCCESS: COLLABORATIVE DESIGN

Avon plans to extend the concept of collaboration throughout the supply chain organization. The company recently conducted a collaborative design workshop that included suppliers, a design firm, and representatives from marketing and the supply chain—40 people in a room trying to design a product. Within three days the team had designed the concept for a new package that was stunning from marketing and design perspectives but also minimized costs at each step of the supply chain. A key part of the process was getting everyone's input.

For example, the back of a truck can hold only so many pallets, but the right box and bottle designs can optimize the number of boxes in each pallet and the number of bottles in each box. If Avon could increase the number of boxes on each truck by 20 percent, the company would save hundreds of thousands of dollars in transportation costs each year. Only the person who loads the truck every day knows these things, but in the past that person's knowledge wasn't considered in the design process. Instead, product costs were locked in early by someone making isolated decisions in the design studio. Explains Watson of the new collaborative design approach, "This isn't about any particular area of the supply chain. It's about making sure that when we design products, we design them with everyone in mind."

The workshop was a major investment of time and people, but Avon expects to save several million dollars over the next few years because of designing the product right—and another $50 million with ongoing use of the strategy.

REORGANIZATION—AND THE CHANGE-MANAGEMENT CHALLENGE

Once the supply chain processes were redesigned, Avon turned its attention to the new organization—and restructured it around the four key processes of *plan, source, make,* and *deliver.* Now, instead of a large number of people from different functions and countries reporting to him, Kitchener has just four direct reports—the four process heads. "Now we have four megaprocesses and four people empowered to drive that across Europe," says Kitchener. "As the person heading this up, I cannot tell you how much less complex it is. It's a far simpler model to manage than the old model."

One of Avon's biggest challenges has been making the concept of a process-driven, collaborative, regional organization in Europe work well on a day-to-day basis. The redesign completely changed the roles and responsibilities of the general managers across Europe. They once managed the inventory in their own markets, for instance, but now that product labeling is postponed until shipment, it no longer makes sense for the GMs to own inventory. Instead, Avon holds it farther back in the supply chain to better allocate it to where demand is greatest. As a result, the metric on inventory days that used to be the general managers' responsibility now belongs to the supply chain organization, along with the other day-to-day supply chain activities. In the new organization, the GMs are primarily responsible for sales. This change, combined with the need for people to work cross-functionally and collaboratively, has been hard to implement because of the major behavioral changes involved. Notes Toth, "It's a cultural change—a cultural revolution, really."

Avon did a lot of work to define primary responsibilities, shared responsibilities, and the supporting metrics. The transformation team realized that a regional, process-based organization demanded very different metrics than a country-based, functionally oriented organization. Setting up metrics early on and monitoring them often were critical to success—and helped keep everyone focused on what was important. These had to be tangible metrics such as operating margin, service improvement, and inventory levels—metrics that linked back to the original business case, metrics that people could be measured against.

Many of the old metrics were backward-looking. Inventory days, for instance, is a good end-of-month measure, but it doesn't help with day-to-day operations. Avon developed metrics that are more operationally focused and can be influenced in the short term. As an example, the company broke down the key drivers of inventory levels. One was supplier lead time, which Avon has taken steps to shorten by giving certain suppliers access to production schedules and making them responsible for delivering materials on time.

By clearly communicating the redesigned structure and accountabilities and defining new performance metrics, Avon began to move the new supply chain organization forward. Says Toth, "Once you change the roles and responsibilities and set up clear KPIs [key performance indicators] for individuals at the country level and at the regional level, it starts to become institutionalized."

Education and training were another critical piece of Avon's supply chain transformation. The company quickly saw that the skill levels in the organization had to be upgraded. Avon analyzed all the critical jobs in the new supply chain and the competencies needed to do those jobs. To fill the gaps, Avon partnered with Cranfield University, one of the leading supply chain business schools in Europe, to develop a customized curriculum. Avon put 75 of its key supply chain associates through the program and offered a shorter version to the senior executives who weren't involved in the redesign. To introduce new thinking, the program brought in several experienced supply chain managers from other leading companies in a range of industries. Avon plans to repeat the program every year with new groups of people to ensure that everyone in the organization understands what a world-class supply chain looks like.

The leaders of Avon's transformation agree that communication is perhaps the single most critical success factor—and the one they most underestimated. Everyone in the organization must understand the change, why it's happening, and his or her role in the new world. Even with the best-laid plans, though, changing a culture and long-held behaviors doesn't happen overnight. "You always read in books about how tough change management is, but the reality is that it's even harder," notes Watson.

Avon was very clear on the fact that its supply chain transformation would be process-driven, not systems-driven. Instead of overhauling its computer systems, the company focused on getting the processes right first. The leadership team felt that doing both at once would be unmanageable. Therefore, aside from creating the central data repository and the Web-based system for suppliers, systems upgrades were put on hold—even though Avon's country-based, entrepreneurial model had resulted in a jumble of systems and no integration.

This lack of integration is starting to cause problems now. Given the growing complexity of the business and the need for greater speed and responsiveness, not having the system and information in place is frustrating. Mindful of these problems, Avon has begun designing a new, global platform to replace the existing system and support the new processes.

In the meantime, the company is savoring the results of its transformation effort. By rethinking the supply chain, increasing efficiency, and taking out costs, Avon will save about $50 million annually—or two gross margin points. Almost half these benefits are a direct result of the company's new approach to working with suppliers: the smaller supplier base, local sourcing strategy, supplier partnerships, and collaboration. Just as important, Avon Europe is far easier to manage now that it has a streamlined organization, upgraded skills, simplified processes, and the right metrics.

"I don't say this lightly, but this has been the most challenging, the most rewarding, and the most fun thing that I've ever done," says Kitchener, a 30-year veteran of the company. "The journey isn't over, though. It's never over."

3

CHAPTER

Core Discipline 3:
Design Your Organization
for Performance

Many companies still think of their supply chain organization as a set of functions that complements manufacturing or as a set of "operations" departments such as receiving, production, and logistics. To provide effective end-to-end supply chain management, however, the organization should include all the core supply chain processes—*plan, source, make, deliver*, and *return*—as well as the supporting infrastructure. That means grouping these processes under one senior manager and, more important, giving that manager a set of cross-functional performance objectives and the resources needed to meet those objectives. This is the key characteristic of the *integrated model* of supply chain organization to be described in more detail later in this chapter.

An integrated organization requires new skills and a new way of thinking about organizational structure. The complexity of today's supply chains and the advent of highly sophisticated technologies have fundamentally changed the skills needed within the supply chain organization. As a result, companies face three primary challenges:

- ◆ Determining how to structure the organization
- ◆ Defining roles and responsibilities
- ◆ Finding the right people with the right skills

Moving to an integrated model doesn't necessarily mean overhauling your existing operations, creating a new department, or "inventing" a new vice president. It does mean ensuring that your supply chain organization is a collection of departments and people clearly responsible for executing and continuously improving each of the core processes. Thus, even if you don't plan to group these departments and people together through a large-scale reorganization, you most likely will need to consider some level of change to your existing organization to ensure that it is able to support integrated, cross-functional process management. This may mean consolidating two departments to eliminate a functional boundary or process handoff, rescoping the responsibilities within a particular group, or realigning existing groups to focus on specific channels or customers.

You also may need to revaluate the skills within your current organization. Certainly, a high degree of fluency with state-of-the-art information systems is a must for virtually any key supply chain position. Technical skills aren't enough, though. Only focused management skills will set your organization apart from the competition. Today's supply chain requires people who can assimilate and interpret vast quantities of data and then make effective decisions. It requires people who have breadth of operational experience and depth of process knowledge, people who have a passion for satisfying customers. It requires people who can embrace new measures as tools to help improve overall performance. And, as if this were not enough, the cross-functional nature of the end-to-end supply chain also demands conflict-resolution skills.

ORGANIZATIONAL CHANGE IS AN ONGOING PROCESS

Your supply chain organization should be evolving constantly, but several conditions may drive more major change. Any significant supply chain improvement effort, for instance, may make it necessary to redefine roles and responsibilities to focus on the right objectives, modify organizational structures to reduce process complexity, or develop new competencies and skills. Similarly, updates to your company's overall strategy may render existing competencies obsolete or give rise to the need for new capabilities. Changes in the business environment, too, may make it necessary to improve specific supply chain capabilities. Or you simply may have to "clean house" or redeploy resources that are underperforming.

Changes in how you evaluate supply chain performance also can drive organizational changes. In a traditional functional organization, metrics often are designed to optimize performance within a specific department or function. But as your supply chain strategy and processes evolve, you'll need to embrace a new set of metrics designed to optimize performance for the company as a whole, as we'll discuss in Core Discipline 5. If you don't restructure and develop your organization in a way that supports these new performance objectives, you'll likely fall short of your targets and sabotage your supply chain strategy.

We rarely see a shift in strategy so major that it drives a fundamental rethinking of needed skills and an organizational overhaul. Because your supply chain organization is responsible for executing your supply chain strategy, you'll need to consider them both in parallel.

Stratex Networks, a leading provider of digital microwave radios, provides a case in point, illustrating how capabilities within the supply chain organization can be developed and improved as the supply chain strategy becomes more focused and corresponding process changes are made. In early 2002, Stratex made a strategic decision to focus on improving its return on assets and customer service levels by elevating order-delivery performance and reducing order-fulfillment cycle time. Among other changes, this meant a fundamental overhaul of the company's operations strategy and a move to outsourced manufacturing. The company embarked on an aggressive schedule for the transfer of production from San Jose, California, to a manufacturing partner in Taiwan.

In parallel with the transfer of manufacturing, Robert Schlaefli, Stratex vice president of global operations, launched an initiative to fundamentally redesign the company's core supply chain processes to support the new manufacturing model.[1] The company needed to maintain strong relationships with several key suppliers while transferring responsibility for most materials purchasing to its new manufacturing partner. Stratex also was concerned about the communication challenges inherent in an outsourcing relationship and wanted to ensure that customer requirements could be collected, integrated, and acted on as quickly as possible.

Many of the new processes were designed to optimize the flow of an order as it progressed through the configuration and manufacturing process—for example, the criteria for accepting a customer order were updated, and checklists were put in place to ensure that all critical information was available prior to order entry, eliminating the delays that occurred when required data had to be researched after the order was already in process. But Stratex still had information gaps between functional groups and confusion about which function ultimately was responsible for order-delivery performance. While regional sales administration, finance, order management, planning, procurement, and traffic were each responsible for a subset of the data included within each sales order, none had ultimate accountability for ensuring that commitments to the customer were made on a timely basis—or kept once they were made.

Stratex quickly concluded that the many handoffs inherent in its current organizational structure would not support the new strategy. The need to improve delivery performance and the decision to outsource production really elevated the importance of the order-fulfillment process. Stratex needed to start thinking about the management and scheduling of orders, the configuration of the product, and the shipment to the customer as one process, not three or more.

Prior to the move to outsourcing, Stratex had a very traditional operations organization, with distinct functional groups responsible for order entry, order management, production, planning, sourcing, and logistics (see Figure 3-1). While the groups interacted frequently, Schlaefli felt that his people were passing information back and forth, as opposed to sharing common information. Communication about delivery schedules between functional groups and when interacting with customers was inconsistent, and both salespeople and customers expressed frustration at being unable to get an accurate order status.

Stratex's solution was to recraft the organization, with a new group focused on managing the entire order-execution process from the time an order is entered to the time the product is shipped to the customer. Stratex created an order-fulfillment team and moved the traffic functions within

FIGURE 3-1

Stratex operations before adopting the outsourcing model.

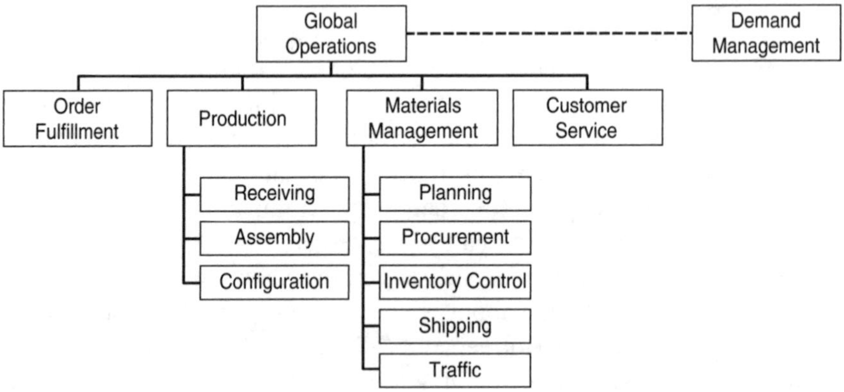

this new group. Links were tightened between customer order management, planning, and procurement by physically moving the groups closer together and requiring that order schedules be confirmed in person rather than via voicemail or e-mail communications between the three groups.

Once the organizational structure was defined (see Figure 3-2), Stratex began to revise the roles and responsibilities within the planning and procurement functions. The change to an outsourced manufacturing strategy meant that Stratex no longer had the luxury of modifying its production schedule as customer requirements changed or were more clearly understood. Instead, it had to provide a forecast of production requirements to its manufacturing partner well in advance of when the products actually were needed. Stratex needed new roles within both planning and procurement. A new supply chain meant buying only a few materials from a limited number of suppliers, but each of these materials was highly complex and quite expensive. Stratex couldn't afford to run out of something or have too much on hand or on order. The company also was concerned about flexibility because a third party was now responsible for production. Stratex needed to focus a lot of attention on demand management and communicating an accurate picture of anticipated demand to all suppliers, not just to its manufacturing partner.

F I G U R E 3–2

Stratex operations after adopting the outsourcing model.

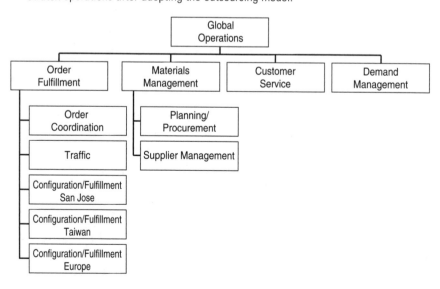

While the new organizational design was not put into place all at once, Stratex kept the end state in view as the company began to use the new processes. "Our new model meant that the buying and material planning tasks were going to blend," says Schlaefli. "You can't just take a tactical buyer who has been placing purchase orders by following system-generated recommendations and suddenly turn him into a planner who needs to be able to make decisions without completely concrete data. We had to do a lot of retraining and, in some cases, some strategic hiring to develop the organization we wanted." Stratex provided on-site APICS[2] training for all buyers and planners and hired several new employees with significant experience in sourcing and master production scheduling processes.

The restructuring was completed over a period of several months, roughly following the schedule of the manufacturing transition. The company met an aggressive schedule to ramp production at its manufacturing partner—with no negative impact on customer service levels. At the same time, the increased focus on the planning process and the associated upgrade of planning skills allowed Stratex to cut inventory liabilities dramatically. The new organization was a key factor in Stratex's ability to realize the benefits of the company's new strategy. "This didn't happen overnight," says Schlaefli. "Having a map of where we wanted to go with the organization made it a lot easier to implement the necessary process changes."

Your organizational design should not be static—it should evolve with your company.

As the Stratex example shows, overall design, combined with clearly defined roles and responsibilities and skilled people, can help a company build an integrated supply chain organization that drives forward its strategy. Your organizational design should not be static—it should evolve with your company.

Sweeping changes to operational processes are not a prerequisite for restructuring your supply chain organization. Organizational changes can improve overall performance even without major process changes. Even relatively minor process changes and an organizational adjustment can generate tremendous benefits.

Consider the case of Smith Bits, which uses state-of-the-art technologies to design and manufacture a full line of drilling bits for the oilfield and mining industries. In late 2002, the company was struggling with rising field inventories despite growing customer demand. At the same time, it was losing sales because the right bits were unavailable and order-fulfillment lead times for sold bits were increasing. Hurt by the lack of product availability and long lead times, sales offices around the world began hoarding bits to ensure product availability to meet customer demand. Often a bit stocked in one region with no demand would not be made available to another region with customer orders.[3]

Smith Bits had a functional organizational structure—sales, engineering, and operations all reported to the division president. Based on our recommendation, the company created a new supply chain organization charged with demand/supply balancing run by a director-level operations manager. Everyone who manages inventory in the sales offices is part of this group, which reports to the vice president of worldwide sales.

Once manufactured, the bits are the responsibility of this new group until they're sold. The group reviews orders that can't be filled locally, reallocates inventory from one region to another as needed, and works with manufacturing to get more bits made, deciding which should be stocked and which should be made to order. The group also sets up weekly demand/supply balancing meetings with manufacturing and helps that organization improve production cycle times by prioritizing field requirements. The results are impressive. By sharply reducing inventory levels, Smith Bits substantially improved cash flow and allowed opportunities for added revenue through several strategic acquisitions.

The Smith Bits example shows how companies can make major improvements in their operations without changing their fundamental strategies. Smith Bits moved the *plan* and *deliver* processes out of operations and created a new supply chain organization. This new group formally linked the *make* and *source* processes through its weekly meetings with manufacturing and by setting up clear responsibilities for inventory levels and customer service. By modifying operating processes and adjusting the organizational structure and roles, Smith Bits was able to gain a strong competitive advantage and raised its customer service level. As Vice President Mike Pearce notes, "The organizational change had a huge impact on how we thought about our supply chain and provided visibility for the first time into how the actions within one region affect customer service in another."

What makes for an effective supply chain organization? Just as there is no universal definition for the supply chain organization, there is no one-size-fits-all approach to creating one. There are, however, several characteristics that increase the odds of success. Based on our observation and experience, an effective organization:

- Supports the overall business strategy
- Provides the skills and core competencies—either internally or through strategic partnerships—needed to execute all supply chain processes
- Has metrics in place to measure performance
- Follows a set of practical design principles

Periodic assessment of how well your organization is aligned with your strategic imperatives is essential. So is regular evaluation of how well each role within the organization is defined. And most critical is the need to verify that the people assigned to each role have the technical and managerial skills to execute their defined responsibilities effectively.

EVOLUTION OF THE SUPPLY CHAIN ORGANIZATION

The traditional operations organization is functionally oriented. That is, key supply chain activities and associated groups report directly to their relevant functional managers. Logistics (receiving, shipping, and traffic management) and manufacturing, for example, may report to the vice president of operations, and typically there would be separate procurement and customer-order management groups (see Figure 3-3). This type of organizational structure was typical in the 1970s and 1980s, and it is still quite common today.

In the 1980s and 1990s, companies began to transition to organizational structures that grouped many, but not necessarily all, core supply chain functions in one department. Many of these companies still had a vice president of operations, but the associated responsibilities expanded

FIGURE 3-3

Functional supply chain organization.

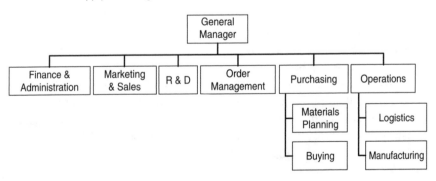

beyond functional areas such as manufacturing and logistics to include managing suppliers and filling customer orders. We call this the *transitional* supply chain organization. In most transitional organizations, order management reports to the sales or sales operations function, not to the vice president of operations (see Figure 3-4).

The term *supply chain* didn't come into vogue until the middle to late 1990s. At that time, we began to see the emergence of positions such as supply chain manager or vice president of supply chain (see Figure 3-5).

F I G U R E 3–4

Transitional supply chain organization.

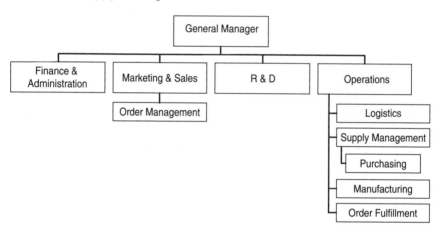

F I G U R E 3–5

Partially integrated supply chain organization.

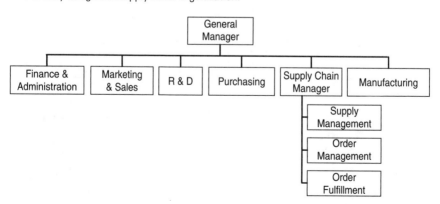

This period also marked the beginning of the now-widespread philosophy of the supply chain as an end-to-end process.

What's in a Name?

The actual titles used within an organization are far less important than the associated roles, responsibilities, and span of control. Although we're using titles such as *operations vice president* and *vice president of supply chain,* your company may choose any title you deem appropriate—depending on the size of the organization, the existing hierarchy, and any policies related to the assignment of job titles.

We started this chapter with a discussion of the integrated model, in which the supply chain organization is a separate function or entity. In this model, a supply chain management group is responsible for cross-functional operational objectives, such as inventory days of supply, order-fulfillment lead time, or customer on-time delivery. In the integrated model, the supply chain manager has full control over the resources needed to execute the supply chain strategy (see Figure 3-6).

At first glance, the transitional and integrated models may look very similar, but the difference is in much more than rearranging a few boxes on the organization chart or renaming functions. The concept of a "holistic" supply chain organization as depicted in the integrated model is relatively new.

FIGURE 3–6

Integrated supply chain organization.

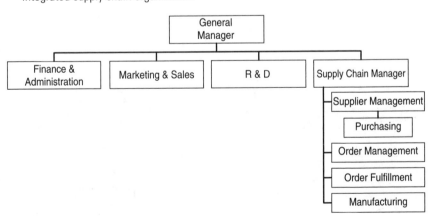

GUIDING PRINCIPLES FOR ORGANIZATIONAL DESIGN

There are many ways to structure an integrated organization, and hundreds of publications on organizational behavior, human resources management, and organizational change management try to offer guidance. But there is no off-the-shelf blueprint for designing an effective supply chain organization. And to compound the difficulty, there is likely to be limited tolerance for an ineffective design because the supply chain runs at the core of the business's ability to generate daily revenues.

The decision to set up an integrated supply chain organization is only the first step of many, but it is a strategically important one with profound consequences. As you plan, design, develop, and implement your new organization, keep in mind these four guiding principles:

+ *Form should follow function—that is, organization should mirror process.*

+ *For every process, assign an accountable function or individual.*

+ *Know, grow, and keep your core capabilities.*

+ *Organize around the skills you need, not the skills you have.*

Let's look at each of these principles more closely.

Form Follows Function

Many companies still use a traditional operations model. Yet improving end-to-end supply chain performance is extremely difficult in an organization with a functional structure and management responsibilities. This is why any integration of your supply chain processes likely will require major organizational change to align your people, processes, and metrics to support your strategy.

Agere Systems is an example of a company that reorganized to support a new top-down planning capability. Agere provides advanced integrated-circuit solutions to manufacturers of personal computers (PCs), wireless terminals, network equipment, and disc drives. In the mid-1990s the company made major investments in supply chain systems for enterprise resource planning (ERP) and advanced planning and order management. With the new systems in place, it was able to do fully integrated, automated planning—everything from high-level supply chain planning to production scheduling for each manufacturing facility—on a daily basis.

The goal was to greatly simplify planning, keep manual intervention to a minimum, and improve customer service while improving asset utilization.

Agere management expected its planners to accept most of the system's recommendations. Instead, they were overriding the system more than 90 percent of the time.[4]

Why? Agere's product-focused business units were responsible for acknowledging orders. Planners within these decentralized business units changed order due dates constantly—in response, they explained, to changing customer needs. In other words, the planners' information was more current than that of the planning system, and overrides were necessary to meet the performance goals for order delivery.

Agere also had a centralized planning group responsible for allocating production capacity to the various product groups. Not surprisingly, this group had a hard time responding to the constant stream of changes in order priority. This turmoil spilled into manufacturing, where production managers had to reshuffle their production schedules constantly to respond to the newest set of priorities—an inefficient approach, to say the least.

When he investigated the root cause of this inefficiency, Peter Kelly, executive vice president, global operations group, found that while some reschedules were indeed due to actual changes in customer requirements, in most cases planners were deliberately "gaming" the system to secure a higher priority for the orders they were managing.

Kelly wanted a planning process that was optimized at the highest level of the supply chain, not one geared to the needs of the various business units. He felt that effective supply chain planning would never occur as long as localized business-unit pressures and incentives drove the planners. To solve the problem, Kelly created a new supply chain planning organization that centralized planning activities and the responsibility for order management.

Within six months, plan overrides had declined from more than 90 percent to less than 50 percent. And as the number of overrides decreased, the time spent by planners on manual calculations and reprioritization was reduced greatly. The planning group became much more focused on ensuring data accuracy within both the planning system and customer orders, dramatically improving shipping performance from 75 to 95 percent and inventory turns by two turns during the next 12 months.

Agere had a clear catalyst for undertaking a major organizational restructuring: a failure to leverage its technology investment and a process-driven operational improvement plan with clear ownership. But you don't have to wait for an adverse event to prod you into refitting the organization to your supply chain processes. Where should you start? First, put aside any organizational charts and focus instead on the activities within your core supply chain processes. Group the major activities, keeping in mind that every participant in each process is both a customer and a supplier and that every supply chain event or task has both an input and an output. Identify the people responsible for executing the *plan, source, make, deliver,* and *return* processes, focusing on the tasks they perform rather than on the name of the group to which they report.

As you begin to sketch the lines around the groups responsible for supply chain planning and execution, remove the real or perceived boundaries between functions and bring complementary skill sets closer together. By setting up a new supply chain planning department, Agere was able to both consolidate planning activities within a centralized group and remove the boundaries between the business units and the supply chain organization.

Be aware that removing the borders between groups destroys the traditional functional organization and may result in managers becoming individual contributors, presidents reporting to managers, or whole groups dispersed and reallocated elsewhere. In some cases you may create an entirely new division organized around supply chain processes.

IBM did just that in 2002, when it established the integrated supply chain (ISC) organization.[5] Within just 12 months, IBM pulled together all the pivotal functions of the supply chain, combining its front-end customer support teams, manufacturing, procurement, and logistics into a new unit. In so doing, it brought together about 19,000 employees in 100 locations in 59 countries. IBM had long used a solutions-based business model—one that combines technology, products, and services—and wanted to adapt its supply chain to support this model. It found that just changing the reporting structure, moving like skills together, and breaking down the walls between manufacturing, procurement, and distribution yielded immediate benefits. The next steps were to establish common goals and objectives, well-defined roles and responsibilities, and a strong management system with clear measurement and accountability.

Kraft Foods North America also created an organization designed around core supply chain processes with the expectation that streamlining the supply chain would reduce the cost of goods sold and improve the company's bottom line.[6] It structured an organization that encompasses all the activities that go into delivering products to customers, from planning and production scheduling to transforming raw materials into finished goods and then packaging and distributing those goods.

The goal of an effective supply chain organization is to optimize the end-to-end order-fulfillment process—not individual functions—all the while achieving the lowest total cost. Kraft willingly invests in

> The goal of an effective supply chain organization is to optimize the end-to-end order-fulfillment process—not individual functions—all while achieving the lowest total cost.

manufacturing, for instance, if it drives equal or greater savings in transportation or warehousing.

As these examples show, designing a supply chain organization is not about inventing new titles or creatively moving the lines and boxes on an organizational chart. It's about form following function. Effective supply chain *process* design tightly integrates a series of disparate processes, whereas effective supply chain *organizational* design tightly integrates the groups and individuals responsible for executing those processes.

Every Process Requires Accountability

A functional or transitional organization is likely to promote activities that optimize performance within specific departments. In some companies, it's not uncommon to find that supply chain metrics are used by one department to highlight the failings of another. These highlighted failings often serve to take focus away from lack of performance or improvement in the "accusing" department. These organizational models also may leave gaps in terms of roles and responsibilities. By contrast, an integrated organization ensures that each essential role is defined and that responsibility for executing each role is unambiguous.

In the integrated organization, it is critical to have a strong leader in charge of the overall supply chain and ultimately accountable for its success. Ideally, a senior-level manager on the executive team, this person mediates between functions and maintains an overall vision of the end-to-end process. Without this leadership role and clearly defined responsibilities throughout the supply chain, it will not deliver its full potential, and in some cases, serious performance problems can arise.

For example, we worked with a company that sells software tools and related hardware in a crowded, competitive market dominated by four major players. Despite the complexity of the products and a lengthy sales process, customers expected immediate product availability once the decision to purchase was made. Our client wanted to differentiate itself through superior order-delivery performance.

Although the products were technical, no custom configuration was necessary. The features and options purchased by the customer did have to be detailed in a custom contract, which a contract specialist had to review and approve. The senior management team reviewed order-fulfillment cycle time on a monthly basis, and functional areas were diligent about monitoring the cycle times associated with the major activities under their jurisdiction.

The shipping department, for instance, was meticulous about tracking the time needed to pick, pack, and prepare an order for shipment. This department also tracked the various reasons why orders could not be processed and prepared a weekly report on those causes, which ranged from material shortages to obsolete product information to incorrect customer addresses.

Other departments used similar metrics to track the time an order sat in their functional area and the causes of any delays. For example, the order-entry group monitored how often orders arrived from the field with incomplete or erroneous information and how often customer orders referenced products that had been phased out or were not yet available. Incomplete or incorrect orders were redirected to the function deemed best suited to resolve the issue. Orders with more than one problem often made multiple loops through the process before all issues could be addressed (see Figure 3-7).

Department managers collected order-fulfillment metrics regularly but used them mainly to justify or explain cycle times that were longer than their functional targets and to redirect responsibility to the group(s) causing the problem. Rarely were metrics used as a tool to analyze the root causes of delays or to correct errors early in the order-fulfillment process. In effect, the metrics masked the problems within each function instead of clarifying them.

Faced with increasingly irritated customers and a sales force that complained about time wasted chasing orders instead of developing new business, the company's executive team turned its attention to the supply chain and set an aggressive goal: to cut the average order-fulfillment cycle time from 25 days to 4 days or less.

We worked with the company to redesign its overall order-management process and eliminate the functional boundaries that resulted in inefficient handoffs. Using a RACI analysis (see the following page), we identified the areas and processes with unclear or ambiguous accountability. It quickly became apparent that no person or function had accountability for the order-fulfillment process as a whole. No group had ultimate responsibility for ensuring accurate customer or product data or for shepherding orders through the fulfillment process (see Figure 3-8 for results of a RACI analysis).

FIGURE 3–7

Order-fulfillment process at Company X before RACI analysis.

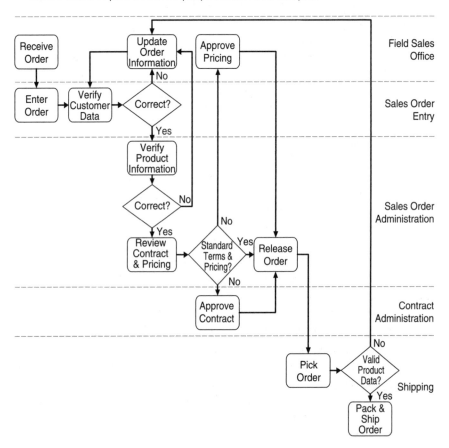

RACI Defined

RACI is an acronym derived from the four potential roles that an individual or function can play relative to a specific activity:

R—Responsible. Designates the person or function responsible for executing a particular activity. The accountable person determines the degree of responsibility. Responsibility can be shared.

A—Accountable. Designates the person or function ultimately accountable for completing the activity. There can be only one accountable person for a decision or activity, and accountability cannot be delegated.

F I G U R E   3–8

What an RACI analysis shows.

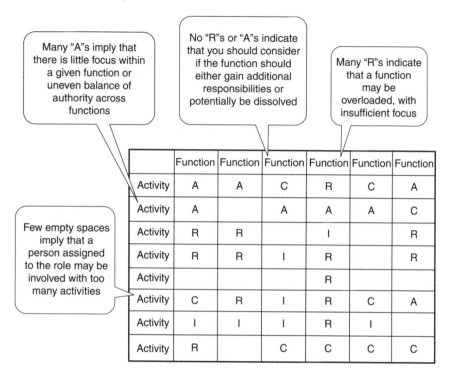

C—Consulted. Designates person(s) or function(s) that must be consulted before a decision or activity is finalized. This is a two-way communication.

I—Informed. Designates the person(s) or function(s) that must be notified of the completion or output of a decision or activity. This is a one-way communication.

The first step was to redesign the order-fulfillment process to minimize errors, backtracking, and delays. The RACI analysis helped us to group, define, and assign accountability for the major activities and related tasks. The new process included checks and balances designed to flag and resolve problems as soon as possible and to prevent the queuing and batching that typified the old process. Most important, the root causes of any problems were identified, and all departments involved in the order-fulfillment process were made aware of necessary changes.

A new customer-order oversight position consolidated several departments—order entry, contract administration, and order management—and had the added responsibility of being the primary liaison between the customer and the company. And the account manager's responsibilities were expanded to include accountability for the accuracy of all customer and product data (see Figure 3-9).

At first, progress was slow. The tendency to shift blame for problems to other functions was a hard habit to break, and some people resisted taking responsibility for their new roles within the organization. After a few months, however, the company began to accept the concept of joint ownership and specific accountability.

As a result, errors were caught and resolved earlier in the process, and cycle times began to decline. The company continued to refine its supply chain processes and developed automated systems to address several of the newly apparent root causes of order delays. For example, a database of nonstandard but preapproved contract language was developed. It helped cut the time needed for contract reviews from over 5 days to less than 1 day. After 10 months, the company had exceeded its initial goal—order-fulfillment cycle time averaged just over 3 days (see Figure 5-4).

FIGURE 3–9

Order-fulfillment process at Company X after RACI analysis.

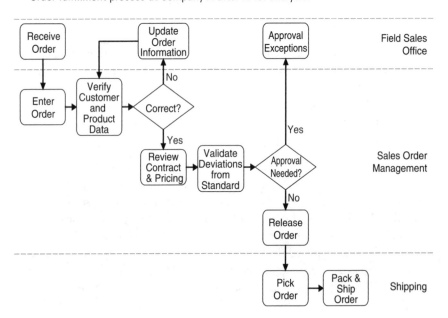

This example shows that as supply chain strategy and associated processes evolve, new metrics can help formalize accountability and drive optimal company performance. The next step is to structure the organization in a way that supports these new metrics and ensures that each person has a clearly defined role with a clear set of responsibilities.

In general, you should choose key metrics and define target performance levels *before* you finalize your supply chain process design. Once you've set performance objectives and the operating processes needed to meet those objectives, you're ready to rethink your supply chain organization, choosing what to do, who should do it, and how. Finally, align your organizational accountability with your key metrics and target levels of performance.

Know and Grow Your Core

Before mapping an organizational design, it's important to lay out both current and desired core competencies. These will serve as a foundation for structuring the organization. *Core competencies* are defined in many ways, but internal capabilities can be considered *core* when they confer a competitive advantage or are otherwise essential for achieving your company's strategic objectives.

Relating your company's core competencies to your supply chain strategy likely will be an iterative activity. Don't try to force-fit existing capabilities onto the needs dictated by your strategy—it won't work. Nor should you let your organization's capabilities limit your company's strategic objectives.

Is a core competency something you *should* be good at? Yes. Is a core competency something you *are* good at? Maybe. How do you know? First, take stock of what you have. In many cases metrics will tell you which activities your company excels at, but don't assume that those activities are core competencies or that subpar performance areas are "not core."

As we saw in Chapter 1, the first step toward making an outsourcing decision is deciding what you're really good at and which areas are—or have the potential to become—strategic differentiators. These are the activities to keep in-house. Other activities may be better performed by third-party providers and their ever-expanding menu of services. For instance, Flextronics describes how it has upgraded its role as "vendor" to that of "virtual manufacturer" to technology companies by offering design, engineering, manufacturing, and logistics solutions.[7] This approach reassures OEM customers that by choosing Flextronics as a partner, they will be free to focus on their other core competencies—such as research and development, sales, marketing, and branding.

By jettisoning noncore activities, companies are promised many benefits: greater focus on remaining activities, economies of scale, buying power, sophisticated planning tools and systems, and access to state-of-the-art production equipment—all without making large capital investments. But what if what's left after outsourcing is insufficient to drive effective performance? We refer to this as *thinning* the core.

In some cases a company becomes increasingly reliant on supply chain partners, and the remaining core begins to shrink in unintended ways. The people left within the company may have little personal experience with core operations processes, such as materials planning, supplier development and management, and demand management. This can result in a vicious cycle: The company continues to lose internal operations talent and becomes less effective. Companies simply may forget how to perform activities once considered essential for day-to-day operations.

Mike McNamara, chief operating officer at Flextronics, sees many companies who have allowed their core to become too thin. "It's important for us to have people within our customers' companies with whom we can 'talk supply chain,'" he says. "We see a lot of companies who are no longer capable of performing some very critical activities."[8]

This is an issue for Flextronics when they work with customers to develop the parameters that will govern the relationship between the two companies—and when they are attempting to execute on a day-to-day basis. "If there is no one within the customer's organization who can develop a long-term demand plan," says McNamara, "it's very hard for us to get set up in the way that will serve them most efficiently."

Companies can easily underestimate the complexity and competence built into their operational processes or misread the ease with which these capabilities can be transferred to supply chain partners. Maintaining strong links between newly outsourced operations and those kept in-house also can be a challenge. Very often the decision to outsource one or more of your core supply chain processes will require that you develop a new core competency—the ability to manage partners effectively.

How do you know what your core competencies are or should be? Remember that all essential supply chain processes must exist somewhere within your supply chain—whether inside your company or beyond your borders in the extended supply chain (the *chain of chains*). Review your company's basis of competition and understand the process elements that must be in place to support it. Ask yourself, "Is this activity critical to competitive advantage, business growth, customer service, or superior offerings?" (See Figure 3-10.)

If the answer to any of these questions is yes, the activity is likely a core competency and one you should keep within your organization and grow. In general, functions such as demand planning, supply-demand balancing, and supplier development need to be nurtured as core competencies because they are so dependent on current customer requirements. Product complexity and supply-base stability also play a role in determining which core competencies should be tightly held; a complex product or an unstable supply base make the transition to a third party more difficult and risky.

While outsourcing providers may offer design-for-manufacturability (DFM) services, be careful what product-development activities you outsource. DFM is a critical link between the product-development function and supply chain operations. The same is true for activities associated with new product introduction (NPI). An NPI coordinator within the supply chain organization is essential. And once these skills are lost, they are extremely hard to rebuild.

In the consumer products market, product development is a critical core competency. The need for a steady steam of new products in response to fast-changing consumer tastes also places tremendous pressure on the supply chain—especially the purchasing function, which must keep the company aligned with the supply base at all times. Dial, the maker of soaps and other consumer products, restructured itself to better focus on its ability to develop and deploy new products rapidly. The company's management team acknowledged that an agile procurement process was a critical piece of the restructuring. Dial redesigned its overall approach to sourcing and procurement, transforming the purchasing function from a

F I G U R E   3–10

Four tests of core competency.

Is this activity critical to:

Competitive Advantage	Business Growth
Customer Service	Superior Offerings

decentralized organization operating at the site level to a central body headed by a senior-level executive. The company combined all of Dial's purchasing and put commodity experts in charge of buying raw materials. The chemical buyer, for instance, is a trained chemist who understands the details of chemical composition. Dial also simplified its supply base, working closely with a smaller number of key suppliers and consolidating its buying power across different business units. Finally, the company developed a system for implementing innovative cost-savings ideas. What was the combined result of these actions? Total savings of $100 million over five years.[9]

Dial is an excellent example of how to build core competencies while developing a supply chain organization. Management saw the need for commodity experts with deep technical knowledge of the properties and characteristics of the materials for which they were responsible. Procurement expertise was identified as an area in which thinning was unacceptable.

To apply a similar approach in your own company, start with a list of key supply chain processes and the core competencies needed to execute those processes. Use your company's longer-term strategy as a guide to establish this list of proficiencies. Summarize the skills that will be needed to create or defend competitive advantage, to help grow the business, and to ensure customer satisfaction. Next, identify any gaps between the skills needed and those already in place. Finally, get consensus on whether to develop these skills in-house through training and targeted hiring or to use supply chain partners to fill the gaps.

GAINING RESPECT FOR THE SUPPLY CHAIN DISCIPLINE

To establish the supply chain as a strategic asset, the leader of the supply chain organization must be accorded status on a par with other members of the executive management team. Many companies remain locked in a traditional paradigm in which sales, marketing, and development are considered the architects of the company's strategic direction, whereas purchasing, manufacturing, and distribution are thought of as tactical executers. While bemoaning high inventories, late shipments, or missed revenue opportunities, few companies see the potential value that effective supply chain management can deliver or view supply chain management as a critical area of expertise. Without the support of the executive team and a clear mandate for the supply chain leader to champion improvement efforts, major business-impacting opportunities are left underexploited.

The development of supply chain management as a core competency and an organizational imperative doesn't just happen—a conscious effort is needed. As a discipline, supply chain management is constantly evolving, and its impact on business performance is growing. Staying on top of best practices in supply chain management is challenging enough; ensuring that the rest of your company does the same is even more difficult.

> # The development of supply chain management as a core competency and an organizational imperative doesn't just happen—a conscious effort is needed.

How do you ensure that an integrated supply chain is viewed as being as critical to business success as product development or marketing and sales? An education and awareness program can be a key driver. Metrics also can be a powerful tool in communicating the benefits of a highly integrated supply chain. Start with a quantitative gap analysis expressed in terms that any executive can relate to—bottom-line impact. For example, research by PRTM's benchmarking subsidiary, The Performance Measurement Group, LLC, shows that best-in-class consumer products companies enjoy a whopping 5.5 percent (of revenue) advantage in total supply chain management cost over median performers. For a $150 million company, that's more than an $8 million difference in cost savings.[10]

Results are the ultimate attention-getter. Following the gap analysis, make a change to your supply chain that delivers a sustainable improvement in costs or service—and use it to get attention. This is what Angel Mendez did at palmOne, Inc. palmOne is one of the world's leading developers of personal digital assistants (PDAs). When Mendez joined the company in 2001 as senior vice president of global operations for the solutions group, he was given the task of transforming the supply chain into a competitive differentiator—no small task considering that palmOne had just been forced to write off nearly $300 million of inventory.

The first item on his agenda: educating palmOne's senior management on the critical role the supply chain plays in executing the company's strategy. "Before I arrived," says Mendez, "palmOne had had eight consecutive quarters where it was difficult to produce enough product to keep up with demand. The mind-set had always been building product, then pushing it to the channel. The supply chain organization was viewed as the means to get the product made. There were really no other expectations."[11]

Mendez aimed to raise the visibility of his organization and garner support from the senior management team. The recession that was in full swing when he joined the company actually proved an advantage. "Sometimes it takes a shrinking economy to get the CEO to focus on the supply chain," he said. "Catastrophe can be a catalyst. Why not leverage this fact to get what you need?" He quantified the financial benefits an upgraded supply chain would deliver to the company and its shareholders. Then he developed a clear roadmap for getting there.

Mendez's roadmap included a fundamental overhaul of the supply chain processes and organization. "We had a lot to do," he noted. "The plan we put in place was iterative. It allowed us to prioritize, get some initial wins, [and] then justify the resources it would take to execute the next step of the plan." palmOne had a weak demand-management process, making it difficult to see the level of activity within the sales channel. Decisions to build product were based on inaccurate forecasts rather than on current market activity. Manufacturing and material costs were high relative to those of other consumer electronics companies. Relationships with key suppliers and customers were strained. And the company used four different service providers to repair returned units, resulting in few economies of scale, a high repair cost per unit, and a highly complex returns-management process.

Still, Mendez didn't "own" all the core supply chain processes. Product groups were responsible for demand management. Repair and support were managed on a regional basis within the sales organization. "The company had always focused on the 'supply' part of the supply chain," says Mendez. "They weren't used to thinking of an end-to-end process. So the supply chain organization was mostly focused on procurement, with enough planning capability to determine what needed to be purchased. And not everyone within the organization was as highly skilled as what was needed for the environment in which we operate."

Mendez used the Supply-Chain Operations Reference-model (SCOR) (see Core Discipline 2), to build the roadmap for his organization and for the group process-improvement efforts. He developed a three-phased plan to be executed over two years. Then he began to restructure the supply chain organization, taking on responsibility for demand management, repair, and product support. He knew that his title of senior vice president made the task easier. "My title helped me cut through a lot of red tape," he says, "but so did the fact that I was able to clearly demonstrate the benefits of an integrated organization."

palmOne's new supply chain organization was set up as a global organization with localized capabilities. Mendez's staff included a director responsible for each of the core *plan, source, make, deliver,* and *return* processes and a well-qualified set of individuals within each group. The skills within the organization reflected the company's strategic imperatives: a demand-management process that could react quickly to current market conditions, a supply base that could provide palmOne with the best value in the materials and services it procures, and ongoing improvements in cost-effectiveness, quality, and customer service.

palmOne's approach is a good example of how to establish the importance of your supply chain organization to ensure that it gets the resources it needs. The best way to gain support and respect for the supply chain as a strategic asset is to prove that it already is one. Simply put, results talk.

Focus on the Skills You Need

Clearly, balancing the competencies you need with the competencies you have is critical to executing your strategy. But what happens when the demand for skills outstrips the supply? Should you change the structure of your organization, change your strategy, or accept the imbalance?

> Clearly, balancing the competencies you need with the competencies you have is critical to executing your strategy.

Common sense tells us that companies with well-trained, knowledgeable people can operate more efficiently, seize market opportunities more readily, and weather economic downturns more effectively. And despite claims to the contrary, state-of-the-art systems and tools that support supply chain management are no replacement for human beings. Although they provide a degree of decision support that was not possible even a few years ago, these systems demand sophisticated users. In fact, today's new knowledge economy requires a new type of supply chain professional—one who can quickly assimilate volumes of information and use it to make sound decisions. In effect, the bar has been raised, not lowered.[12]

Simply put, behind every world-class supply chain are world-class people. The same "total cost of ownership" principles that apply to your material assets also apply to your human assets. Procter & Gamble (P&G) is a case in point. P&G built an organization that merges manufacturing, engineering, purchasing, and customer service.[13] The company sees these functions as an integrated system whose principal purpose is to move materials from suppliers to customers while adding value along the way.

P&G hires highly qualified, flexible people and pays them well, reasoning that it will get more for its money than by hiring lower-cost people with limited skills and higher turnover. In short, a more expensive workforce provides a lower total cost of ownership.

As you design your organization, keep in mind that technologies don't deliver success—people do.

New technologies such as the Internet are transforming traditional business functions. But it's important to remember, as you design your organization, that technologies don't deliver success—people do. To get the most out of new technology, you'll want to find and develop people who understand how to leverage it to improve operations and the performance of such routine activities as purchasing, customer service, and logistics management.

Advanced Fibre Communications, Inc. (AFC), understands this well. The Petaluma, California–based telecommunications equipment manufacturer is the leading provider of broadband access solutions for the global telecommunications industry. And, although AFC had enjoyed eight years of steady growth, it still operated like a startup when Jeff Rosen joined the company in 2000 as vice president of operations. "The organization was set up to be effective in a startup mode," explains Rosen, "but the processes in place were increasingly strained. Everything was done manually, and there was no focus on building processes and systems that would allow the company to scale."[14] AFC's focus on tactics and day-to-day execution was wholly consistent with the company's strategy for many years. However, the market was changing, the strategy was changing, and the supply chain had to adapt to new business imperatives—immediate product availability, high service levels, and higher product margins.

Rosen knew that he had to upgrade his organization and the systems used for supply chain planning and execution. He also knew, though, that he had to prove himself before he could get approval to make broad changes to his team. Thus he developed a plan to "get some wins and put something on the table to get attention." His first efforts targeted the procurement group, where he replaced some people with more experienced commodity managers. These new hires were tasked with building cost models for key materials, restructuring the supply base, and negotiating with existing vendors to secure better pricing. Rosen avoided making very senior hires. "Reasonably experienced was fine for what we needed," he explained.

As a result of these initial efforts, customer service levels and time margins began to improve. These improvements caught the attention of AFC chairman, president, and CEO John Schofield, as well as the company's board of directors. Over the next two years, Rosen was given more responsibility and more resources to continue upgrading the supply chain organization. He replaced many of the people who were focused on day-to-day transactions with people who could design entirely new supply chain processes. "My strategy was simple," says Rosen. "Start by hiring smart people capable of designing highly effective processes, [and] then let them run the process they helped architect." His first key hires were chartered with defining new processes for procurement, asset management, planning, and order management.

Once the basic processes were in place, Rosen brought in several very senior managers tasked with putting in place a mind-set of continuous improvement. He also began a systematic update of the systems that supported AFC's supply chain processes. Like many telecom companies, AFC outsources production to a contract manufacturer and uses sophisticated information systems to provide forecast data and to closely monitor the status of customer orders.

Rosen notes that the outsourcing strategy and the new software tools shaped the skills his organization needed. "When I started, I had a lot of people who were good at day-to-day transactions and putting out fires. Many of them were uncomfortable with the idea of using technology for processes they were used to doing manually. I needed people who were not afraid to use technology to do their job."

Over a two-year period, Rosen completely restructured the organization, merging procurement and materials planning and forming an umbrella organization that included *plan, source, make, deliver,* and *return* processes. Old positions were eliminated and new ones created. Rosen chose his team carefully. Today, his "cost per head" is somewhat higher than in the past, but there are far fewer people, and each one provides critical skills the organization formerly lacked.

Matching the right people to vital roles is no easy task. Many managers are reluctant to jettison an employee who has served the company well, for example, even if his or her skill set does not meet the needs of the redesigned supply chain organization. Other companies view the prospect of finding, recruiting, hiring, and training the people they really need as too complicated or time-consuming, so they transfer someone who did well in one position but is a poor fit for the slot being filled. It's important to resist the temptation to force-fit a valued employee into a role for which he or she is not qualified.

Even worse than making wrong fits is designing an organization that is too strongly influenced by the skills and interests of existing employees. We worked with a computer peripherals company that was moving to an outsourced production model. The company engaged two contract manufacturers, each responsible for a major product line. The supply chain vice president created two relationship manager positions, knowing that managing each of these new relationships would be a full-time job.

Not surprisingly, several current employees saw the new positions as an excellent opportunity. Although the new jobs called for a more sophisticated set of skills, the vice president found himself lobbied aggressively by internal candidates. He also was under tremendous pressure to "just get someone in here." He ended up hiring both an internal candidate and an external hire—a seasoned industry expert who had been managing a contract manufacturing relationship for several years. Not surprisingly, the "home grown" relationship manager struggled with his new responsibilities. After six months, he was replaced by a more qualified individual.

The lesson? Your supply chain strategy and associated processes will fail to move your company forward if you don't have the right people. Effective execution demands the right skills and capabilities. Define your organization around the end-to-end supply chain processes, identify the skills you need for each role, and then go shopping—both inside and outside your company. Don't let the "inventory on hand" limit the success of your organization.

NEXT-GENERATION ORGANIZATIONAL DESIGN

The end-to-end supply chain typically needs management skills and roles that did not exist previously (see Figure 3-11).

Given the relative newness of some of these positions, your human resources department may not know how to find the people you need or how to screen them effectively without some support from your organization. To ensure that you have the right people in the right positions, put together a description of your supply chain strategy, a description of each key role, a clear definition of available career paths, and a comprehensive hiring plan.

This is not to say that every reorganization requires a major workforce turnover. Most supply chain organizations have only a few extremely critical roles—before or after an overhaul. These are the jobs that require specific qualifications, and you shouldn't settle for less. Current employees, with appropriate retraining or coaching, can fill most of the other roles in your new organization.

F I G U R E   3–11

New roles for end-to-end supply chain management.

New Role	Key Required Skills
Outsourcing Partner Relationship Manager **Make**	• Ability to negotiate strategic alliances and partnerships • Ability to drive best-in-class performance from supply chain partners • Ability to inspire individuals within various organizations to work collaboratively
Global Commodity Manager **Source**	• Ability to manage across continents • Ability to manage ongoing relationships with key suppliers and to execute the global supply chain strategy for products purchased from these suppliers • Ability to structure the supply base to achieve the lowest total cost of ownership • Ability to manage suppliers through objective measurements and regular generation of formal supplier scorecards
Customer Relationship Manager **Deliver**	• Deep understanding of the customer's business and channels • Sufficient understanding of supply chain operations to ensure implementation of core processes that support customer requirements
Supply Chain Process Improvement Manager **Plan**	• Thorough understanding of supply chain best practices • Ability to inspire individuals within multiple functions to work collaboratively • Ability to recognize opportunities for process improvement and appropriate automation
Supply Chain Performance Analyst **Plan**	• Thorough understanding of supply chain metrics and appropriate methods for target-setting • Ability to institutionalize metrics-driven reviews and continuous improvement programs

Owens Corning Profile: Reorganizing for "a Bright Future"

The "big squeeze" of its core industry segments—cost inflation and price deflation—led Owens Corning to rethink its supply chain organization and processes in order to understand the impact of these elements on its ability to be competitive and customer-facing enterprisewide.

Based in Toledo, Ohio, Owens Corning (OC) has manufacturing facilities in more than 25 countries and 165 distribution centers. It's a $5 billion market leader in building-materials systems and composites solutions known for its innovative portfolio of products—it invented glass fiber and glass-fiber insulation over 50 years ago.

Approximately 80 percent of the company's revenues come from its building-materials portfolio of products and systems that are sold through distributors, contractors, and large national retailers mainly in North America. Composites account for the remainder of revenues and are used in the automotive, telecommunications, electronics, and construction industries in a global market.

As big as it is and as well known as its brand is, however, OC has faced increasing competition within key markets because of globalization and industry consolidation in recent years. "We must be able to compete on more than price," notes Sue Hatfield, the company's director of strategy and integration for supply chain and technology. "Our greatest challenge is providing low-cost flexibility to meet increased customer demands."

This is a turnabout for the industry. Building products is a process manufacturing industry and is highly asset-intensive, making use of assets

131

and production efficiency the primary success factors for competing in the marketplace. Traditionally, flexibility has not been considered a key factor but increasingly is becoming one.

OC is organized into business units, each with its own commercial, sales, and supply chain processes and facilities. Having many business segments within the business units, the company struggled as supply chain requirements got more demanding. In the past, the company had a substantial level of redundancy in processes and personnel across business units and had inherited multiple legacy software applications that were poorly integrated. These factors created a lack of data integrity/integration at the enterprise level. This was seen as a key contributor to the increasing problems that OC was experiencing, such as inaccurate demand forecasts, poor planning, overall customer dissatisfaction, and high-cost supply chain operations.

THE TECHNOLOGY SOLUTION WASN'T ENOUGH

In the mid-1990s, the company deployed SAP's enterprise resource planning (ERP) product across its global enterprise. At the time, OC believed that a common global technology platform would resolve many of the business issues relating to its product-driven, make-to-stock manufacturing environment. This was important because these process issues affected OC's forecasts, materials management, production scheduling, ability to meet deadlines, and cost containment. According to Hatfield, "Our forecast accuracy was not good, we didn't have the right linkage to production schedules, and we weren't doing the right level of demand-supply balancing. Our planning problems were having downstream effects on our customers, impacting on-time delivery and order fill-rate performance."

The SAP system eliminated 500 legacy systems, achieving one of the company's prevailing goals—to keep it "simple, common, and global." OC then implemented SAP's advanced planning and logistics software. However, the information technology applications only brought so much benefit. As David Johns, senior vice president and chief supply chain and information officer, notes: "The progress made was in the areas of back-office operations, logistics, and

> A new SAP system eliminated 500 legacy systems and achieved one of OC's prevailing goals: to keep it "simple, common, and global."

materials management. But where we still lacked real integration was with our manufacturing and our sales and operations planning processes."

> OC wanted to see a $250 million improvement in income from operations (IFO) over three years.

It became apparent that a more customer-centric, enterprise-level approach using best practices and standards adopted by top-performing companies was needed to meet strategic goals. The biggest goal was "to operate as one company." This would prove to be no small order. A supply chain transformation initiative would become one of five top strategy principles championed by OC's new chief executive officer, Dave Brown. OC wanted to make significant gains in customer service levels and a $250 million improvement in income from operations (IFO) and working capital over a three-year period. It wanted to create a brighter future for its employees and stockholders.

Lifting supply chain transformation to the strategic level was just the beginning of the three-year plan. As Hatfield explains, "What we needed to do was to get better in each supply chain process (*plan, source, make, deliver*), change our mind-set from manufacturing efficiency to supply chain flexibility, and integrate our customers and suppliers into our supply chain. We also had to expand our thinking beyond the functional level to the enterprise, integrated supply chain level."

> "We needed to change our mind-set from manufacturing efficiency to supply chain flexibility," says Sue Hatfield.

ORGANIZATIONAL CHANGES

A first step was to integrate the functions having an impact on the customer experience—materials management, logistics and warehousing, customer service/call centers, receivables management, customer and product master data integrity—within a single group. Today, 350 employees report to this department, headed by Vice President of Customer Supply Chain Operations Meg Ressner.

"We intentionally put 'customer' in front of our organization's name to make sure that we were really driving the culture of the supply chain to be end-to-end and externally focused," she says. "The other thing we're trying to do is distinguish the process of supply chain from the organiza-tion that operates many of the processes." Ressner's group sits inside a broader organization called Supply Chain and Technology Solutions (SCTS), headed by David Johns. The reason for the differentiation? "We've been trying to help our company see that the supply chain is a business process that touches everybody in the company. SCTS focuses on the processes, by operating them, deploying technology that supports them, or encouraging process innovation and enhancements."

OC has recognized the value in combining the technology and supply chain process functions in one organization.

OC has recognized the value in com-bining the technology and supply chain process function in one organization. Johns explains the rationale: "We wanted to lever-age the resources we have across the enter-prise, do things faster, and improve the service we can provide." The company also wanted to be more flexible in its response to customers. Because OC had had a "do everything for everybody" mentality a decade ago, company costs were too high, and, as Johns says, "We weren't really able to grow, because we didn't have a consis-tent, coherent strategy."

"In those earlier days, we did understand that 'simple, common, and global' were key operating principles—and they remain so today—but now we understand that flexibility is the key competitive advantage," Johns says. He contrasts this customer-facing perspective with OC's his-torical focus on manufacturing efficiencies: "Our philosophy as a 60-year-old manufacturer was long product run times. And that strategy had all sorts of implications. But today, with a focus on flexibility, we're looking at market-driven lead times for product delivery and our ability to quickly respond to big changes in demand."

THE VISION THING

In order to ensure that it could respond more flexibly to customer demand, OC conducted an end-to-end supply chain assessment using PRTM's "stages of process maturity model for supply chain excellence" as a refer-ence point (see Chapter 6 and Appendix B). OC found that it was at early stage 2 of functional excellence in process maturity yet aspired to achieve solid stage 3 status, designated "enterprise integration." The company used the Supply-Chain Operations Reference-model (SCOR) to create a context for understanding the relationships among business strategy, supply chain configuration, supply chain practices, and technology. It knew that it needed to define the value proposition before it could get buy-in by all stakeholders. "The transformation vision provided a common, overall road-map," says Hatfield, "and provided an umbrella for enterprise-level improvement projects."

The supply chain organization identified four areas for immediate improvement: fixing the end-to-end planning process within materials management and instituting a sales and operations planning process in every business, leveraging warehousing and transportation at an enterprise rather than an individual business level, improving overall service performance with customers, and building greater manufacturing effectiveness and flexibility.

At the start, OC benchmarked its then-current performance levels against similar manufacturing organizations in three areas: customer service and responsiveness, cost performance, and asset performance. It set priorities and targets for customer-facing processes such as on-time delivery to request—a downstream result of greater alignment between demand and supply planning processes. Increasing the effectiveness of its 10-step sales and operations planning (S&OP) process also enabled OC to reduce costs by operating in a more integrated way across global operations.

Early results have included lower inventory levels and higher inventory quality, improved on-time delivery and order fill-rate performance, and reduced logistics costs. OC estimates that it will generate more than $165 million in value within the initial three years of the plan.

FROM PRODUCT TO MARKET FOCUS

Another goal was moving the organizational mind-set and execution capabilities from a commodity-based product focus to a solutions-based market focus, even though, as Meg Ressner confirms, OC has customers of both types: "It's true that our customer demands are evolving," she says, "and we must have the capability to deliver on all those demands, which means you have to have a flexible platform." To this end, account teams, transparent to the customer regardless of their request for service, were organized around specific high-value/high-volume partners. The intent is to align the right set of people, skills, and processes around customers' requirements. This might mean self-service for some customers, supported by portal technology or electronic data interchange (EDI) transactions for order management and fulfillment. It might mean a dedicated customer account team for other customers. As Ressner notes, even though OC is exploring use of the Internet for ordering and other customer-facing activities, the company also realizes that many of its major distributors and retailers have an emotional comfort level with their customer service representatives from OC.

The challenges are manifold. Customers want more customized service and more flexibility. They want tailored solutions that take cost out of their supply chains. "Many customers want us to be their partner—where we leverage the full resources of OC to help their business grow," says Hatfield. In customer alliances, this means that OC needs to become more integrated into its customers' supply chains—to understand what its customers are demanding and to create the processes that will ensure that demand is filled on time every time.

THE MECHANICS OF TRANSFORMATION

A key challenge of putting supply chain issues on everyone's radar screen was to redefine and educate employees on what the integrated supply chain meant for OC down to how each employee's role and responsibility fit into the supply chain. Says Hatfield, "We embarked on a whole educational process. One of the most effective things we did, as simple as it sounds, was to hire a design firm to draw an illustration of all the high-level supply chain processes at OC. When they were finished, it was clear that the supply chain is centered on our customers and really encompasses almost everything that we do. Everyone has a role, and the key to success is integration."

The supply chain organization realized that it would take three components to effect the transformational change it was aiming for: the people component, the process component, and the technology component. The people component would require education about the value of the supply chain to create "fully engaged employees"—those who would be trained and certified to execute processes with a high level of accountability for performance. A process architecture would have to be created with the unified goal of providing exceptional customer experiences. And last, the technology would have to be "fit for purpose": the enablement of higher levels of performance through greater visibility of information at all levels of management.

Once viewed as the primary driver of business processes, technology was now seen as an enabler of larger, more strategic goals. Evidence of this shift is apparent in the type of employee hired for the information systems organization. Don Kosanka, OC's chief information officer, explains: "The IS folks that we have are really not the technical folks you find in typical IS organizations. They have a really good understanding of the business processes that we operate, and their value comes in helping figure out where technology can enable each process to become more efficient, precise, or accurate. We outsource the more routine technical skill sets required to operate the IT infrastructure."

Kosanka is an example of the shift in thinking at OC. As he says, "When I first joined the firm 25 years ago, fresh out of college, I thought technology was the important driver. After a few years here, I shifted my view to process. Now I see the equally critical importance of people. Without every employee's buy-in, you can't execute the process or realize the value in the technology. So you might say I've moved to a much more integrated approach."

What's especially different about today's perspective on the role of technology, says Kosanka, is that "we actually try to solve our process challenges without technology, if possible, and use technology when it's required and when it actually enhances the project so [that] it justifies the investment."

Kosanka has used IT to take costs out of the supply chain. "Our total investment in IT over the last seven years has dropped every year, and as a percentage of sales it has dropped even faster," he says. "While we've decreased the amount spent in the infrastructure, we've been maintaining or growing our investment in applications to help the business units operate their processes better. Basically, we've done a good job of managing our costs to get higher performance for lower costs. We now have just a handful of major systems that we use." OC achieved these gains primarily by outsourcing many operational aspects of the IT infrastructure, from help-desk and data-center operations to network management.

Now the organization looks at technology very differently from even seven years ago. Ressner refers to the common set of technology and process elements as an enterprisewide toolkit. "Flexibility comes from using that toolkit and recognizing the unique characteristics of a particular market segment or customer. Without having the process and IT foundation in place that we have today, it would be difficult, if not impossible, and certainly much more expensive, to customize an approach."

GREATER COLLABORATION WITH SUPPLIERS

As it builds better partnerships with distributors and retailers, OC has developed a new perspective on its suppliers. "We have a point of view that

"We want to be our customers' best supplier and our suppliers' best customer," says David Johns.

our suppliers are as important to us as our customers, so just as we want to be our customers' best supplier, we want to be our suppliers' best customer," explains David Johns. "We are trying to make our systems, our processes, etc., as transparent as possible with our suppliers and our customers, by eliminating as many inefficiencies as possible in our dealings and taking the costs out of our shared supply chains."

The company has established programs and metrics for vendor relationship management and supplier development. Although its sourcing organization is separate from the supply chain solutions organization, the two departments leverage resources in support of common goals. For example, both groups collaborated on creating a portal structure that would facilitate interaction with vendors.

HORIZONTAL INTEGRATION

OC also has developed project review boards to help enforce the alignment and integration of key business processes, such as customer operations, materials management, sourcing, production, research and development, IT, and logistics. Each has representation from the three functional areas of technology, process, and operations to jointly assess and monitor IFO benefits, working capital savings, return on net assets (RONA), supply chain performance metrics, and overall allocation of people and capital resources for approved initiatives. A new "stage gated" approach ensures that before resources are assigned to specific projects, each has to pass a stringent test for business value.

This is another one of the building blocks to OC's "one company" mantra these days. Currently in the process of coming out of a financial restructuring process, it is reinventing its processes and internal organizations to give customers the experience of a single company that is poised for the increased competitiveness of the future.

4
CHAPTER

Core Discipline 4: Build the Right Collaborative Model

Collaboration is the cornerstone of effective supply chain management. As companies continue to narrow their strategic focus to a smaller number of core competencies, the skills and talents of outside partners become more critical. This creates a growing reliance on resources that you may not control directly and on strategies that you may have no hand in developing.

A recent survey of more than 100 international business leaders found that as companies migrate toward more extended supply chains, collaboration becomes their most strategic activity.[1] Despite its importance, there is little consensus about what collaboration means. If you asked 100 supply chain executives for a definition, you'd likely get 100 different answers. Certainly most would agree that collaboration is important, that technology and relationship building are critical components, and that companies with effective collaboration skills are likely to have a competitive edge. However, few executives would be able to offer a clear, unambiguous definition.

Why is it so hard to define *collaboration*? Because it can be many things and involve many types of partners. It can refer to a wide range of joint activities, from information sharing among business units to complex, long-term product development and marketing projects. We define *collaboration* as "the means by which companies within the supply chain work together toward mutual objectives through the sharing of ideas, information, knowledge, risks, and rewards."

Why collaborate? Very simply, an effective collaborative relationship can have major strategic and financial benefits. It can accelerate entry into a new market, increase flexibility, and provide access to expertise not available within your own company. It can deliver cost savings or increased revenues—or a combination of both. Collaboration is a business arrangement that changes the overall dynamics between two or more partners. Drivers of collaboration include the desire to access

* A technology owned by another company
* A technology that is too capital-intensive for one company to invest in alone
* A competency that is too costly to acquire, develop, or maintain
* A new market effectively closed off by high entry costs or preconditions (trade barriers, legislation, etc.)

Collaboration changes the most fundamental of all economic models— the relationship among cost, volume, and profit (C/V/P). For example, a company that needs specialized, capital-intensive equipment for production of a key component might have a C/V/P model with high fixed costs and low per-unit variable costs, as shown in Figure 4-1. This company needs a high volume of sales to be price-competitive and profitable. If an economic recession cuts into volume, the company could soon be operating at a loss.

FIGURE 4-1

C/V/P model with high fixed costs.

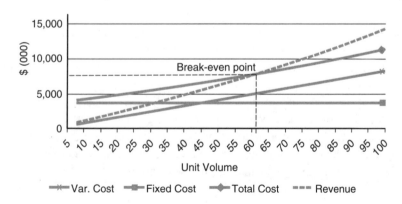

Collaborating with a partner that focuses on the production of specialized materials similar to the component might allow this company to offload some of its fixed costs, as shown in Figure 4-2, but with an accompanying increase in variable costs associated with the increase in the level of external sourcing. To make this approach pay off, the company must be willing to share any proprietary technology needed to manufacture the component, and its collaboration partner must be willing to invest in developing the additional capabilities needed to produce it. Since breakeven volume is lower, the company can compete across a wider range of volumes—albeit at the expense of gross margin at high volume.

Ongoing collaboration on product designs and production planning can make the company even more agile while continuing to add volume to the specialized manufacturer's business. Both collaboration partners will benefit economically.

As you can see, collaboration is *not* an altruistic activity. While it may seem a best practice to provide "seamless integration" and "extended visibility" to your supply chain partners, the fact is that true collaboration is very difficult, and there's no point in doing it unless you can achieve financial or strategic gain. For collaboration to be truly successful, therefore, it must deliver quantifiable economic benefit to all partners.

> True collaboration is very difficult, and there's no point in doing it unless you can achieve financial or strategic gain.

F I G U R E   4–2

C/V/P model after outsourcing some fixed costs.

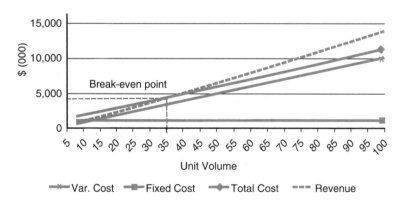

Despite the highly touted benefits shown in Figure 4-3, supply chain collaboration has the dubious distinction of being one of the most sought after but disappointing aspects of supply chain strategy. What's going on? To start with, the promise of effective, efficient collaboration is based on Internet technology and its ability to provide new levels of visibility and information sharing. The Internet bubble of the late 1990s gave rise to hundreds of software products that promised seamless interaction and endless visibility among supply chain partners.

Do these tools work? Some do, and some don't. Technology doesn't ultimately determine the success or failure of a collaborative relationship. Nor do the underlying processes that govern the use of technology—at least not on their own. Successful collaboration requires two additional components: sharing information and sharing benefits.

Information is at the heart of any collaborative relationship. To collaborate effectively, all partners must provide timely, accurate, and complete information—whatever is needed to achieve their mutual objectives. And each partner must respect the confidentiality and security requirements of the other. Mutual trust is key to a successful collaboration. Just as important, each partner must commit to a joint sharing of benefits—not necessarily an equal sharing but an equitable sharing. The success or failure of a collaborative relationship depends on clearly identified mutual gain.

FIGURE 4-3

Commonly cited benefits of collaboration.

Customers	Material Suppliers	Service Suppliers
• Reduced inventory • Increased revenue • Lower order management costs • Higher gross margin • Better forecast accuracy • Better allocation of promotional budgets	• Reduced inventory • Lower warehousing costs • Lower material acquisition costs • Fewer stockouts	• Lower freight costs • Faster and more reliable delivery • Lower capital costs • Reduced depreciation • Lower fixed costs
• Improved customer service • More efficient use of human resources		

COLLABORATION IS A SPECTRUM

Potential collaboration partners in supply chain management can be classified in three broad groups—customers, materials suppliers, and suppliers of services that support supply chain operations, such as manufacturing and logistics. Although each group requires a slightly different management approach, the relationships are established and maintained in similar ways.

Not all collaborations are created equal. Relationships between supply chain partners can have very different characteristics and still be considered collaborative in nature. And the results of collaborative relationships may vary widely from one set of partners to another. Figure 4-4 offers a framework for differentiating the various types of collaborative relationships and defining the basic characteristics of each. The horizontal axis plots the relative number of relationships, whereas the vertical axis measures the relative depth of collaboration. Within this framework, we define four levels of collaboration:[2] transactional, cooperative, coordinated, and synchronized.

Note that the boundaries between the different levels of collaboration are blurred. This is so because collaboration is a continuum, not a set of clearly delineated management practices. Note, too, that the dimensions of the two axes are inherently subjective and are used simply to

F I G U R E 4–4

The collaboration spectrum.

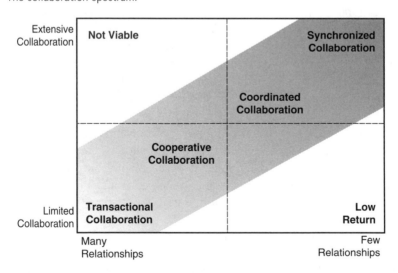

provide a clear graphic view of the collaboration spectrum. Other models use different criteria, such as level of investment or dependence on technology, to describe the depth and breadth of collaborative relationships. It's possible to create a matrix using any combination of these criteria or even to apply a multidimensional approach.[3]

The point is not to worry about picking the right labels for your collaborative relationships but to examine the various characteristics that differentiate each partnership. First, choose the degree to which each characteristic contributes to the likely success of the collaborative relationship, and then put a plan in place to achieve it. Every customer-supplier relationship can involve some level of collaboration. The fact that you're buying from a specific supplier or selling to a specific customer implies a relationship between your two companies, but it doesn't necessarily mean that you are collaborating. And just as not all relationships are created equal, not all collaborations are created equal.

Before setting off to systematically establish collaborative relationships with your supply chain partners, take the time to understand the degrees of collaboration along the spectrum and your company's specific needs. Often, a small number of deeply collaborative relationships is preferable to multiple relationships with a wide range of partners. Later in this chapter we'll discuss how to decide which degree of collaboration to set up with each supply chain partner.

Transactional Collaboration

Transactional collaboration aims for the efficient and effective execution of transactions between partners. This isn't to say that transactional relationships between supply chain partners offer no strategic value. However, partners in a transactional relationship rarely focus on reducing supply chain management costs or increasing revenues. The focus is usually on improving the ease at which transactions are conducted—for example, by eliminating the need for constant renegotiation. Transactional collaboration usually applies to customer-supplier relationships in which common or maintenance, repair, and overhaul (MRO) materials are purchased, and the decision to deal with a supplier is based mainly on price. With less strategically important supply chain partners, companies tend to focus on minimizing the effort associated with day-to-day transactions rather than on developing long-term relationships.

Transactional relationships rarely require sophisticated information systems. Indeed, many companies involved in this type of relationship lack the systems and infrastructure needed to provide and respond to information electronically. Because of this, many transactions are manual.

An example of a transactional relationship is any time a customer and a supplier agree to a set price for a specific product over a set period of time or until a certain purchase volume is reached. The buyer gets a fixed price over the life of the agreement in exchange for purchasing a minimum quantity of products; this also helps the seller's production planning. Transactional collaboration is the most basic and by far the most widely used collaboration model.

Cooperative Collaboration

Cooperative relationships have a higher level of information sharing. Supply chain partners may provide automatic commitments and confirmations or share information on forecasts, inventory availability, purchase orders, or order and delivery status. Usually, one partner posts information that the other partner reviews and acts on—

> Cooperative relationships have a higher level of information sharing.

a one-way communication in which data are sent either manually or electronically ("pushed") from one partner to the other or published in a manner that's accessible by the recipient ("pulled").

In a cooperative collaboration, the type and format of data provided usually are standardized. While more sophisticated technologies are available, electronic data interchange (EDI) is the primary method of communication used today, through either a proprietary EDI network or the Internet. For companies without an EDI capability, Internet-based supplier portals or extranets are an excellent alternative. Most of these tools enable document and content management and include embedded workflows to automate the routing of documents, forms, and certain data and tasks.

Coordinated Collaboration

In a coordinated relationship, supply chain partners work more closely together and rely more on each other's capabilities. As such, a coordinated relationship requires a two-way flow of information between partners and tightly synchronized planning and execution processes. Because the infrastructure and processes needed to support this type of information sharing are more complex than in the cooperative model, coordinated collaboration usually is reserved for more strategically critical supply chain partners.

Coordinated collaboration requires a high level of negotiation and compromise.

Unlike transactional and cooperative relationships, coordinated collaboration requires a high level of negotiation and compromise. Given the more strategic nature of these partnerships and the high level of data sharing, proprietary systems are needed for exchanging information. Because of this complexity, a coordinated relationship requires a long-term commitment by both partners and is rarely undertaken lightly. Putting the required processes and tools in place takes time and money; the expectation is that both parties will benefit from the expected efficiencies created as part of the ongoing execution of the relationship.

Vendor-managed inventory (VMI) programs are a commonly used method of coordinated collaboration. In a VMI relationship, the supplier is responsible for making sure that the customer never runs out of materials. While some VMI programs are manual—the supplier walks through the customer's site to monitor inventory levels—most programs in place today are automated. In some cases, the supplier can remotely manage inventory at the customer's site based on forecasts and usage. In other cases, the supplier uses current consumption rates and inventory levels to determine if more inventory is needed. In either case, effective data transmission is the key to successful VMI, a hallmark of coordinated collaboration.

Synchronized Collaboration

The greatest degree of collaboration on the spectrum occurs at the upper right quadrant of our framework—synchronized collaboration. In this model, the collaborative relationship moves beyond supply chain operations to include other critical business processes. Partners may invest in joint research and development projects, supplier development, and intellectual property (IP) development. The sharing of both physical and intellectual assets may even extend to shared personnel. Synchronized collaborations are often called *strategic alliances*.

In a synchronized relationship, information is developed jointly rather than just transmitted or exchanged. Moreover, synchronized collaboration tends to focus on a

In a synchronized relationship, information is developed jointly rather than just transmitted or exchanged.

strategic vision of the future rather than on near-term planning and tactical execution. Long-term commercial commitment is a hallmark of this type of collaboration.

Development projects that consider supply chain requirements when developing the product strategy are good examples of synchronized collaboration. A company that includes key materials suppliers or manufacturing partners as an integral part of its development team is far more likely to have product designs that are compatible with best-in-class supply chain performance. Unlike other types of collaboration, in which partners are apt to exchange product data, synchronized relationships usually include a shared product data management system.

FINDING THE RIGHT PLACE ON THE SPECTRUM

Each relationship with a supply chain partner has its own place on the collaboration spectrum. As you architect your collaboration strategy, you must identify which partners are best suited for each type of relationship. The collaboration spectrum offers a set of options—there's no "right" or "wrong" place to be along the diagonal. But there are areas within the matrix that should be avoided when choosing a collaboration model (see Figure 4-4).

First, there's the area labeled "Low Return." In this quadrant, companies collaborate on a limited basis with a set of supply chain partners. The investment and risk involved in this model are relatively low—and so is the return. While financial benefits certainly can accrue from limited collaboration, the "Low Return" model is not a commercially effective basis for a collaboration strategy, for the benefits are not worth the required investment.

The second area to avoid is that labeled "Not Viable." In this quadrant, the objective is deep collaborative relationships with many supply chain partners. Interestingly, developers of collaboration tools often describe this as the optimal model, asserting that advanced technologies enable collaboration that is both broad (many supply chain partners) and deep (extensive collaboration with each). While this level of integration is possible theoretically, it's not practical—mainly because aligning a large group of partners with your business objectives is extremely difficult.

Despite the hype around technologies that claim to support flawless integration among supply chain partners, most of today's collaborative relationships are transactional or cooperative. They tend to focus on basic supply chain activities—typically procurement and manufacturing. And even though transactional and cooperative relationships are considered "collaboration," they rarely deliver the benefits of lower inventory levels, better customer service, more efficient use of human resources, and faster, more reliable delivery. Why not? Because the investment required of each partner is low, and the resulting value is not enough to advance either company's strategy, enable entry into new markets, or provide access to new technologies or skill sets. Transactional collaboration and cooperative collaboration simply deliver modest improvements in how day-to-day transactions are executed.

This is not to say that transactional and cooperative relationships are without value. They're merely a first step in developing more complex, strategic relationships that create a true bond between partners. Advanced collaboration needs a greater investment, continuing maintenance, and ongoing vigilance against circumstances that could harm the relationship.

As companies move away from the traditional model of vertical integration, the need for deeper collaboration with select supply chain partners intensifies. Deciding to divest an internal competency doesn't eliminate the need—it simply moves the source of the competency beyond your company's direct control. As we saw in Core Discipline 3, the ability to manage these external relationships successfully can become a critical competency.

It's a major challenge to balance what's theoretically possible, what's needed to support the business strategy, and what's practical in terms of managing day-to-day operations. The fact that the collaboration spectrum is different for every company means that what's "optimal" in terms of number and type of collaborative relationships varies widely. Although most companies today are still a long way from their optimal range, the number of cooperative and coordinated relationships is growing (see Figure 4-5). The ability to reach an optimal state of collaboration is limited by the availability of partners prepared to work with you.

THE PATH TO SUCCESSFUL COLLABORATION

Your success depends on the ability of both you and your partner to execute according to your mutual agreement. While every partnership is different, the following guidelines for success apply to all:

- Master internal collaboration before trying to work with external partners.
- Define the appropriate degree of collaboration for each partner segment.

F I G U R E   4–5

The evolution of collaboration.

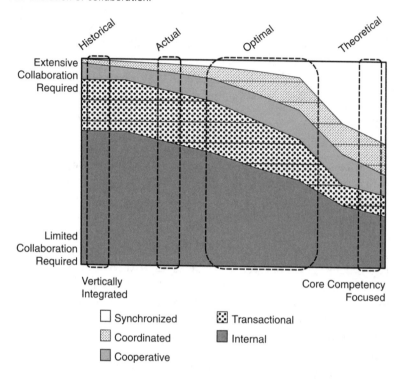

- ◆ Be sure that each party has a stake in the outcome of the collaboration. Share benefits, gains, losses, and risks.
- ◆ Be prepared to share information you once considered proprietary. Mutual trust is integral to successful collaboration.
- ◆ Set clear expectations for each party.
- ◆ Use technology to support your collaborative relationships.

Master Internal Collaboration First

If you can't collaborate within the four walls of your own company, your chances of success with external partners are small. Internal collaboration helps to test your company's "readiness" to achieve common goals by aligning processes, systems, and organizational structures—all in a low-risk environment. And internal success provides proof positive that the benefits of collaboration are real.

A key requirement of effective collaboration is shared metrics, but all too often these are missing.

The fact is that many companies don't collaborate particularly well, even internally. Departments or functions may be unwilling to compromise, even if a proposed concession is for the greater good of the company. The idea that successful collaboration will result in lower overall costs or improved service levels can be difficult to substantiate, so it may be viewed with skepticism. A key requirement of effective collaboration is shared metrics, but all too often these are missing.

Internal collaboration actually can be more difficult than external collaboration due to a range of complicating factors. For instance, a drive at the highest levels of a company to institute accountability for performance at the business unit or functional level can hinder effective collaboration. Moreover, complex systems for setting transfer prices and cross-charges are designed to allocate costs fairly across the company as a whole but often promote functional performance at the expense of enterprisewide cost performance. And reward structures that link individual compensation to business-unit performance can reinforce business-unit autonomy. These measures can be counterproductive, eliminating many of the key benefits of collaboration: economies of scale and scope, greater efficiency, knowledge sharing, and less duplication of effort.

Articulating the benefits of collaborating with external partners also may be easier than making the case internally. Collaborating with a customer, for instance, can increase revenues and deliver greater customer satisfaction. Collaborating with suppliers can decrease costs, shorten response times, improve reliability of supply, and lower inventory levels. Internally, the benefits may not be as clear.

Why forecast by item instead of product family, for instance? The greater the level of detail, the easier it is for the supply chain organization to plan for material supply and ensure product availability. For the sales group that prepares the forecast, though, this added detail may seem like extra work with no clear benefit. The supply chain organization needs to quantify the inherently qualitative reasons for changing the process and to get the sales force to buy into it.

Finally, business units or functions may have incompatible information systems. Without a common data platform, shared functionality, and standardized metrics, these disparate systems can block effective collaboration.

Despite these challenges, internal collaboration is worth the effort. It can confer a competitive edge—and lay the groundwork for external collaboration. First you'll need to dispel the perception of internal collaboration as a zero-sum game, where one department's gain is another's loss. This means modeling and clearly articulating the benefits to your company as a whole and making sure that your existing infrastructure doesn't discourage collaboration because of a real or perceived negative impact on a function or business unit.

Logitech is a company where the need for internal collaboration is obvious. It's an international market leader in personal interface products such as computer mice, keyboards, interactive entertainment peripherals, and audio products. The company has a very strong brand presence, selling its products in tens of thousands of retail outlets in over 100 countries, as well as on hundreds of Web-based retail sites and through relationships with original equipment manufacturers (OEMs). Logitech excels at high-volume manufacturing and distributes its products worldwide. The company's supply chain strategy mirrors its emphasis on award-winning designs and price performance and has led to the creation of a highly efficient company-owned manufacturing facility, as well as relationships with numerous supply chain partners, including original device manufacturers (ODMs) and packaging houses. The company's primary manufacturing facility and the majority of its suppliers are located in Asia.

Logitech's product line is both broad and deep. This complexity, combined with the fact that most production is done in a region of the world far removed from many of the end customers, places tremendous emphasis on the need for excellent planning and efficient processes to move products from manufacturing sites to regional distribution centers.

As is typical of many sellers of retail products, Logitech relies on attractive packaging to catch the customer's eye. "Packaging is very important to us," explains Nolan Perry, director of project management services. "The package is really an extension of the product itself. It needs to showcase the product while projecting an image consistent with our strategy of high quality and ongoing innovation." For many products, this means form-fitted, clear packaging that highlights the product's look and feel from any angle. The package also needs to be well suited to retailers' displays, for it may need to stand on a shelf or hang from a rack.

This emphasis on appearance can conflict with "efficient" supply chain operations. Moving product from Asia to other regions of the world is facilitated by easy stacking on pallets and optimization of the quantity that can be accommodated in a standard shipping container. Gray Williams, Logitech's vice president of worldwide supply chain, says, "Unfortunately, what is good for the retailer isn't always good for product distribution. Retail packages come in odd sizes and shapes, and this can make them hard to fit on a pallet or in a shipping container. Sometimes, a very small adjust-ment in the packaging dimension can make the difference between fitting 200 units on a pallet or fitting 250."

This sounds like an easy change to make, but at Logitech, decisions about the look and feel of packaging are the domain of marketing, not the supply chain group. As Perry notes, "Everyone understands the need to keep operations costs low, but not if it means the products don't sell as a result." Not only that, but once a product has been sold in a particular pack-age, it is very difficult to modify the design. "Retailers see a packaging change as a whole new product," says Perry, "so they may want to exchange anything they already have on hand for the 'updated' version of the product. That can be extremely expensive for us. We need to get it right the first time—and that wasn't always happening."

The process for packaging design was never intended to be serial, with a handoff from marketing to the supply chain group after the design was finalized; it just evolved that way. The solution for Logitech was close collaboration between the supply chain and marketing functions and early involvement of the supply chain group in the product development process. It also meant compromises on both sides. "Our job is to take the desired packaging design and find the most cost-effective way to source and distribute it," says Williams. "It isn't to second-guess the design. But we want the marketing team to be open to making concessions that can make distributing the product more efficient."[4]

A focus on collaboration between the marketing and supply chain organizations resulted in packaging that allows Logitech to get products to customers as efficiently as possible while remaining a reflection of the innovation and quality of the products within.

Define the Appropriate Degrees of Collaboration (i.e., Segment)

A world in which your company is tightly linked to all its supply chain partners—customers and suppliers alike—is highly appealing but virtually impossible and not likely to be very cost-effective. Intensive collaboration is complicated, challenging, and costly, requiring a major investment in resources, processes, and systems. Moreover, not all customers are equally profitable and not all suppliers are equally valuable. And many potential partners may not be capable or even willing to support the level of collab-oration you want. Therefore it makes sense to segment your partners before embarking on a collaboration program—much like marketing profession-als segment their target customers.

This means deciding on a segmentation approach. No doubt you have a list of customers, suppliers, or commodities that you consider "key" or "strategic." But what factors cause you to label them as such? Size of company? Price of materials or services? Their dependence on you—or you on them—as a buyer or supplier? Their value to you in terms of revenue generation?

Segmenting supply chain partners is critical to effective collaboration. No matter how much or how little value they contribute to your company, all potential partners have an appropriate place along the collaboration spectrum. Basing your decision of whom to collaborate with on a simple ranking of who your most valuable suppliers, service providers, and customers are is inherently risky.[5]

A better approach is to consider several partner-selection criteria weighted according to your specific needs:

- *Strategic importance.* How essential are the potential partner's size, business volume, technology, expertise, materials/ components, or market position?

- *Cultural fit.* How compatible are your people and values, and how well will you work together? Are you equally committed to the relationship, even though business conditions may change? Is there mutual trust?

- *Organizational fit.* Can the partner respond quickly and fully to requests for information and materials? Is the partner flexible enough to adapt to changes in demand or supply? Are the roles and responsibilities in place for managing a long-term relationship?

- *Technology fit.* Are your systems compatible and easily integrated? Do you have the same degree of technical sophistication? Are you equally willing to share technologies and innovative solutions? Can your partner provide accessible, integrated data?

Choosing partners is made much more complex by the need to assess the selection criteria along two dimensions: the category of relationship (customer, material supplier, or service supplier) and collaboration type (transactional, cooperative, coordinated, or synchronized).

The best approach is to create an assessment framework before approaching any partners. Start by listing the conditions that a partner must meet to be considered for each collaboration type. To make sure that you're being objective, develop criteria that are clear and unambiguous. Know how many partners of each type you want to have, based on the needs of your business or previous experience with collaboration. Then rank the prospective partners by how well they meet the different criteria. You may create a list of "must haves" and eliminate any partners that fail to meet these criteria.

Alcatel, a global manufacturer of telecommunication products and services, applied a deliberate segmentation strategy when it set up collaborative relationships with several major customers and suppliers. In the company's own words, a relationship with Alcatel "can enable a partner to focus on its own core competencies rather than worrying about the reliability of its telecommunications infrastructure."[6]

In late 2001, in the midst of a contracting telecommunications equipment market, Alcatel management conducted a comprehensive assessment of its existing planning process. The assessment showed that component suppliers often relied on outdated information from Alcatel in their own production plans. The problem stemmed from a serial, disjointed forecasting process that involved multiple supply chain partners. Alcatel fed its customers' forecasts into its demand-planning cycle. Planning data were then provided to the company's contract manufacturers, who had their own planning processes. Finally, up to six weeks after the customers' forecasts were received, the data—by then out of date—were sent to component suppliers. Moreover, the participants in the process all applied their own interpretations of what actually was needed. By the time responses were received from suppliers, the perceived reality and the accompanying supply plan had very little relationship to the original marketplace demand.

The company had a clear opportunity to better match supply with demand by improving collaboration with its supply chain partners. Notes Burt Rabinowitz, Alcatel's vice president of sourcing and procurement, "We realized that our supply chain can only respond when it is synchronized with the supply chains of our key trading partners. We needed to jointly address the 'pinch points' in the supply chain—the points at which information flows from one supply chain partner to another. To do that, we needed to involve our key trading partners."

The management team developed a short list of companies considered highly important because they either provided a large volume of business or supplied unique or critical materials to the company. The team then ranked prospective collaboration partners based on three primary criteria: business volume, technical sophistication and innovation, and partner loyalty and willingness. The partners chosen included a major customer and its primary contract manufacturer, primary electronics distributor, and several suppliers of custom ASICs (application-specific integrated circuits) and optical devices.

To initiate the relationships, Alcatel management invited executives from each prospective partner to participate in a business outlook forum. The executives discussed the impact of the severe market changes on their business and how their companies could better collaborate to streamline processes and lower costs. Another goal of the forum was to assess more subjective criteria—including cultural fit and seeming willingness to commit to a collaborative relationship.

"We knew that the key to greater supply chain flexibility would be to better understand the process handoffs and then augment the existing systems with deeper, collaborative processes," says Danny Wade, senior vice president for quality. Wade notes that applying this approach to all customers and suppliers would not have been practical. "We were very deliberate in crafting our 'guest list.' We needed to make sure each partner recognized that we were all in this together, and we needed to avoid unnecessary complexity."

By the end of the forum, each executive had committed to finding better ways to collaborate and to developing a conceptual design for a coordinated collaboration model to address forecasting, order management, inventory visibility, and performance measurement. The model would include roles and responsibilities, process flows, business interfaces, and operating rules, in addition to information technology (IT).

Then Alcatel senior managers worked with the partners to define the detailed guidelines needed to support the conceptual design. Finally, Alcatel piloted the collaboration model with a key product that created demand for the partner companies, had market momentum, and required the coordination of both internal and external manufacturing operations. Some of the partners helped Alcatel with supporting IT solutions to augment the process guidelines, including new reports, additional logic, and Web-enabled views into work in process. All partners agreed to share data, synchronize their planning calendars, and respond to standard demand requests within three business days.

The new collaboration model reduced planning cycle times by 50 percent and sharply reduced end-to-end inventories. "We're able to better match our supply to our customer's demand," says Mike Quigley, chief executive officer of Alcatel USA. "More important, by involving customers in the problem definition, solution, and pilot, we increased their commitment to broader improvement initiatives. They're excited about working with us, and we're enjoying a closer business relationship—one based on facts, not feelings."[7]

Share Benefits, Gains, and Losses

Our definition of collaboration includes the concepts of mutual objectives and of sharing risks and rewards. Formal gain sharing is a well-known way to distribute the financial benefits of a business relationship. In gain sharing, each partner agrees to work toward lower overall costs and to share the savings. The specifics usually are detailed in a legal contract.

Gain sharing can be a highly effective incentive for continual cost reduction and improvement of services, and there are numerous approaches for implementing a gain-sharing strategy. While we have seen many examples of effective partnerships based on gain sharing, a collaborative relationship can be mutually beneficial even when it is not based on tangible cost savings.

Consider the relationship between Dow Corning and Cabot Corporation. Dow Corning is equally owned by the Dow Chemical Company and Corning, Inc., and is one of the world's largest producers of silicon and silicone-based technologies, offering more than 7000 products and services.[8] Cabot is a $1.5 billion plus global specialty-chemicals company. Its primary products are carbon black, fumed silica, inkjet colorants, plastic masterbatch, oilfield drilling fluids, and tantalum capacitor materials.[9]

In the world of specialty chemicals, one company's by-product is another company's key ingredient. Such is the case with Dow Corning and Cabot, and the two companies have established a collaborative relationship that demonstrates clearly how each company's results can be tied to its trading partner's performance.

Dow Corning is a major producer of purified silicon for the silicon wafer industry using a process that results in a by-product known as silicon tetrachloride or chlorosilane. Silicon tetrachloride is a key ingredient used in the manufacture of fumed silica, one of Cabot's key products. Dow Corning uses 20 different grades of fumed silica as a key "filler" ingredient in its sealant (silicone caulking) product line.

The relationship between the two companies is so strong that two of Cabot's primary plants are located directly adjacent to Dow Corning's, and material is transferred between the two entities through a shared infrastructure. To make the process work properly, Dow Corning and Cabot production managers meet to discuss production plans on a daily basis. Dow Corning managers identify the expected amount of silicon tetrachloride that will be made available and the amount and grade of fumed silica that will be required. In response, Cabot identifies the amount of silicon tetrachloride that it will be drawing from Dow Corning and the grades of fumed silica that will be available. If sufficient quantities of the desired grade are not available, both sides negotiate until a mutually acceptable solution can be developed. The production schedules for each company are then adjusted in response to these inputs.

An additional indication of how tight this relationship is can be found in how each partner pays for the material used. Each company monitors the volume of product flowing between the factories. At the end of each month, the aggregate data are reviewed, any discrepancies are reconciled, and a summary invoice is produced. Since prices are set during negotiation, only the volume requires reconciliation.

An Example of Mutual Gain

Today's technologies offer the opportunity to manage business in ways previously thought impossible or, at the very least, implausible. Even though a capability may be technically feasible, setting up a process that leverages that capability is not always necessary. Indeed, in many cases it is not at all appropriate.

Many effective collaboration strategies are not reliant on technology. Despite the hype associated with business-to-business (B2B) solutions that seems to envelop many supply chain professionals, most companies find that many of their prospective partners simply lack the technical sophistication required to participate in a collaboration process that is based on the use of complex information systems. Remember that transactional relationships are still considered collaborative; just because your systems are not "seamlessly integrated" with every sheet-metal shop and plastics molder who supplies your manufacturing operation doesn't mean that you are not working collaboratively. In fact, relationships all along the collaboration spectrum may be extremely effective but make little or no use of the advanced capabilities offered by supply chain collaboration systems vendors.

Jamba Juice is a San Francisco–based retailer that operates stores in 25 states throughout the United States. The menu at Jamba Juice stores is simple; the chain sells made-to-order all-natural smoothies, as well as a variety of freshly squeezed juices, baked goods, and other snacks. All items are created with the goal of balancing "great flavor" with "powerful nutrition."[10]

Jamba Juice's suppliers include large fruit and vegetable growers. The company establishes long-term contracts in order to ensure availability of supply. "We can't strike a deal with Mother Nature herself," explains Joe O'Neill, Jamba Juice's chief financial officer, "so we have to get creative when it comes to getting as close as possible to guaranteed availability of the produce we need." And Jamba needs a lot of produce—the company uses more than 10 million pounds of frozen strawberries, 6 million pounds of frozen bananas, and 27 million pounds of fresh oranges every year.

While this may sound like a huge quantity of fruit, Jamba Juice competes for the growers' attention with many other companies, such as beverage manufacturers who sell fruit-based products and large producers of other products with high fruit content, such as pies and jams. In addition, the same growers who supply fruit for these companies also sell to supermarkets and restaurant industry distributors.

Strawberries are a particular challenge in that they are a very popular choice among supermarket shoppers. The supermarket channel also offers the greatest margin for the growers, so it is no wonder that of the 1.4 billion pounds of strawberries produced each year within the State of California, approximately 75 percent are harvested for the fresh market, whereas only 25 percent are frozen for the processed market.[11] There is a common perception that a strawberry's size is directly related to its taste and sweetness, with bigger berries considered sweeter and riper. In actuality, a strawberry's flavor is determined by growing conditions (such as weather), stage of ripeness when harvested, and variety. Despite this reality, much of the agricultural research done by grower consortia is focused on breeding fruits that will be appealing to the retail grocery shopper. This means larger strawberries.

The same strawberries that are so appealing to the retail grocery shopper cause major headaches at Jamba Juice. "They're just too big," explains Anne Kimball, Jamba's director of supply chain management. "They are difficult for our blenders to handle, they don't fit in the scoops we use, and the inconsistency in the size results in variability of texture, flavor, and color of our smoothies."

Since Jamba Juice does not have the ability to influence the development of these new strawberry varieties, they have turned to their processors for help. Frozen fruit processors are the produce industry's equivalent of contract manufacturers: They wash, sort, and package frozen fruits and then sell them to distributors.

Strawberries must be frozen as soon as possible after picking to ensure that the best flavor and appearance are retained. In most cases, the berries are sliced, pureed, or kept whole for freezing. Processors have specialized equipment for these three options. And Jamba needs a fourth "form factor"—berries that are broken up into fairly large chunks but still maintain their fruit identity to the retail customer, who could watch his or her smoothie being created.

"I know it sounds simple," says Kimball, "but this required a creative process for ensuring that there was a sufficient quantity of frozen berries coming off the processing line that met our growing volume requirements." Jamba's supply chain and R&D organizations worked closely with Cleugh's Frozen Foods, Inc., to develop a proprietary technology to break up the berries prior to freezing in a way that suits the in-store production process. "This was not a small investment by Cleugh's," notes Kimball. "However, their ability to ensure that we had fruit that could be portioned solidified our existing partnership with this long-term supplier partner."[12]

The relationship between Jamba Juice and its strawberry packer is a great example of coordinated collaboration. It's an example that is not at all reliant on the availability or use of sophisticated information systems.

Trust Your Partners, but Protect Your Interests

Effective collaboration is based on building relationships and on sharing both information and the benefits gained as the relationship progresses. This means that you can't ask your partners for something without giving them something in return: That "something" can be price concessions, value-added services, or in most cases, information. If you're willing to set up an infrastructure to automatically send purchase requirements to your suppliers but don't want to provide your sales projections for the next nine months, ask yourself why not. Sharing information requires trust; it may be that you don't have the necessary confidence in your partner.

There's a good reason that many companies are skeptical about making highly strategic information available to collaboration partners: Trust is violated all the time! Confidential pricing data make their way into the hands of competitors, engineering specs are copied, or the "best" supplier terms and conditions are found to be less favorable than those granted to other customers.

Take the experience of a leading network equipment company with healthy margins—due in no small part to its extremely aggressive supplier management. The company demands the lowest price on its key components and insists that these pricing arrangements be kept confidential. To shield prices from competitors, it buys these key components through a central procurement group, which delivers them to a contract manufacturer. The company had established a close relationship with a major supplier and was confident that it was getting the lowest price on an important electronics component—until it acquired a company and found that it had been buying the same component from the same supplier for 10 percent less! This occurred despite a commitment from the supplier that the price being paid by the network equipment company was the lowest offered to any customer.

Violations of trust related to pricing are not news to Greg Frazier, executive vice president of Avnet Supply Chain Services (ASCS). He sees examples of failed collaboration "all the time." ASCS is the services arm of Avnet Electronics Marketing, a global distributor of electronic components. Frazier's organization provides end-to-end supply chain services to original equipment manufacturers (OEMs), electronic manufacturing service (EMS) providers, and electronic component manufacturers. Frazier notes that the pricing problem may stem from the definition provided by the supplier, which may have promised the lowest price, but with fine print clarifying "for a company exactly your size, serving your exact customer base." Notes Frazier, "In many cases the idea that a 'best price' exists is an illusion."

The fact is that trust does get violated. Instead of using this as an excuse to avoid collaboration, set up your partnership so that you'll be protected.

The concept of protecting a company from a confidentiality breach also has matured in the last few years. As more companies share forecasts, production levels, delivery schedules, pricing, and product data, security of information becomes a critical issue—and no longer just an internal one. Your collaborative partnerships typically should include a contract or confidentiality agreement that provides a level of legal data protection that transcends the "fuzzier" concept of trust. While a structured contract can minimize risk, don't assume that it will provide a source of legal recourse should the relationship fail. Instead, use the contract as a tool for clarifying how the relationship will be governed and for specifying roles and responsibilities.

Another concern is transmitting data. Although many technologies can encode data to arrive uninterrupted and uncompromised, the risk of technology failure is very real. As a result, more companies are using comprehensive, pricey security services to minimize this risk. These often require that partners follow certain security practices that specify password types, for instance, and limit access to networked servers and workstations. Although approaches vary, business and IT executives scrupulously analyze their partners' security as well as their own. [13]

To help companies manage information security risk, the International Organization for Standardization (ISO) created ISO/IEC 17799, a comprehensive set of controls that dictates best practices in 10 critical areas ranging from security policy to business continuity management. Some companies require that their collaboration partners adhere to ISO/IEC 17799. Because the standard is a framework for best practices in information security rather than a methodology, these companies generally use it to frame the specifics of what they require of their partners. These specifics may include such measures as disaster-recovery plans or the consistent use of antivirus protection within all network-connected devices.

Eliminating all information-security risk is virtually impossible. Your company's supply chain is dynamic. New customers and suppliers are added constantly, and the level of collaboration in current relationships is always evolving. To set the right level of security, first identify the situations that would cause the greatest business disruption. This might be the unavailability of critical systems, loss of data integrity, or disruptions in ongoing communications with your partners. Then assess and put in place the steps or tools needed to minimize the odds of these events occurring.

Use Technology to Support Your Collaborative Relationships

Technology allows you to communicate with your supply chain partners. It breaks down barriers between companies, improves the flow of information, and converts data into useful information. Given the conceptual appeal of end-to-end supply chain management and the ready availability of technology to make it happen, then, why have companies been so slow to embrace real collaboration? We think the answer is simple: They've not been ready.

At the peak of the Internet bubble, many software companies believed that if they installed the right supply chain applications and systems, sales would follow. But things didn't work out that way. Many companies expected to reap the promised benefits without doing the preliminary legwork—the analysis, process redesign, and alignment with the new applications needed to gain the full functionality.

Most early e-commerce systems addressed large, long-term collaboration issues such as extended forecasting, demand creation, and operations planning. Many of these were top-down initiatives driven by executives with equity positions in the companies whose technologies they were advocating. And many purveyors of systems and tools made promises they simply couldn't keep. At many companies their processes were too immature, the needed data weren't available, or they were unprepared for the new, collaborative ways of working that the new technologies theoretically could enable.

Moreover, no single e-business standard for transactions and messaging emerged to rally a critical mass of users. Collaboration tools had to translate multiple data formats, adding to their complexity and further limiting their appeal. In short, the world was not ready for the richness of technology available.

As a result, many of the early B2B "portals" were simply databases for pushing information. Company A would publish data to a site and then notify Company B that the information was available—or assume that Company B would check the site on a regular basis. Company B would view the information, download it to its own system, and choose whether or not to take action. In effect, the Internet became an expensive, sophisticated enabler of electronic data interchange (EDI). The most common application became online auctions for buying and selling products and materials. Why? Because these applications didn't demand the systems and data integration needed for true collaboration.

After the dot-com collapse, many collaboration tools addressed a narrower focus—supply chain execution rather than long-term planning. This narrowed focus mitigated the risk of information sharing, helped automate many manual processes, and allowed companies to work in real time.

> Today's collaboration tools focus on supply chain event management and on relationships between customers and suppliers.

Today's collaboration tools focus on supply chain event management and on relationships between customers and suppliers. As technology advances and companies become better prepared for the rigorous data maintenance needed for supply chain collaboration, the promise of these new applications may soon become a reality. It's important to use these tools sensibly. While they can improve the flow of information and aid decision making, they can't compensate for suboptimal processes or the expertise of a seasoned supply chain professional. A good collaborative system can gather data and make recommendations based on a predefined set of business rules, but it can't gauge the applicability of those rules to the current situation or calculate the effect of an inappropriate demand on a supply chain partner.

Nonetheless, technology is a critical element of most coordinated and synchronized collaborative relationships and many cooperative relationships. Remember that technology is an enabler, not the driver of success. To make your technology investment pay off, make sure that your organization is set up to leverage it. This may mean changing your organization's structure, processes, incentive plans, and performance measurement.

Involve your suppliers and customers in the selection and development of processes and systems. Or at the very least, solicit feedback from them and allow them to influence or enhance the design. Make your technology solution a foundation of service excellence—not an excuse for poor service.

Don't Forget to Compromise

Unless you're Dell or Wal-Mart, don't expect that your requests for customer or supplier collaboration will be met with an immediate flurry of positive activity. When you invite another company to be a collaboration partner, you're asking it to make fundamental changes in how it operates. The farther you go along the collaboration spectrum, the more you're asking of your partner. Only the largest and most powerful companies are in a position to force changes. Other companies must be prepared to sell prospective partners on the idea of collaboration.

We've already made the point that the goal of a collaborative relationship is to realize strategic or financial benefit. As obvious as it sounds, collaboration for the sake of collaboration is simply not worth the effort. Collaboration isn't about shifting costs from one supply chain partner to another. It's about setting up the supply chain to lower overall costs and then sharing the savings. This means that you must be willing to compromise.

> Collaboration isn't about shifting costs from one supply chain partner to another. It's about setting up the supply chain to lower overall costs and then sharing the savings.

Avnet's Frazier sees many electronic-component suppliers and contract manufacturers forced into collaborative relationships at a level that they're not prepared to support. "It's one thing to share forecasts electronically," he notes, "but when these companies are asked to do sophisticated logistics, it can be hard to take on these added tasks and still profit from the relationship."

Frazier's company works with component manufacturers that prefer to sell their products through Avnet rather than directly to the end customer. "Many of these companies have a hard time making money selling direct," he says. "It isn't a matter of competency; it's a matter of strategy and scale. These companies are in business to sell electronic components, not to manage other companies' supply chains."

Many of these component manufactures sell to OEMs that outsource production to contract manufacturers—often multiple contractors in multiple locations. A component manufacturer selling to five OEMs, each with five manufacturing partners with five manufacturing facilities, must support 125 different manufacturing sites. "That means 125 forecasts coming in each week," Frazier points out. "Without major investments in people, systems, and infrastructure, this is a very difficult model for most component manufacturers to support."

Often, OEMs or EMS providers develop the "master plan" for a collaborative relationship—a plan that optimizes their own benefits. Suppliers are expected to provide value-added services as the cost of continuing to do business. Yet, if you expect your suppliers to provide additional services and to take on additional risk at no additional cost to you, your chances of getting them on board are small. And even if you do succeed in getting them to "sign up," you may find that they're unable to meet the requirements you've set for them. Instead, work closely with your partners to develop a value proposition they can understand and buy into. Create an agreement that fairly values the added services you want them to provide—and pay them an appropriate premium.

Successful collaborators make a major effort to bring their partners up to speed. Some of the best practices involved in offering a compromise include providing a technology solution to them at little or no cost and working closely to get them up to speed with any new technology. Purchasing a license and having it installed at your supplier, however, is not collaboration.

Finally, be sure to set up a way to monitor the results of your collaborative relationships. Work with your partners to establish a set of metrics that is consistent with the value proposition and can be updated and reviewed on a regular basis.

NEXT-GENERATION COLLABORATION

A critical aspect of collaboration is the need to capture and react to changes in a partner's planning data. Most of today's collaboration tools are built on centralized databases. Since it can take hours to assimilate and process data collected from numerous sources, companies often make decisions based on historical data. If you're an international company with headquarters in the United States, that might be where you keep your central database. The tools need the data to be centralized in order to do global analysis—otherwise, they are just optimizing local information. To get the data into the database, they have to be "piped in" from all over the world, which can take several hours. Thus, even though you think that you can run real-time analysis, you can't. This is the reason companies run their analysis using information from yesterday (or earlier). Before centralized databases, analysis took a lot less time but was suboptimal because it only used a portion of the available data.

The next generation of collaboration takes us "back to the future"—to the late 1990s, before the bubble burst, when Internet technology promised complete visibility of operational information across the entire supply chain network. In many ways the future is already here. Most of the technology needed for end-to-end visibility already exists and has for some time. However, you can't fully leverage this technology until the process maturity at your organization catches up. Most companies are not there yet, but they're getting there fast.

> In the next generation of supply chain collaboration, technology advances will be overshadowed by changes in individual attitudes.

In the next generation of supply chain collaboration, technology advances will be overshadowed by changes in individual attitudes. There'll be an evolution toward collaboration as a joint investment rather than the more one-sided, "if we build it, we can make them use it" attitude that characterizes many of today's collaborative efforts. Changes will include the following:

- ◆ Companies will focus on collaborating to achieve long-term customer satisfaction rather than internal cost reductions.
- ◆ Distributed data architecture will become the most common platform for collaboration tools, allowing companies to respond in real time to planning and execution data.
- ◆ Companies will explore the security policies of their collaboration partners more closely, and new technologies will enable in-depth electronic audits of security provisions.
- ◆ True integration among disparate systems will become a reality, allowing companies to monitor all their production and logistics assets from a central system.
- ◆ Instead of simply automating routine transactions, systems will be able to look ahead, predict unplanned events, and trigger the correct response as needed.

- Software applications will be extended to multiple tiers of suppliers and distributors. While collaborating with multiple customers and suppliers will be the norm, companies will still reserve deeper planning and forecasting efforts for a select set of partners.

- Collaboration with materials suppliers will continue to be transaction-focused, whereas relationships with service suppliers will be more strategic and focused on planning.

- Applications will be built on top of an Internet-based architecture hosted externally.

- Collaboration increasingly will focus on the front end of the supply chain, with heavy emphasis on collaborative forecasting and replenishment models.

- Use of industry-standard tools, such as RosettaNet PIPs and CPFR, will become the dominant forms of collaborative communication in the electronic and consumer products sectors.

As a management discipline, collaboration is still in its infancy. We believe that it will change the economics of all companies as business practices, rules, and conventions are adjusted to reflect the realities of integration and increasing visibility across supply chains. Collaboration will allow smaller companies to compete with larger companies, making scale less critical as a competitive differentiator. Collaboration will become an essential discipline—and an inevitable part of your supply chain strategy. See Figure 4-6 for a collaboration guideline.

FIGURE 4-6

A collaboration guideline.

❏ You may have a grandiose vision for the future, but your chances of success are small if you try to go for "collaboration nirvana" from the start. Start with tactical improvements.

❏ Focus on a single, unambiguous vision for your collaboration strategy, including clear goals and a purpose.

❏ Clearly understand your company's current and future desired core competencies, and ensure that the collaboration strategy is wholly consistent.

❏ Start small, focusing on a limited set of capabilities, on selected partner candidates, and on selected tasks.

❏ Recognize that early efforts can be supported by a manual infrastructure (phone/fax/email); more extensive efforts will certainly require more advanced supporting systems. So pay close attention to how the systems will need to evolve.

❏ Let your business drivers and economic realities shape the nature of your collaborative relationships and the way they will be managed.

❏ Advance your technological capabilities only to the level that you expect your partners to be able to manage.

❏ Assess the organizational changes that will be needed to support collaboration on a larger scale in parallel with your initial efforts.

❏ Align your company's compensation and reward structure to the goals of the collaboration strategy.

❏ Effectively manage your collaboration partners; have a comprehensive metrics program in place that allows you to monitor their performance—and your own—on a regular basis.

❏ Don't take people out of the equation. Stories abound about companies who "flipped the switch" on new collaboration tools, only to find that the system was recommending actions that made no sense from a business perspective. As your effort gets underway, make sure your organization is populated with skilled professionals that can monitor progress and make necessary midcourse corrections.

U.S. Department of Defense Profile: Making the Tail Smaller and the Tooth Stronger

As the U.S. military enters the 21st century, the Department of Defense is recrafting its approach to warfare. It's creating a new blueprint called the Force-centric Logistics Enterprise (FLE) which will take the best practices of business and integrate them with the best practices of the military, creating a more vital partnership than ever for more agile supply chain performance.

"There is no parallel in commercial industry for what we do today. If we were a private enterprise, we would be number 1 on the Fortune Global 500," noted Diane K. Morales, U.S. deputy under secretary of defense for logistics and materiel readiness, at the time of our interview. She was responding to a question about the scope of the largest supply chain in the world—that of the U.S. Department of Defense. At our request, she continued with the stats: "Our dollar volume of business is more than double that of Wal-Mart, which is currently number 1 on the global Fortune list. Our supply chains cost nearly $80 billion a year to operate. We employ over 1 million people and deliver more than $400 billion in value to our customers.

"Every U.S. soldier, sailor, aviator, and Marine is a customer, and every American citizen is a stockholder. We have an active and vocal 535-member board of directors [the House and the Senate]. And we're number 1 in our marketplace—the dominant market position that our stockholders demand."

We get the picture. Yet, although mighty indeed, the U.S. Department of Defense's (DoD's) supply chain apparatus is facing a transformation on a scale never before attempted. Morales's invocation of Wal-Mart ($246.5 billion in annual sales) is appropriate. Besides shoelaces and toothbrushes, frying pans and motor oil, though, the DoD has to supply missile subassemblies, vehicle engines and transmissions, microcircuits, x-ray machines and magnetic resonance imaging (MRI) equipment, aircraft frames, heavy industrial machinery, and jet fuel, to name a few of the 4.6 million items stocked by the Defense Logistics Agency (DLA). Every SKU must be delivered on time—no stock-outs, no rainchecks—in whatever quantities the customer requires, wherever the customer happens to be in the world at any particular moment.

That "customer," as we all know, is what the military calls a "warfighter." And he or she is liable to be anywhere, anytime these days. As Morales notes, the pace and modus operandi of warfighting have changed considerably even over the past decade. "In 1991, in Desert Storm, General Norman Schwarzkopf wanted 60 days of supplies on hand before he would launch an assault with a quarter million troops. In Operation Iraqi Freedom (OIF), General Tommy Franks wanted just two weeks' worth of supplies for 150,000 troops."

WHEN PUSH COMES TO PULL

Morales has spearheaded one of the biggest transformation programs ever launched at the DoD. It was called the Future Logistics Enterprise during its policy-planning phase and was renamed the Force-centric Logistics Enterprise (FLE) during the implementation phase. She describes the program as "an integrated plan to transform logistics to a more flexible force to meet the requirements for agility and responsiveness." The characteristics of this vision for a modernized logistics capability are fivefold:

- ◆ *Speed.* General Tommy Franks's battle plan called for a lightning advance on Baghdad, for instance. Never before has an army advanced so far so fast: The army covered more than 300 miles in 22 days.

- ◆ *Flexibility.* When Turkey balked at supporting a second front from the north in Iraq, the United States advanced successfully, solely from the south, changing its strategy in a matter of hours.

- ◆ *Precision weaponry.* In the Gulf War, 8 percent of weapons used were precision-guided. In OIF, that figure was 66 percent.

◆ *Increased reliance on unmanned aerial vehicles.* These are useful for both surveillance and combat.

◆ *Joint operations.* Coordination of the different service "components" is essential for effectiveness in today's defense environment. In OIF, 78 percent of the sorties flown were in direct support of special operations forces.

Of course, the Army, Navy, Air Force, and Marines are not fighting any battle alone. They are dependent on what's called the "tail": the vast infrastructure that supplies them, from product development of weaponry and machinery to transportation and other services sustaining them. As Morales says, "Traditionally, defense logistics has been thought of as supply, transportation, maintenance, and supporting information systems and infrastructure. But actually, it's supply chain management, integrated weapon system support, and integrated, shared data (the knowledge environment), plus materiel readiness." Since the scope is so broad, the concerns range from rightsizing the infrastructure to rightsizing the inventory and from transforming the overall logistics processes to demanding performance standards and accountability from a very young military force.

> **Because of the scope and speed required to transform the military to a higher state of readiness, tomorrow's defense supply chain will be very different from yesterday's.**

Because of the scope and speed required to transform the military to a higher state of readiness, tomorrow's defense supply chain will be very different from yesterday's. To use the parlance of supply chain management, it will move from a push to a pull model of customer order fulfillment. One of the most critical of its characteristics is a shift from vertical integration to a strategy of virtual value-chain management based on deep collaboration with customers, partners, and suppliers.

The "tail" that supports the "teeth" of the military is drawing on best practices from private industry. It is creating greater partnerships with the private sector than ever

> **Today, the "tail" that supports the "teeth" of the military is drawing on best practices from private industry.**

before. It's being organized differently because more horizontal processes are being instituted incrementally. The end state will be the largest enterprise system in the world. It is designed to be more flexible, transparent, and simultaneous—to be an agile infrastructure. It will, in itself, be a lean, mean fighting machine. It won't get there overnight, but the FLE has been the launching pad for total transformation.

Unfortunately, the DoD cannot mimic the private sector in transforming its supply chain to effect these changes, for the scope and significance of its activities and obligations vastly exceed those of any private enterprise. It must answer to changing legislative mandates and, unlike private enterprise, to the changing mandates of different presidential administrations. Its very motive—readiness or preparedness rather than profit—forces it to cope with logistical complexities and uncertainties unknown to private business.

THE BLUEPRINT FOR CHANGE

The FLE defines three drivers of change:

- *Total life cycle systems management.* This type of management is well established among manufacturers of complex products and among advanced industrial users of complex, mission-critical capital equipment but not so developed in the military.
- *End-to-end distribution.* This initiative is aimed at providing faster and more reliable delivery by synchronizing the flow of materiel across the entire supply chain—from factory to foxhole. It calls for breaking down the barriers and seams between the "stovepipes" or "silos" among the organizations involved in demand planning, acquisition, sourcing, positioning, and transportation (e.g., DLA, and the U.S. Transportation Command, or TRANSCOM, etc.). This may well be the biggest challenge of the plan.
- *Enterprise integration.* All the aforementioned initiatives require the close integration of information systems and processes among all the entities in the national defense supply chain. DoD must have interoperable information systems that deliver comprehensive operational data, aggregated information, and logistical "situational awareness."

These initiatives obviously have far-reaching consequences for logistics, personnel, weaponry, technology, and supplier relationships throughout the DoD—for the "components" (i.e., the Army, Navy, Air Force, and Marines), as well as for the policy-making offices. As Morales describes it, "We must build processes from the supplier base (both public and private) through the distribution agents to enable rapid movement of materiel. We must collaborate and build partnerships with industry to achieve this responsive, end-to-end delivery capability. This involves real-time information and tools such as radio frequency identification (RFID) tags to track assets and more accountability and integration in the lifetime support of weapons systems."

Transformation at the DLA

Execution will not be for the faint of heart. A case in point is the Defense Logistics Agency (DLA). The DLA has served for over four decades as the DoD's "logistics combat support agency." With its nearly $25 billion in sales and services for fiscal year 2003, it would occupy the no. 65 spot on the Fortune 500, just ahead of New York Life. The agency operates in 48 states and 28 foreign countries and is staffed by 21,000 civilian and 500 military personnel.

> With its nearly $25 billion in sales and services for fiscal year 2003, the DLA would occupy spot no. 65 on the Fortune 500.

"We run the world's largest warehouse distribution system," says Vice Admiral Keith W. Lippert, the DLA's director. "We also run a defense energy support center that supplies all the fuel for the Department of Defense. We run a national defense stockpile composed of strategic materials that we gradually sell into the market if they're not needed. The stockpile is big enough that we have to watch the world markets, because we can end up affecting world prices through our volume of sales."

Admiral Lippert addresses the shift in thinking as it affects his agency: "DLA was put together to manage consumable items that were common to all the services. What DLA did—and this dates back to 1962— was to buy material, put it in a warehouse, and then basically say to its customers, 'OK, I bought it, so you had better come get it.' The shift we're going through right now is toward understanding our customers' requirements and being responsive to them, even when there are problems in the industrial base [that affect us]." In other words, the DoD is extending the supply chain to include the customer's customer and the supplier's supplier.

Lippert is a member of the Joint Logistics Board (JLB), which Morales established and which oversees the FLE. The JLB consists of the most senior-ranking logisticians from the four service branches, the U.S. Joint Forces Command, the DLA, and TRANSCOM. Three working groups have been created to expedite the FLE's initiatives: The Best Business Practices Group (*"Reengineer for Success"*), focused on logistics architecture and process reengineering; the Program Implementation Group (*"Do It Right"*); and the Change Management Group (*"Make It Stick"*). Assisting all three groups is an advisory team drawn from industry.

THROUGH THE LOOKING GLASS: LIFE CYCLE MANAGEMENT

"I look at the FLE as a cross within a circle," explains Morales. "The vertical bar is the requirement for integrated weapons system support over the life cycle of a weapons system, which is something we don't have today." To reach this goal will require accountability, says Morales. "Today, we don't know what the lifetime cost of supporting a single weapons system is, for example. No one person is accountable. You have the program manager who is responsible for the design, development, and fielding of a weapons system. The system then gets thrown over a fence to somebody else to sustain it over its lifetime. Reliability, maintainability, and mobility have not been key considerations, yet they have to be built into a system.

"We then need to have the people who are accountable for building those features into a given weapons system also be the people accountable for the sustainment of that system over its lifetime. Once we have these dual accountabilities, we'll see better up-front decisions being made."

Morales refers to end-to-end distribution as the horizontal line of the cross within the circle. This line encompasses a spectrum of partners: industry partners, coalition partners, public-sector partners—partners who range from the supplier, the manufacturer of the part, all the way through to acquisition, contracting, and the fulfillment agents who actually deliver that weapons system to the warfighter. "The horizontal line includes the operational planners who develop the system requirements. It includes the financial community,

> Right now, the DoD is building the partnerships, protocols, and systems that will get us to the goal of end-to-end capability, says Diane Morales, who launched the FLE initiative.

and it includes the acquisition community. The point is that you have a world of partners who are being called on to deliver this end-to-end capability. It's the extended supply chain," Morales says.

"Nobody owns all the partners," she continues. "There is no single manager of this supply system or owner of that system. Right now, the DoD is building the partnerships, the protocols, and the systems that will get us to the goal of end-to-end capability. And we're starting to see some amazing successes in this area."

THE INTEGRATED ENTERPRISE INITIATIVE: FROM EXCESS TO ACCESS WITH INFORMATION TECHNOLOGY (IT)

Enterprise integration is the circle around the cross and the enabler of integrated weapon system support and end-to-end distribution. The fast-track evolution of the DoD's data enterprise from hundreds of cold-war legacy systems and their hundreds of millions of lines of code to state-of-the art information systems and processes integrated across the national defense supply chain has been one of the most ambitious programs in the FLE agenda.

Laura Faught, cochair of the Program Implementation Group, one of the FLE's "triangle groups," and assistant deputy under secretary of defense for logistics systems management, talked to us about the process and progress of logistics systems modernization: "First, and most obviously, we developed the overall enterprise data strategy collaboratively with parts of our logistics domain. A basic lesson in change management is that you don't stuff an architecture, especially a process-oriented architecture, down the throat of an $80 billion supply chain. We pulled in from across the DoD logistics domain, business process owners and key stakeholders from the Defense Logistics Agency, the Army, Navy, Air Force, Marines, Joint Forces Command, and TRANSCOM. This gave us an anchoring in our customers' perspectives, just as the SCOR model anchored us in a process orientation."

Faught says her group leveraged the IT community's technical views of the standards and focused on architecture, data strategy, portfolio management, and "a scalable, repeatable process to ensure that we're very smart acquirers of commercial technologies to support our system and process integration." She thinks the key to success in

> "You don't stuff a process architecture down the throat of an $80 billion supply chain," says Laura Faught.

integrating systems is data strategy: "Our basis is motherhood and apple pie: It's to have accurate and operable data available to whoever has authorized access to it, whenever they need it." This meant a single point of entry into the logistics data enterprise, as opposed to all the point-to-point interfaces provided by the legacy systems. The DoD accomplished this in a test case with the Joint Strike Fighter. "It's a matter of transparency: access to accurate data as the weapon moves through its life cycle," says Faught.

The work of Faught's group evolved into an enterprise integration toolkit that has wide applicability beyond logistics: "It's a framework for how anyone can develop the business case, how you can select and do contracts with the integrators and the commercial off-the-shelf (COTS) software vendors, how you can do your blueprinting, how you can map the whole life cycle of this process or of that project," says Faught. "In it, you have an entire set of compliance criteria tied back to all the architecture products at the component level."

Application of IT Principles at the DLA

The DLA has built on the work of Faught's group and its "integrate the enterprise" mandate. As Admiral Lippert explains, DLA runs on a system called the *Standard Automated Materiel Management System* (SAMMS). It's a system that was designed in the 1960s and implemented in the early 1970s. SAMMS is written in COBOL, and it has about 6 million lines of code associated with it. It's probably five generations behind the systems at world-class private-sector companies. The DLA tried on five different occasions to replace the system and failed five different times, according to Lippert. "So we're now on our sixth attempt to replace it, and this time we're going to succeed," he asserts.

The new system went up in August 2003, with 170,000 of the 4.6 million items the DLA handles, on a SAP backbone solution, an enterprise resource planning system that's being customized for the DLA's volume and requirements. SAP is the core for financial management and requisition fulfillment, but the DLA is using an application from Manugistics as a bolt-on for demand planning, and a separate system, called the *Procurement Desktop 2* (PD2), for procurement.

"Collectively, this is the biggest development in our business in 34 years," says Lippert. "I think we're on schedule for the new system to pay for itself by 2008 or 2009 through fewer IT people, reduced inventories, better forecasting, and better data accuracy than we've ever had before."

Lippert speaks proudly of the executive information system that has been instituted at DLA as well: "I get a daily update of key statistics on my PC, as does the entire management team. The results are color-coded: red, yellow, or green, depending on whether we're on plan, or behind plan, or starting to fall behind plan. One of the first things I do in the morning, after I get through my e-mails, is click onto this thing and find out exactly how we did yesterday."

The DLA handles 45,000 requisitions and issues 8,000 contracts *a day*, on average. To improve its performance, it has simultaneously embarked on programs of strategic distribution, competitive sourcing, and strategic supplier alliances in addition to business systems modernization. Are the programs working? And if so, how well? The agency is is aggressively implementing performance metrics and benchmarking to answer these questions. DoD always has struggled with what metrics the staff should be looking at to measure performance within the logistics operation. It realizes that it's important to get the right metrics—the transformational metrics—so the current effort is to develop what's called a "balanced scorecard." The Joint Logistics Board is working together to finalize the metrics to implement this scorecard.

The bottom-line results are already impressive: By paying attention to the metrics and taking corrective actions, the DLA has reduced its back orders by 22.2 percent since October 2001 and has achieved the lowest cost recovery rate (operating costs as a percentage of total sales) in its history. The agency is also operating at close to an all-time low in terms of personnel—just under 22,000 people—versus an all-time high of three times that from 1989 to 1992. "We're working to improve the tooth-to-tail ratio," notes Lippert.

THE END-TO-END INITIATIVE: CREATING POLICIES FOR CHANGE

The champion for the end-to-end initiative is Alan Estevez, assistant deputy under secretary of defense for supply chain integration and the chair of the FLE's Best Business Practices Group. Estevez characterizes the biggest challenge in supply chain integration as getting supplies to the end customer without his having to even order them: "Why should my soldier out on the battlefield—who is out in dust and dirt and getting shot at and fixing things so [that] he can keep fighting the enemy—have to worry about ordering if he can pull the supply he needs and then have the back-fill for that supply just show up?"

To effect this kind of change, Estevez has been working on revisions to the military's 4,140 materiel management regulations. The revisions call for accountability on all sides for delivering supply to customers wherever they are in the world. Everyone is accountable. There are no handoffs of

"It's not about end-to-end *distribution* but about end-to-end *supply,*" says Alan Estevez.

responsibility, as in the past. "It's not about end-to-end *distribution* (which implies sequence) but about end-to-end *supply,*" says Estevez. The mechanism for this accountability is performance agreements—with original equipment manufacturers (OEMs) and suppliers and internally with customers. The metrics that Estevez is looking at—*time-definite delivery, customer wait time* (a measure of the velocity in the pipeline), etc.—have everything to do with the end customer, not with the distribution network. Three pilot programs have shown that calibrating to the customer can pay off: with the Naval Air Systems Command and Naval Sea Systems Command and their depots, with the Army's installation activities for the Black Hawk helicopter and the Abrams Tank, and with the Air Force/DLA collaboration on supply for the F15, F16, and KC135.

With the imprimatur of the Joint Logistics Board, Estevez's group is also using a balanced scorecard to track performance to key metrics. One of the quadrants of the scorecard—the anchor quadrant—represents the warfighter perspective. There are two high-level metrics in that perspective. One is getting the combat capability to where it needs to be, and the other is force readiness and the operational availability of weapons systems. However, there's also a quadrant for "sustained capability" that goes beyond the warfighter's perspective, says Estevez. That quadrant takes into account such matters as development cycle times for weapons platforms—concerns that would not have been considered supply chain issues in the military world before FLE. They're indicative of the new end-to-end perspective.

Part of the policy set forth by the Best Business Practices Group calls for "mobility force structure." More than any other single concept, this explains the critical role that logistics play in supporting warfighters today. Earl Boyanton, assistant deputy under secretary of defense for transportation policy and previously a career transportation officer in the Air Force, describes it as "a three-legged stool: airlift, sealift, and prepositioning."

"Just as combat units have force structure—the Army has so many divisions, the Navy has so many carriers, and the Air Force has so many air wings, fighter wings, and bomber wings—we think of mobility force structure in the same way. How many air mobility (airlift and aerial refueling) wings do we need, how many transport ships? In Iraq, prepositioning—

where you have everything from combat equipment like tanks and helicopters to consumables all stashed in places other than the United States, a sizable portion of them on ships in different oceans of the world—allowed more rapid reaction and less reliance on airlift and sealift to get materiel to a distant location. All of that paid off dramatically."

Much of the afloat prepositioning Boyanton is talking about uses specially commissioned 900-foot-long medium-speed ships with large roll-on, roll-off ramps to more efficiently load and unload the military's wheeled and tracked equipment. These ships, crewed by civilian merchant mariners, were procured by DoD after Operation Desert Storm, when the military realized that greater flexibility and quicker reaction were imperative and could be realized through increased afloat prepositioning.

Boyanton thinks that another major factor for success during the Iraq engagement was in-transit visibility. And this, we learn, is related to advanced technology. With a fast-moving force, the challenge on the logistics side is to keep up and keep it supplied without putting too much of a "logistics footprint" on the ground. One of the ways this was accomplished in Iraq was with RFID tags, which can be read by a computerized interrogator. General Franks had requested that all materiel entering the central command theater of operation in ocean containers or on aircraft pallets have a robust data tag so that military personnel at any point in the distribution process could read it without having to access a remote database or physically break into cargo to find out what was "in the box."

The challenge for the future, says Boyanton, will be providing in-transit visibility "from source to foxhole." In addition to enabling the customer and other materiel managers to determine status at any time, the military needs to collect consumption data to be recorded in such a way that it automatically triggers resupply, similar to point-of-sale data collection and inventory/reorder triggers in the consumer products industry. The abiding question for the DoD FLE plan is: "Where is the end of the supply chain for this purpose?" Each of the military services has somewhat different practices, and situational variables can cause modifications within those practices.

Special Partnerships with Commercial Transport

Part of Boyanton's responsibility is the Civil Reserve Air Fleet (CRAF) and the Voluntary Intermodal Sealift Agreement (VISA). Each of these programs gives the DoD a contract-based authority to mobilize U.S. flag civilian air and ocean transportation resources, respectively. The air and ocean carriers that make up CRAF and VISA were employed extensively on a voluntary basis during the operations in Afghanistan and Iraq after 9/11. In addition, a portion of CRAF was formally mobilized to support the force buildup prior to OIF.

Boyanton describes the contribution of DoD's commercial transportation partners, including highway, rail, and integrated carriers such as FedEx and UPS, as well as ocean and air, as "nothing short of outstanding— we simply can't do without them."

However, long-held perspectives here are changing as well. Says Boyanton, "Part of our job right now is convincing people [in the military] that they have the transportation options they think they don't have." These misunderstandings stem from what has been a kind of schizophrenia in transportation policy. For example, there's this presumed "rule" that if you're a DOD shipper and you're shipping to a customer overseas, you need to move your air cargo, the priority stuff that qualifies for air movement, through DoD's organic air transport. "But that's contradictory to what we're doing right now with the supply chain," says Boyanton. "We're telling sources of supply to collaborate with their customers and all prospective fulfillment agents to pick the supply chain design that adequately fulfills the customer's requirements for time-definite delivery. I'm having to disabuse the notion that cargo that moves by commercial air transport is leakage from the defense transportation system. Commercial air transport is emphatically a part of the DoD's air transportation capability."

During peacetime, the DoD maintains its fleet of cargo aircraft—the C17s and the C5s—and aircrews, aerial ports, and a worldwide air mobility infrastructure to respond immediately to the orders of the President and Secretary of Defense. This readiness requires constant international flying for training and to exercise the system. Thus international air transport capacity is created in the process. "We need to carefully rationalize our decisions of when we bypass that capacity in favor of another option," explains Boyanton. "On the other hand, the providers of that capacity, TRANSCOM and the Air Force's Air Mobility Command, need to offer best-in-class service and reliability to convince suppliers and customers that they are a viable supply chain."

THE CRITICAL ROLE OF PERFORMANCE-BASED AGREEMENTS

What supports the immense number of decisions that have to be made is performance-based agreements (PBAs). Boyanton's new policy documents, like Estevez's, will make one point crystal clear: "The customer and the source of supply will design the supply chain for whatever is best for that customer's requirement. The decisions will be made by the participants to the agreement."

Boyanton cites a sterling example of the success of this approach. It's a weapons system known as JSTARS on a 30-year-old platform called the C135, a Boeing 707-type airplane equipped with this highly sophisticated radar suite that provides ground-situation information such as movements of vehicles and helicopters, much as the AWACS provides air-situation information. There's a performance agreement between the integrating contractor who put the electronics on the plane and the Air Force, as well as with the OEM who manufactured the electronics.

"When JSTARS deployed for Afghanistan, they had a 100 percent sortie rate," says Boyanton. "They generated 148 sorties during the combat phase of OIF, and all of them launched. A 100 percent launch reliability rate is unheard of for such a complex weapon system. Now, what was responsible for the success? I believe it was the PBA in addition to some very dedicated and skilled Air Force people at the far end of the pipe that were saying, 'We're going to get this airplane off come hell or high water. We're going to find a way to make sure this mission flies.'"

IN SUMMARY

Although Diane Morales stepped down as deputy under secretary of defense for logistics and materiel readiness in January 2004, the life of the FLE likely will be a long one. Its characteristic will be continuous change. How will anyone know whether it has been successful? Morales summed it up for us: "The greater logistics community will be measuring success through the balanced scorecard. It balances the risks among operational requirements, cost-effectiveness or affordability, and performance by the service providers."

Some of the measures of success will be

- Increased capability at no transformational cost
- Increased weapon system operational availability
- Consistent, reliable, time-definite delivery of support to the customer
- Efficient supply chain business operations

The defining change in perspective is the accent on effectiveness over efficiency. As Boyanton puts it, "Effectiveness says we're going to get the job done because that's our job. And sometimes it's going to cost more than if we did it the most efficient way. To some degree that's done to mitigate risk to the supply chain—but we can't completely eliminate risk because you never have enough resources to be in a zero-risk game. Our job in logistics is to make as certain as we can that the operator, the shooter, has at his disposal everything he needs. But also, as we implement standard processes—integrate the enterprise—we will achieve efficiencies because we'll all be operating from a common set of business rules and information at the enterprise level."

THE MARINES TAKE ON THE FLE

The U.S. Marine Corps, which throughout its history has practiced the art of doing more with less, is actively engaged in numerous logistics modernization and transformation initiatives. Focused on providing more effective support to the war fighter, these efforts range from improving internal supply chain practices to participating in joint and DoD enterprise logistics improvement initiatives—such as the Force-centric Logistics Enterprise (FLE).

We talked with Susan C. Kinney about the Marines' logistical direction and initiatives. Kinney is deputy director of the logistics plans, policies, and strategic mobility division, Headquarters, U.S. Marine Corps (HQMC).

"The increasing number of dynamic threats to national security objectives dictate a leaner, more focused logistics effort from the Marine Corps, one that replaces footprint with precision and volume (the 'iron mountain') with information and speed," she says. Why? "Because we learned that setting that iron mountain and working from that point were no longer good enough; it's too difficult to sustain the forces from that vantage point today," she says. "This has never been more apparent than in recent conflicts, where Marines have been forced to maintain supply lines extending 500 or 600 miles. If you are going to move that far inland, you have to be lighter. So we're looking, in our acquisitions programs, to make less of a footprint so that we can become more agile."

In fact, the Marine Corps is moving toward the concept of sea-basing, replacing those mountains of iron with information and speed. Major Ken Lasure explains how the concept worked in Afghanistan: "Due to political considerations, we couldn't maintain a permanent presence on the beach in Pakistan or operate during the daytime. As a result, we had to establish a temporary beach support area three to four times a week and shuttle equipment and supplies from the ships to an airfield in Pakistan at night, and then we'd fly it forward. But at the same time, we were muscling through some significant communication challenges. More often than not, the only way I could talk to our personnel in Pakistan was when that LCAC [Landing Craft Air Cushioned—a hovercraft that transports personnel, equipment, and supplies ship to shore] went ashore and I was able to grab someone and say, 'I need you to do this.' Nevertheless, the sea-basing operations enabled us to adjust to the access limitations and still move inland 400 to 500 miles—something the Marine Corps really isn't designed, sourced, or organized to do."

To make the logistics chain organization operate more responsibly end to end, the Marine Corps has now blended the functions of distribution, transportation, materiel management, and supply management under one umbrella. It is mapping its logistical and supply chain processes at the enterprise level for the first time in its history. To do this, it has depended on the Supply-Chain Operations Reference-model (SCOR) described in Chapter 2.

Mapping the processes across the enterprise was no easy matter. As Keith Rineaman of the Log[istics] Vision Center explains it, it all starts with the customer, the supported unit—the Marine battalion that needs products or services. They go through a process called request management, involving the identification of needs; they then pass those demands to a supporting unit, which is their first line of logistics support, their "bellybutton," as the Marines call this single point of contact.

A role called *order management* accepts all those demands from supported units and turns them into orders and then manages those orders through to fulfillment. The order manager sources orders to a set of functional units or activities within the supporting unit. It could be inventory, maintenance, food—or any product or service. And they have their own functional management and execution roles and processes. The processes include activities at the wholesale level, where there are depot operations, and in commercial industry through the procurement role.

These processes create an "operational architecture" that is role-based. After documenting the processes, often it's necessary to restructure. Thus there's the need to define new roles and make policy changes, doctrinal changes, organizational changes, and information technology changes.

Then there's the special attribute of the Marine Corps: It moves in groups, in what's called *Marine Air Ground Taskforces* (MAGTFs). As Kinney explains, "When you go into a situation, you go with a MAGTF. You don't go anywhere without the whole group. There is no splitting aviation or logistics off by itself, for instance." Because of the special role of the logistics element, it has become a fifth element in the MAGTF, historically comprised of four elements: a command element, a ground combat element, an air combat element, and a combat service support element. The fifth element is now considered the supporting establishment. A MAGTF can range from 100 people to a Marine expeditionary force, which could be 18,000 strong.

What will be the metrics of success for the FLE program in the Marine Corps? Having just finished its process reengineering, the Corps is now readying to buy empowering applications and other IT, using the enterprise integration toolkit developed through one of the three "triangle groups" of the FLE. The attributes it expects all its programs to have are reliability, responsiveness, flexibility, expense containment, and asset utilization. All these are embedded in the SCOR model. However, the Marines have added a sixth attribute: readiness. "It wasn't in the SCOR model [developed for industry], but it's obviously critical to the DoD," says Gavin McCarthy of the Log Vision Center.

5
CHAPTER

Core Discipline 5: Use Metrics to Drive Business Success

Most people agree with the adage, "If you can't measure it, you can't fix it." Yet few metrics programs actually provide a clear picture of overall performance, pinpoint the root of performance problems, or identify improvement opportunities. The reason is simple: Establishing a robust— and useful—performance measurement program is difficult! Just getting agreement on what to measure, how to define the chosen metrics, and how often they should be measured can be a major effort. And getting management to agree on the fundamental purpose of a metrics program can be the most contentious activity of all.

Think about the metrics your company uses to determine its operational health. Like many companies, you may have functionally focused scorecards for customer service, purchasing, and manufacturing already in place. Few companies, however, track cross-functional supply chain metrics, even though actively monitoring these metrics for management purposes is a key component of an integrated supply chain organization (see Chapter 3).

Most corporate metrics focus on financial impact and outcomes. This isn't surprising because financial reporting must be done on a regular basis. Financial metrics are also relatively easy to obtain once the books are closed for any given period. Moreover, regulations such as the Sarbanes-Oxley Act of 2002 oblige companies to be thorough about ensuring the validity of their financial data and diligent about documenting the controls and procedures used to arrive at those numbers. (Sarbanes-Oxley requires that officers of U.S. public companies certify the accuracy of their financial statements and the effectiveness of the associated disclosure controls and procedures. As such, it requires that companies establish and actively manage sound internal controls.)

Indeed, many executives laud the Sarbanes-Oxley Act for enforcing good business practices and providing external validation for company initiatives.[1] The strict reporting requirements give managers more and better information that can make business processes more efficient and cost-effective. Some executives even regard the Sarbanes-Oxley Act as a leverage point in making the case for process improvement.

Yet, while financial metrics can help to gauge the impact of process changes on a company's financial health, we think they're inadequate when it comes to measuring supply chain performance. Why? Since most financial measures are historical, they don't provide a forward-looking perspective and can be very difficult to tie to operational effectiveness. Nor do they provide insight into strategic nonfinancial performance indicators such as order-delivery performance and customer service levels.

What exactly is a *metric*? The *Merriam-Webster Dictionary* defines a *metric* as "a basis or standard of comparison." Note that by this definition, a stand-alone number or value is *not* a metric. A number or value only becomes a useful management tool when compared with another number or value. This is the premise of an effective performance measurement program.

WHY MEASURE?

Is measuring supply chain performance really that important? Absolutely. For starters, the right set of metrics can tell you how well each *plan*, *source*, *make*, *deliver*, and *return* supply chain process is performing, highlight where there's room for improvement, and help you to diagnose problems and decide where to focus your improvement efforts. Metrics also can be a powerful management tool by letting people know what is expected of them and allowing you to track progress—or lack thereof—over time.

Supply chain metrics can be difficult to define and even more difficult to measure. At the highest level, supply chain operations are expected to contribute to a company's financial performance. Supply chain metrics, therefore, have three important objectives. First, they must translate financial objectives and targets into effective measures of operational performance. Second, they must do the opposite—translate operational performance into more accurate predictions of future earnings or sales. Finally, they must drive behavior within the supply chain organization that supports the overall business strategy.

Even if you don't measure nonfinancial metrics on a regular basis, you can be sure that your customers do. For instance, they'll take into account how good your service was on their last order when deciding whether to order again. This is just one way that nonfinancial performance metrics can be leading indicators of future financial performance.

Measurement is the only way to understand whether process performance is improving or worsening and whether action is required. All too often companies learn about performance problems or the failure to meet stated objectives after the fact—when revenues fall short of targets, customers take their business elsewhere, or margins fall below expectations.

> Measurement is the only way to understand whether process performance is improving or worsening and whether action is required.

Our research and experience show clearly that companies with good supply chain management skills have higher levels of process maturity that lead to better supply chain performance overall. They avoid the difficulties associated with "steering by the rear-view mirror" and can take steps to correct problems early—before they become overwhelming.

This chapter will examine the universe of supply chain metrics, their definitions, and the ones that apply to supply chain performance management. We'll also provide guidance on how to gain a comprehensive view of overall supply chain performance and pinpoint opportunities for improvement.

It's important to draw the distinction between performance *measurement* and performance *management*. Performance measurement is about putting in place the right metrics to assess the health of your supply chain. Performance management uses those metrics to support your company's strategic objectives. Your metrics program is an effective management tool if it includes the following three activities on an ongoing basis:

- *You integrate quantitative targets into plans and budgets.* If cutting distribution costs is a priority, for instance, budget assumptions are adjusted to integrate the specific cost-reduction targets.
- *You establish meaningful targets at the individual and departmental levels that link to overall corporate objectives.* For example, if you plan to drive lower delivery costs, a distribution center's targets might aim for a lower percentage of express versus standard deliveries. To track process changes, you might measure the adoption rate of new practices that drive lower premium freight costs, such as adherence to order cutoff times.
- *You have well-defined mechanisms and processes in place for tracking progress and managing performance.* Performance exceptions are identified easily and drive appropriate actions that involve the right individuals and organizations in a timely manner.

MANAGING PERFORMANCE WITH METRICS

To make these activities a regular part of your company's supply chain management process, you'll first need to define an approach to supply chain performance management. We've found that the most effective approaches share these characteristics:

- Supply chain metrics are linked to the business strategy.
- Supply chain metrics are both balanced and comprehensive.
- Targets are set based on both internal and external benchmarks.
- Targets are aggressive but achievable.
- Metrics are highly visible and monitored at all levels of the company.
- Supply chain metrics are used as a continuous improvement tool.
- Metrics are implemented via a formal implementation plan.

Let's look at each of these characteristics more closely.

Link Your Metrics to Your Business Strategy

Traditional supply chain metrics focus on efficiency and productivity. Improvements in service levels, costs, and inventory levels are the desired outcome of an operations strategy and are measured accordingly. A more strategic perspective looks at these measures as *enablers* of business objectives such as growth within a specific segment or market, accelerated product development, or immediate product availability. When aligned with key business objectives, the supply chain becomes an added source of competitive advantage.

For example, a leading maker of personal computer (PC) peripherals developed a business strategy focused on low cost, constant innovation, and a make-to-stock approach for fast order fulfillment. Each business unit was expected to manufacture at the lowest possible unit cost and have products available for shipment within two to three days of receiving a customer order. Supply chain metrics tracked on a regular basis included product cost, delivery performance, and fill rate.

To compete based on cost, the company set up plants in locations with low labor rates and developed long-term contracts with carriers to ship the products by sea to local distribution centers. Although most of the manufacturing sites were in Asia, most of the company's business was in North America and Europe, so products took up to five weeks to reach the distribution centers. This made achieving the strategic objective of fast order fulfillment a major challenge. Accurate forecasting was critical but extremely difficult in the highly volatile peripherals market. And constant product introductions and phase-outs made it even harder.

As a result, the company had to depend increasingly on flexibility within the supply chain. One of the few levers available was shipping products by air rather than sea. This nearly tripled transportation costs but was necessary to maintain customer service levels. The need to rework products to better align them with current demand when they arrived at the local distribution centers also boosted costs.

The product managers didn't see these added costs as an issue: The transportation and rework costs appeared as expenses charged to the operations function. As such, they did not affect the product-cost metric.

Of course, the total cost of managing the supply chain increased significantly because of these unplanned expenses. To address this problem, the management team began measuring total supply chain management costs on a quarterly basis (see Figure 5-1). The team also examined how the supply chain strategy affected costs related to order management, materials acquisition, inventory carrying, and planning—not just the cost of goods sold.

The management team worked closely with each product group to communicate the importance of total supply chain management cost. Product costs were still measured regularly, but the entire company was asked to focus on the new total-cost metric. As a result, product managers saw for the first time the huge expense associated with expediting shipments

FIGURE 5-1

Components of total supply chain management cost.

Total Supply Chain Management Cost	
Order Management	• New product release, phase-in, and maintenance • Customer order creation • Order entry and maintenance • Contract/program and channel management • Installation planning • Order fulfillment • Distribution Transportation, outbound freight, and duties • Installation • Customer invoicing/accounting
Materials Acquisition	• Materials/commodity management and planning • Supplier quality engineering • Inbound freight and duties • Receiving and materials storage • Incoming inspection • Materials process and component engineering • Tooling
Inventory Carrying	• Opportunity cost • Shrinkage • Insurance and taxes • Total inventory obsolescence—raw materials, WIP, and finished goods • Channel obsolescence • Field service parts obsolescence
Finance and Planning	• Supply chain finance costs • Demand/supply planning costs

Management Information Systems (MIS)	• Plan
	  – Product management
	  – Finished goods demand/supply planning
	• Source
	  – Sourcing/materials acquisition
	• Make
	  – Manufacturing planning and execution
	• Deliver
	  – Order management
	  – Logistics and distribution
	  – Channel management
	  – Field service/support

Source: The Performance Measurement Group, LLC—definitions used in benchmarking studies

because of forecast inaccuracies. This was the catalyst needed to move forward with a major initiative to improve the forecasting process, which greatly improved forecast accuracy—and reduced reliance on supply chain execution to make up for planning errors.

This example is not unusual. Measuring operational metrics in isolation is a common—and often counterproductive—way to use performance-related data. A more effective approach is to start with your company's strategic goals and work backward to identify the supply chain performance metrics that support those goals.

Make Sure Your Metrics Are Balanced and Comprehensive

The goal of performance management is to drive desired behaviors—not across-the-board excellence. This may sound obvious, but many companies have a hard time agreeing on where performance excellence is critical and where it's merely "nice to have."

Consider the classic triangular balance of customer service, cost, and quality. Which is most important? Least important? The natural tendency is to say that all are equally important and that inferior performance in any of the three areas is not an option. Excellent customer service costs money. So does superior quality. And cost cutting usually means shaving dollars allocated to improving product quality or service excellence. This is the classic dilemma of managing supply chain performance. If you want to pursue balanced objectives, you need to cover multiple performance perspectives and then select your metrics accordingly. An effective metrics program must include a balance of

> If you want to pursue balanced objectives, you need to cover multiple performance perspectives and then select your metrics accordingly.

+ Internally focused and customer-facing metrics
+ Financial and nonfinancial metrics
+ Functional and cross-functional metrics
+ Metrics designed to measure innovation and continuous improvement

In the chapter on strategy (Discipline 1) we talked about the need to constantly look for ways to improve and differentiate your supply chain performance. Once you have decided on the appropriate path forward, the next step is to decide how you'll know if you're meeting your objectives. This assessment forms the basis of your performance-management approach. A necessary step in this process is determining where average performance is acceptable and where superior performance is a must.

For the computer peripherals company discussed earlier, the objective of reducing total supply chain management cost may result in a supply chain configuration that forces a trade-off between low product costs and high fill rates. Achieving best-in-class performance for both is unlikely because each requires a different focus and configuration. The company must choose among higher transportation costs for specific products, higher finished goods inventory levels, or slower order fulfillment.

We worked with a large telecommunications company whose first attempt to develop a comprehensive set of metrics resulted in the selection of 21 key performance indicators. The management team had spent a lot of time winning commitment to the program, making the metrics highly visible, and even modifying individual performance objectives to support the chosen targets. Then the team realized that not one metric focused on the customer. Instead, the program focused on such metrics as market penetration, inventory levels, and cost data. In the end, the team kept the 21 performance indicators they'd worked so hard to develop but added a set of metrics focused on customer satisfaction, with an emphasis on delivery performance.

As you begin to structure your performance-management program, consider including metrics that align with the four dimensions of the well-known balanced scorecard approach:[2]

- The *financial* dimension includes metrics such as cost of goods sold, labor rates, transportation cost per mile, value-added productivity, and asset turns. As we noted earlier, financial metrics are relatively easy to measure but don't provide a complete picture of how well your supply chain is performing.

- The *internal* dimension includes metrics such as forecast accuracy, production quality, production flexibility, and internal cycle times. These metrics assess operational performance but are not tied to specific financial results.

- The *customer* dimension includes metrics such as on-time delivery to commitment, order-fulfillment cycle time, fill rates, and perfect order fulfillment. Customer-oriented metrics are designed to show how your company performs from the customer's perspective.

- The *innovation and learning* dimension is the most difficult to define because metrics in this area quantify your company's effectiveness at learning new skills. Setting goals for employees who are APICS-certified or have completed Six Sigma training is an excellent way to establish meaningful metrics for this dimension.

How often should metrics be monitored? This depends on the life cycle or clock speed of your business, but monthly reporting is fine for most top-level metrics. This usually allows you to spot trends before they become problems and avoids overreporting with little value. Detailed operational metrics should be monitored and reported at least weekly, if not daily. Often these are key customer-facing metrics such as fill rate or delivery-to-commit performance.

While invoiced costs, such as warehousing and transportation, should be tracked on a monthly basis, costs related to internal headcount should be reexamined during the budgeting cycle, the frequency of which may vary from one company to another but typically is on an annual cycle. Despite making large investments in supply chain planning tools, most companies track inventory and delivery performance only on a monthly basis. These metrics should be tracked at least weekly—if not daily—to ensure excellent customer service.

Creating the capability to use existing metrics more effectively also can be an important lever in gaining organizational support. Increasing the frequency with which you monitor an existing metric is an excellent way to leverage already available infrastructure while improving its effectiveness.

Base Performance Targets on Both Internal and External Metrics

Benchmarking—both internal and external—can provide valuable data for improving supply chain performance and has two main benefits. First, external comparisons place your performance in an industry context, which helps to identify supply chain improvement opportunities. And second, internal benchmarking helps you to identify which of your business units, regions, or locations are the best performers. Then you can pinpoint the underlying practices that make the difference and adopt those practices across the company.

Companies typically use external benchmarking to study business practices of industry competitors as a basis for improving their own performance. Benchmarking is *not* just the study of another company's performance levels—it's about the practices that lead to those performance levels. An effective benchmarking effort will help you to understand what level of quantitative performance is possible and, more importantly, what practices can deliver this level of performance.

Besides external competitors, we believe that companies should study noncompetitors in other industries—provided that they have similar supply chain characteristics. Why look outside your own industry? Because often what works in one industry can be applied successfully to another. But be careful which companies you compare yourself against. You should compare yourself to peers—companies with similar production processes, distribution channels, or other dynamics that allow a valid comparison. Otherwise, it's less likely you'll be able to set realistic targets.

External benchmarking requires collecting performance data—often highly sensitive data—from other companies. Many companies are reluctant to provide such data directly to competitors or even to noncompetitors. To get around this roadblock, consider participating in benchmarking surveys managed by independent third parties. These benchmarking service providers specialize in defining relevant supply chain metrics and working with participating companies to ensure that the data collected are unambiguous and accurate. When choosing a service provider, look for one that offers a thorough assessment of the supply chain practices associated with best-in-class performance. This link between practice and performance is the key to understanding how to change your supply chain to reach new performance levels.

Many companies make the mistake of thinking that participating in a benchmarking survey is the same as conducting a benchmarking assessment, or they want to have access to a supply chain database without any plans to participate in a survey. As Michelle Roloff, general manager of PRTM's benchmarking subsidiary, The Performance Measurement Group, LLC, notes, "The benchmarks are only as good as the data the organizations submit. We want survey responses from companies that are using benchmarking to change how they do business. This means they're willing to invest the time needed to collect accurate information from a variety of sources."

An external benchmark is only useful if a company knows how its own organization is performing in the same area. An effective benchmarking program starts with a thorough understanding of your own processes and level of performance. This means generating a comprehensive set of internal metrics.

Internal benchmarking doesn't depend on sensitive data from other companies. Instead, it involves measuring the performance of comparable functional areas, processes, and facilities within your company using consistent definitions. For instance, you might compare the performance levels of a set of manufacturing facilities, warehouses, distribution centers, purchasing organizations, or order-management groups. In an internal benchmarking program, best-in-class functions are identified, and their benchmark metrics become the basis of performance targets for similar functions within the company.

Although internal benchmarking can be easier than collecting external data from competitors, most large companies are extremely complex, with multiple regions and business units. If your company does not have common processes, information systems, and underlying data across business units, internal benchmarking can be a major undertaking. Even so, it's the right place to start.

Once you've agreed on what to measure and how to define the metrics, collecting internal benchmarking data is relatively simple. Since internal organizations operate within the same corporate structure, there's usually minimal controversy about whether or not the basis of comparison is relevant. You should monitor your internal benchmarking effort closely—on rare occasions, internal benchmarking can result in unproductive competition among business units or divisions. In extreme cases, business units may try to "game the system" to deliver winning results. If you see this, you will need to take immediate action to reset behavior.

Once you've generated your internal metrics and collected relevant benchmarking data, the next step is external benchmarking—comparing your company's performance against that of other companies. You may choose to limit your comparison to companies within your own industry or extend your comparison to companies in other industries. Some benchmarking services offer custom comparison populations, where you can select a specific set of companies that share similar business characteristics, such as product complexity, geographic distribution, or manufacturing strategy.

Analyze the performance gaps between your company and your comparison group. Pay special attention to strategically critical areas that have subpar performance. Follow this gap analysis by investigating the causes of any performance issues and assessing the business practice changes that will be necessary to close the gaps. To do this effectively, make sure to benchmark both qualitative and quantitative data. Qualitative data include an assessment of the business practices that the comparison population uses to run its businesses.

External benchmarking can be a very powerful tool when making the business case for supply chain transformation because an external view often is needed to justify making major internal changes. To minimize potential skepticism about the relevance of the comparison population, you'll need to do a thorough analysis to ensure that the external benchmarks are meaningful. Your benchmarking service provider can help you to choose a relevant population, especially if you're looking beyond your own industry.

BASF Corporation used a combination of internal and external benchmarking to drive process improvements throughout its operations. The BASF Group, headquartered in Ludwigshafen, Germany, is one of the world leaders in the chemical industry, with more than 160 subsidiaries and affiliates. In 2003, its North American Free Trade Agreement (NAFTA) operations in the United States, Canada, and Mexico set up a task force to assess the core supply chain operations of its 13 business units, identify any performance gaps, and develop a plan to close those gaps. The task force planned to use both internal and external benchmarks to compare the performance of each business unit against other BASF businesses and a customized external population.

At first, the business unit leaders were somewhat skeptical about the proposed approach and expressed concern that the benchmarks wouldn't provide a meaningful comparison. As Mary Scheibner, the NAFTA director of supply chain consulting, explains, "Each of the business units is unique. Each produces different products through different manufacturing processes and sells to different customers. So we needed each business unit to feel confident that the population to which they were being compared was appropriate."

To address this concern, BASF used a "bundling" approach to create meaningful comparison populations. The 13 business units were grouped into two high-level categories based on their primary manufacturing process—continuous or batch (see Figure 5-2). Then each unit completed a PMG supply chain scorecard (see generic scorecard shown in Figure 5-3). Similar external companies were chosen to create a comparable benchmark population for each of the two bundles. The performance of each business unit was compared against two groups—the BASF units with the same manufacturing process and the population of similar external companies.

Each business unit got a report comparing its performance with that of the two different comparison groups. The results were used to set performance-improvement targets. Scheibner worked closely with senior management to establish aggressive but reasonable targets for each unit. "This was a huge effort, so we needed to come up with a fairly simple approach," she notes. "We looked at each business unit's percentile-based

F I G U R E   5–2

BASF benchmarking population.

Continuous Manufacturing Population			Batch Manufacturing Population			
	BASF Business Unit 1	BASF Business Unit 2	BASF Business Unit 3	BASF Business Unit 6	BASF Business Unit 7	BASF Business Unit 8
Continuous Manufacturing Bundle	BASF Business Unit 4	BASF Business Unit 5		BASF Business Unit 9	BASF Business Unit 10	BASF Business Unit 11
				BASF Business Unit 12	BASF Business Unit 13	Batch Manufacturing Bundle
	Comparison Company A	Comparison Company B	Comparison Company C	Comparison Company G	Comparison Company H	Comparison Company I
	Comparison Company D	Comparison Company E	Comparison Company F	Comparison Company J		

performance compared with the benchmarking population and set a target of 25 percent improvement." For example, if a unit ranked in the 50th percentile for inventory performance, the target was to achieve a performance level consistent with the 75th percentile. Business units that were already at the 75th percentile level or higher for a given metric were off the hook.

This top-down approach provided a relatively straightforward way to set stretch targets. Notes Dave McGregor, BASF's senior vice president of logistics, "Historically, business units have taken a bottom-up approach to incrementally improving productivity. The benchmarking data are allowing us to link theoretical opportunities with proven supply chain practices to achieve breakthrough performance."[3]

Set Aggressive but Achievable Targets—and Tie Them to Actions

If you plan to use metrics to determine how your supply chain is performing, you must set a target for each metric. Only a target gives you a basis for tracking whether performance is improving, holding steady, or getting worse.

Don't aim to be best at everything—no company can excel at every key metric. Unattainable goals are more likely to result in behaviors that disrupt rather than enhance a company's performance. Instead, start by agreeing on your overall strategic objectives, and acknowledge that previous targets may not align with those objectives.

FIGURE 5–3

Typical supply chain scorecard.

		Performance Versus Comparison Population					
Key Perspectives	Metric	0–20% Major Opportunity	20–40% Disadvantage	40–60% Median	60–80% Advantage	60–100% Best-in-Class	Your Org.
Customer-Facing Metrics	On-Time Delivery to Request %			82.1%		97.3% ◭	96.3%
	On-Time Delivery to Commit %			91.1% ◭		99.2%	92.8%
	Order Fulfillment Lead Time (OFLT): Primary Manufacturing Strategy (days)		◭	7.9		2.4	11.0
	Upside Production Flexibility: Principal Constraint (days)			49.0	◭	5.5	25.0
Internal-Facing Metrics	Total Supply Chain Management Costs (% of revenue)			10.3%	◭	4.7%	6.9%
	Total Returns Processing Costs (% of revenue)			0.9%		0.2%	66.6%
	Inventory Days of Supply			64.2	◭	23.6	39.0
	Cash-to-Cash Cycle Time (days)			76.3	◭	22.3	43.6
	Net Asset Turns			2.0		9.1 ◭	5.9

◭ Your Organization

We noted earlier that a balanced set of metrics is critical to an effective performance-management program. The same is true for performance targets. While optimizing supply chain performance isn't a zero-sum game—a performance improvement in one area doesn't have to be at the expense of another—it's true that to reach a target in one big area, you might have to accept a lower metric in another.

It's also true that you can improve the performance of numerous parts without improving the performance of the whole—an idea that can be hard for companies to grasp. Sometimes compromises at the functional level are needed to improve overall performance, but this can be a bitter pill to swallow for managers of those functions: It may appear that their own performance is declining.

There are many ways to set performance targets. Perhaps the simplest is to develop specific percentage-improvement goals based on historical and baseline performance. With this method, you simply measure performance in a specific area over a specified time period, determine the baseline, and set a target for improvement. But be sure to link the target to a specific change in strategy or execution. Too often targets are based on the assumption that because a certain level of performance is possible— as indicated by benchmarking data—it is a logical, attainable goal.

For example, a telecommunications equipment company was dissatisfied with the service its key suppliers were providing and embarked on a program to improve supplier on-time delivery. The company measured the performance of 25 key suppliers over a three-month period and found that on-time delivery ranged from 70 to 80 percent. It then set an objective of achieving average on-time delivery of 95 percent for these key suppliers within six months.

After six months, supplier performance hadn't improved noticeably. The manager of the procurement group explained that the 95 percent target wasn't tied to any specific program. The company had just assumed that improving performance by about 5 percent per month was a reasonable goal. Later, after benchmarking delivery performance within the telecom industry, the company found that the top performers were achieving supplier delivery performance of only 87 percent. Using these data, the company set a long-term goal of 95 percent but also set interim targets tied to specific practices shown to be lacking by the benchmarking program. These included the use of joint service agreements, increased use of electronic data interchange (EDI), and upgraded supplier certification programs.

We advocate setting "stretch" targets, but we also caution against setting unrealistic goals, which can hurt morale and breed cynicism. The best approach is to combine historical analysis and baselining with internal and external benchmarking and—in some cases—an assessment of what is realistic given specific business conditions and planned process improvements.

Make Your Metrics Highly Visible and Monitor Them at All Levels

You've probably experienced a performance-management program that got off to a great start and then failed. In our experience, the most common reason for failure is a lack of attention paid to the program once it's off and running. Consistent measuring and reporting will help you to avoid this problem.

One of the most successful metrics programs we've seen was put in place by the supplier of software tools and related hardware we first discussed in Chapter 3. The company's customers were very unhappy with how long it took to get their orders. Order fulfillment averaged 25 days, whereas 2 to 3 days was a reasonable expectation; the sales force cited long order-fulfillment cycles as the primary cause of the company's inability to meet its growth objectives. A supply chain analysis revealed the source of the company's slowness—too many functional handoffs throughout the order-fulfillment process. As a software provider, the company didn't have to deal with most traditional manufacturing issues, such as supplier performance and manufacturing cycle times. Instead, processing customer orders, getting them through the contract negotiation cycle, and packing them for delivery were the major issues.

To improve supply chain performance, the company set targets for each functional area involved in order fulfillment. Then, in an effort to break down functional barriers, it set up a highly visible system for tracking order-fulfillment cycle time overall. Convinced that e-mail updates or Web site postings would lack the necessary impact, the chief financial officer (CFO) placed huge scoreboards in high-visibility areas—near the executive offices, in the local sales office, and in the shipping area—and manually updated the cycle-time scores each week. Since the cycle-time metric was made up of data from every function involved in order fulfillment, many people were involved in data collecting and were well aware of the progress toward the goal of four days or less.

In an unexpected twist, the strategy of high-visibility tracking nearly derailed the project at the beginning. The metrics allowed the project team to look at each activity in the order-fulfillment process, eliminate those which didn't add value, and create a new process designed to do away with many of the handoffs between functions. The heightened scrutiny of people and the added burden of manually tracking each exception and cause of delay actually slowed the process down, and at first, cycle time increased from the historical average of 25 days.

After the first several weeks of posted results, many project team members feared that the initiative would fail. "It's going the wrong way," was a frequent comment. Despite concerns that the highly visible data would discourage people and make them resistant to change, the CFO insisted on continuing to update the scoreboards. Each board showed both the order-fulfillment cycle time and a rolling average of the most recent four-week period. This second metric was added as a way to smooth the results and reduce the perception that a one-time backslide was the sign of a negative trend. After about a month, when the first elements of the new process were put in place, the results were immediate and significant. After two months, average cycle time had been cut by nearly 10 days, and after 10 months, the stretch goal of two days was nearly a reality (see Figure 5-4). An added bonus: The boards have proven effective as a sales tool. Sales reps show them to customers as proof of the company's focus on customer service.

This example shows clearly the need for demonstrated commitment by leaders within your business. Identify a set of "metrics champions" early on and work closely with them to secure their commitment. They will serve as the advocates for performance management. To take their role seriously, they will need to actively monitor relevant metrics and take immediate action if the program is not being executed as designed.

You also should define the decision-making processes and work-flows resulting from the metrics program. Measurements are only useful to the degree that they enable timely decision making. All too often action stops at the point at which the measurement is made. Successful performance management must include specific actions to be taken when

FIGURE 5-4

Order-fulfillment cycle time for Company X.

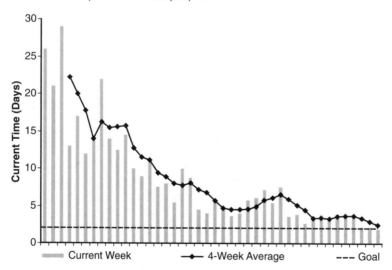

> **Measurements are only useful to the degree that they enable timely decision making.**

a measurement falls outside a defined tolerance level. Processes and workflows should show which decisions are to be made, by whom, and within which limits.

Use Your Metrics to Drive Continuous Improvement

Gathering comprehensive benchmarking data takes time and effort. And since most benchmarking services charge a fee for participation and database access, there's usually an out-of-pocket cost as well. Logic would say that any company willing to make this sort of investment would highly value the resulting information and make every effort to leverage it. Yet, a recent survey of hundreds of companies found that few had used their supply-chain metrics to drive strategic management practices, and most had failed to realize a full return on investment from their benchmarking efforts.[4] This is true of many companies. Too often they review the benchmarking information but don't use it to move the company forward. Over time, the data-collection effort no longer may seem worth the benefits achieved.

Develop an Implementation Plan

There are four major steps to putting a performance-management program in place:

1. *Set supply chain strategy objectives.* Start with your company's business strategy, and then develop supply chain objectives that support this strategy.

2. *Choose supporting metrics and targets.* Identify the specific metrics and targets that you'll use to track progress toward your supply chain objectives.

3. *Identify supporting initiatives.* Develop performance-improvement programs to help meet the supply chain objectives.

4. *Implement the programs.* Collect data and develop tools for reviewing the data and to support decision making.

Set Supply Chain Strategy Objectives

Create supply chain objectives and priorities that support your company's business strategy. Although senior management may agree with the supply chain strategy overall, opinions may vary as to which supply chain performance criteria are most important. This is where a standard framework for performance management, such as the Supply-Chain Operations Reference-model (SCOR), can come in handy.

If necessary, interview senior managers or conduct workshops to validate the supply chain priorities. Articulate the key objectives expressed during these sessions and then validate them with the entire management team and with other stakeholders inside and outside your own organization.

Choose Supporting Measures and Targets

Once you've agreed on the key objectives of your supply chain strategy, choose the metrics you'll use to gauge progress toward those objectives. The best place to start is with an assessment of current performance levels. Then use a tool such as PMG's supply chain performance scorecard to define a list of metrics and ensure consistency. Group the metrics according to which aspect of the business strategy they support. Use the standard definitions to determine the baseline performance level and internal and/or external benchmarking to set near- and long-term targets. As mentioned earlier, choose aggressive but achievable targets.

Start with a few metrics and insist on widespread use before adding additional metrics. Metrics to consider as a starting point include SCOR level 1 metrics, such as inventory days of supply, delivery performance, order-fulfillment lead time, and cash-to-cash cycle time.

Identify Supporting Initiatives

Start by looking at all existing initiatives, their expected impact, and how well they're aligned with the objectives of your supply chain strategy. Eliminate any initiatives that are redundant or misaligned, identify gaps that might prevent achieving the stated objectives, and develop programs to address those gaps. Then update your performance targets, tying targeted improvements to specific activities to clearly show the cause and effect. Getting management support for these improvement programs is critical.

Implement the Programs

Almost every performance-improvement program will require systems support. You may choose to design and build an in-house system or buy a data warehouse, an enterprise resources planning (ERP) module, or a stand-alone solution that offloads data from your ERP system. Knowing the specific data sources is critical when choosing the right system tool. So is understanding how your performance-management approach will link to other efforts and metrics used in other core functions. Never develop a performance-management system in a vacuum.

Understand and respect your organization's capabilities, and strike a balance on business criticality when introducing new measurement requirements. Products and geographic regions can be brought online progressively. A metrics program does not have to be initiated simultaneously for all regions, channels, and products.

Establishing the measurement frequency up front can help to avoid costly reimplementation of data structures. This does not preclude providing reporting on a less frequent basis, a tactic that may be useful if the organization is not ready to exploit more real-time information. Focus on fast "clock speed" metrics on a daily or weekly basis and report the remainder as part of your balanced scorecard. Also determine the appropriate level of visibility. The goal should be visibility all along the supply chain, including a sufficient amount of drill-down capability to understand performance differences by, for example, originating factory and warehouse.

Identify all required data sources, and make the data accessible. For example, if you choose to monitor the percentage of orders delivered on time to the customer's request, you will need the ability to capture the customer request date. Some transactional systems do not have a field for this information, and many systems, while capable of tracking this date, are not programmed to do so.

A gap analysis of data elements and data sources is a vital first step to ensure that existing data are accessible to decision makers. If you are like many companies, you may have large amounts of data buried within multiple, disparate systems. An information systems architecture for both applications and infrastructure is needed to pull data from different sources and enable timely decision making. To simplify both data gathering and reporting, design the data-capture and reporting infrastructure using standard data and metric definitions.

Take the time to understand the performance-management software market. It is made up of many discrete tools and components, enterprise suites, and packaged applications, including such categories as reporting, business intelligence, advanced planning and scheduling (APS) analytics, supply chain event management, and supply chain performance management. As you evaluate the system tools available, resist the temptation to create an all-encompassing data warehouse to enable "slicing and dicing" for root-cause analysis and resolution. Integrating extensive sets of lower-tier metrics can lead to an overly complex implementation and should not be seen as a prerequisite for an effective metrics program.

The remainder of this chapter provides guidance on how to choose the right metrics and build an infrastructure that supports ongoing measurement.

WHICH METRICS?

When faced with a universe of metrics, companies tend to choose more than they actually need. This is especially true when one or two key metrics are first put in place—providing visibility into operational capabilities and results for the first time. For companies used to backward-looking metrics and rear-view-mirror steering, data that can offer insight into cause and effect of key supply chain processes are extremely powerful. The natural inclination is to want such data for all processes.

As an example, let's look at order-fulfillment cycle time. The macro-level metric used by most companies measures the elapsed time between when a customer order is entered and when the associated product is shipped. Orders go through numerous "gates"—an order may be received, verified, entered, priced, credit-checked, released, picked, packed, and shipped—and it is possible to measure the elapsed time between each gate and the next. From the customer's perspective, though, the clock starts when he or she issues the order and stops when the product is received; customers are not particularly interested in the interim stops the order may take along the way. Because of this, it probably doesn't make sense to measure each gate-to-gate cycle. Instead, choose larger "process sets," such as the time between order receipt and order release. And if the results indicate a performance issue, consider adding additional granularity at that point.

You also should avoid using a predefined set of metrics designated as being "right" for your business. No predetermined set of metrics is appropriate for all businesses. Earlier in this chapter we discussed the need to align metrics with strategic objectives. Since a supply chain strategy is based on a company's overall strategic direction and core competencies, you'll need to carefully choose the metrics that make sense as signals of performance to your objectives.

> Since a supply chain strategy is based on a company's overall strategic direction and core competencies, you'll need to choose carefully the metrics that make sense as signals of performance to your objectives.

The metrics you use will evolve as your supply chain processes mature and will vary based on how functionally focused your supply chain is. Clearly, it's futile to establish aggressive targets for cross-enterprise collaboration if your company is still struggling to move beyond a functional focus (see Figure 5-5).

Even if your company focuses only on functional processes, metrics based solely on functional performance are inappropriate. Besides encouraging functional silos, measuring functional performance alone can promote functional excellence at the expense of overall supply chain excellence. For example, the customers of a large telecom company were demanding lower prices. In response, the company pressured its procurement group to lower the cost of materials by negotiating better prices with suppliers. The buyers negotiated substantial discounts by committing to higher-volume purchases for some materials and finding lower-cost suppliers for others. On a monthly basis, the purchasing group posted the results of its efforts—a declining cost per unit of materials.

After a few months, however, it became clear that the focus on reducing materials costs was having a negative effect elsewhere in the

FIGURE 5–5

Focus of metrics to solve performance problems.

Supply Chain Characteristics	Focus of Metrics
Functional Focus Lack of functional policies/processes and basic operations management leads to unpredictable product quality and supply.	Performance of specific functions or departments
Process Focus Although processes, systems, and disciplines are in place to optimize functional quality, cost, and cycle times, cross-enterprise performance may be suboptimized.	Performance of specific processes within or beyond a functional area
Enterprise Focus Supply chain processes are integrated, aligned across all subprocesses and levels of management, and display world-class performance and continuous improvement.	Performance of cross-functional processes
Cross-Enterprise Focus Integration of both internal and external processes allows enterprise partners to focus on their customers, supply chain partners, core competencies, and on creating value.	Performance of cross-enterprise processes and designated external processes

business. Buying in volume caused inventory levels to increase. And manufacturing yields were dropping—a problem traced back to lower-quality materials purchased from the low-cost suppliers.

The moral of this story is clear: Exclusive use of functional metrics can drive unwanted behaviors and interfere with overall strategy execution. Functional metrics aren't bad in and of themselves, but they can hurt overall performance if not combined with cross-functional measurements that enhance the end-to-end supply chain.

Choose Metrics That Support Your Strategy

In Chapter 2, we discussed the importance of organizing around cross-functional processes and breaking down functional silos to support the end-to-end supply chain. Your metrics program must do the same—break down the barriers and handoffs between functions by using cross-functional and process-based performance measures to supplement functional metrics. Functional metrics then become useful tools for diagnosing the causes of performance problems.

The first step in choosing the right metrics is to assess your company's supply chain maturity. The next step is to review your overall strategic objectives and any plans you have to move to the next stage of maturity—cross-process excellence, for instance, or cross-company excellence. Then you can begin to structure a balanced set of supporting metrics, including top-level metrics that evaluate whether or not your supply chain is supporting your company's overall strategy.

Our design of the SCOR model was influenced heavily by our work with hundreds of companies in establishing appropriate approaches to supply chain performance management as part of operations strategy and performance-improvement programs. This work allowed us to establish one of the world's most comprehensive databases of supply chain metrics and associated best practices, which, in turn, became the foundation for PMG's supply chain management database. These metrics and practices are embedded in the SCOR model and are leveraged widely by all industries today.

PMG's Supply Chain Management Benchmarking Study, an ongoing survey of supply chain practices and performance, is based on the same work that led to creation of the SCOR model and uses the same hierarchical construct. At the highest level, the SCOR model provides quantitative measures of performance under 5 key attributes and 13 specific measures.[5] SCOR level 1 metrics typically are associated with executive-level concern (see Figure 5-6).

FIGURE 5–6

Performance attributes and associated level 1 metrics, SCOR, version 6.0.

Performance Attribute	Performance Attribute Definition	SCOR Level 1 Metric
Delivery Reliability	Supply chain performance in delivering: • the correct product • to the correct place and the correct customer • at the correct time • in perfect condition and packaging • in the correct quantity • with the correct documentation	• Delivery performance • Fill rate • Perfect order fulfillment
Responsiveness	How quickly a supply chain delivers products to the customer	• Order fulfillment lead time
Flexibility	How quickly a supply chain responds to marketplace changes; agility in gaining or maintaining a competitive edge	• Supply chain response time • Production flexibility
Cost	The costs associated with operating the supply chain	• Cost of goods sold • Total supply chain management cost • Value-added productivity • Warranty/returns processing cost
Asset Management	How effectively a company manages assets to satisfy demand. Includes fixed assets and working capital.	• Cash-to-cash cycle time • Inventory days of supply • Asset turns

Note that the SCOR level 1 metrics include both internally focused measures (total supply chain management cost, value-added productivity, warranty/returns processing cost, cash-to-cash cycle time, inventory days of supply, and asset turns) and customer-facing metrics (delivery performance, fill rate, perfect order fulfillment, order-fulfillment lead time, supply chain response time, and production flexibility).

SCOR level 1 metrics are designed to provide a view of overall supply chain effectiveness. Explains Michelle Roloff, "While it is virtually impossible for one company to perform at a best-in-class level for each of the level 1 metrics, strong performance in targeted areas is a reflection of overall supply chain health and therefore a very good indicator of return on supply chain spending."

While level 1 metrics are appropriate for monitoring performance at a high level, they are less useful for diagnosing the causes of performance problems. More detailed performance measures that provide details on tactical execution provide a better understanding of these problems. In keeping with the SCOR model's hierarchical structure, each level 1 metric is associated with a group of level 2 and level 3 metrics. These lower-level metrics can be used to diagnose the causes of any performance problems that appear at level 1. Before you start, make sure that you create an overall architecture for your performance-management program—determine which level 1, level 2, and level 3 metrics you will monitor. (See Appendix C for a comprehensive list of level 2 and level 3 metrics.)

Measure Yourself as Your Customers Measure You

The metrics embedded in the SCOR model are consistent with the premise of the supply chain as an end-to-end process. As such, each metric is considered from the perspective of customers and suppliers—not just from an internal perspective. The supply chain scorecard is necessarily prescriptive. It provides detailed definitions for each metric and specific recommendations for how to collect the needed data.

> The metrics embedded in the SCOR model are consistent with the premise of the supply chain as an end-to-end process.

In many cases a company may stray from the standard definitions. This may be done to ease the burden of data collection, to influence the behavior of an internal or an external constituent, or—consciously or unconsciously—to make performance seem better than it really is. While it may be appropriate to "tweak" the standard definitions, always make sure that your metrics are consistent with what your customers and suppliers would use.

We worked with a global automotive parts company that spent more than two years making sure that each of its business units adopted a consistent measurement for delivery performance to its primary customers—retail chains and stores. With daily deliveries and an official policy that all products would be available to customers within one day of ordering, "on-time delivery" was based on the percentage of products received by customers within one day of the order being placed. However, while the business units reported good results, customers were complaining about delivery performance, and a customer satisfaction survey showed that the company was performing worse than its competition.

A closer look revealed that the order desk used a default of next-day delivery except when a product was not available. Products were considered available if they were either in a local distribution center or scheduled to arrive the next day. Customers who ordered a product that was not available were given an estimate of when it would be delivered.

Of course, customers expected delivery the next day or on the estimated date provided by the order desk. They measured on-time performance based on these dates, as did the industry association that reported customer satisfaction data. The company, on the other hand, based its calculations on the assumption that only products that were not available at the time the order was placed had missed their target. Missed "next day" deliveries were not tracked, nor were failures to meet the estimated dates provided when the requested products were not available immediately. In addition, business units calculated their performance on a per-item basis, whereas customers based their measurement on whether or not the entire order was received on time.

Following this analysis, management established two new metrics for order-delivery performance. The first was on-time delivery to commit, defined as the percentage of complete orders received by customers on the delivery date that the company committed to. When a later delivery date was requested by the customer, the commit date was updated accordingly. The second metric, order-fulfillment cycle time, tracked the elapsed time between when an order was received by the company and when the product was delivered to the location specified by the customer.

Interestingly, by analyzing the discrepancy between performance as reported by the business units and performance as reported by customers, the company made a valuable discovery: Customers valued an accurate delivery date for their entire order more than they valued 24-hour turnaround. This insight led the company to reassess its entire service-level strategy.

CASE IN POINT: PERFORMANCE MANAGEMENT AT 3COM

In 2003, 3Com Corporation, a leading maker of networking products, set out to develop a way to use performance management to help execute its business strategy. The company's sales, marketing, product management, research and development (R&D), and supply chain operations are centralized and support all product lines. 3Com hoped to develop an infrastructure that would allow the leaders of each of these functions to

- Align the organization's activities and priorities with overall corporate objectives
- Monitor key performance indicators
- Provide timely information for better decision making and responsiveness

3Com put together a project team, along with a cross-functional steering committee, to provide executive oversight. Before starting, the company went through a major strategic planning effort. Ari Bose, chief information officer (CIO) and chair of the steering committee, explains, "We wanted to make sure that we had a clearly defined business strategy that was bold and forward-looking. And the functional heads had to clearly understand the strategy so [that] they could execute against it."

Once the strategy was set, 3Com focused on aligning each function. Using the balanced scorecard framework, each function set up actions and metrics along the four key dimensions of customer, financial, internal ("operations"), and innovation and learning ("people"). Each function's objectives and actions were designed to support the overall company strategy, and key initiatives were derived from the corporate goals. For example, the service organization had an initiative to upgrade its capabilities to support 3Com's reentry into a specific market segment, and the operations organization had an initiative to move manufacturing to a contract manufacturing partner. Each functional scorecard rolled up into an overall worldwide operations scorecard (see Figures 5-7 through 5-11).

The supply chain organization chose a set of metrics that measures critical aspects of performance and also supports the business goals, as well as more detailed metrics that provide broader visibility into the health of the function. Performance metrics include delivery predictability, stockout percentage, order cycle time, and supply chain costs. These costs can be broken down into materials costs, overhead costs, and period costs, which have even further detail.

Figure 5-9 shows the graphic format that 3Com uses to emphasize the key targets at various levels of the scorecard. To identify the root causes of any problem areas, the company analyzes lower-level metrics in the drill-down option of the supply chain scorecard (see Figure 5-10).

FIGURE 5–7

3Com's approach to performance management.

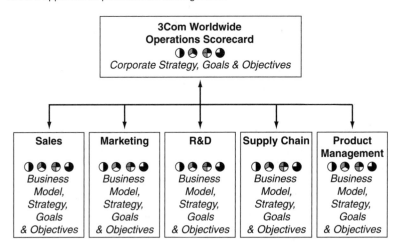

FIGURE 5–8

Setting up a balanced scorecard at 3Com.

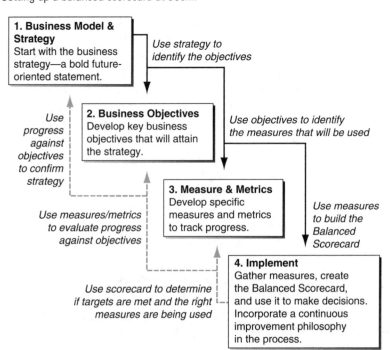

FIGURE 5–9

Supply-chain scorecard for 3Com.

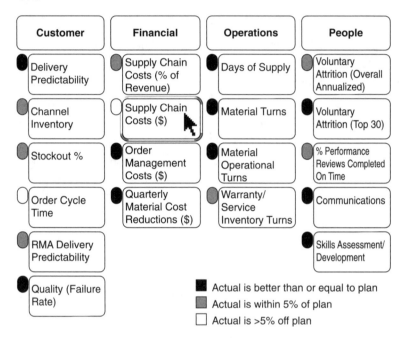

Today, the worldwide operations scorecard resides on every 3Com executive's desktop and is used daily to monitor performance at both a corporate and a functional level. At weekly executive staff meetings, each functional area takes turns making a presentation that includes the summary scorecard and an update on key initiatives that align with overall corporate objectives. "This process has really helped our supply chain organization focus on what's important," says Jim Ticknor, 3Com's vice president in charge of supply chain operations. "But even more, it has helped all the groups see how their activities and decisions affect other areas of the company."[6]

NEXT-GENERATION PERFORMANCE MANAGEMENT

Like 3Com, many organizations are moving away from a piecemeal approach to performance management and toward a more holistic approach. This means that supply chain performance management will become an integral part of an overall performance-management strategy—what Gartner calls "corporate performance management" (CPM).

FIGURE 5–10

Submetrics of supply chain scorecard for 3Com.

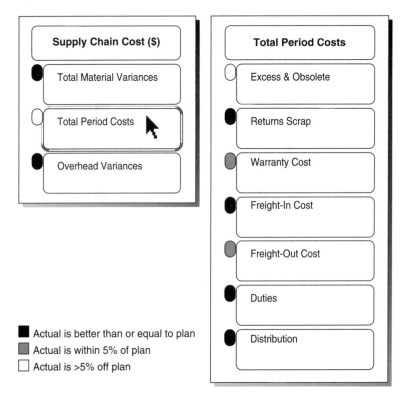

CPM describes the methodologies, metrics, processes, and systems used to monitor and manage an organization's overall business performance.[7] It's more than software. It includes the processes for managing corporate performance, the methodology for choosing the right process metrics, and the processes for managing those metrics. It also blends data from ERP, customer relationship management (CRM), product life-cycle management, human resources management, and business intelligence systems, providing necessary and valuable links between the disparate points of internal operations.

Supply chain performance management is a key element in overall corporate management-performance strategy, which also must include the processes and tools that will enable links with supply chain partners.

While CPM solutions are evolving quickly, there's no silver bullet or system that offers one-stop shopping. This means that your company

FIGURE 5–11

Regional/product group scorecard for 3Com.

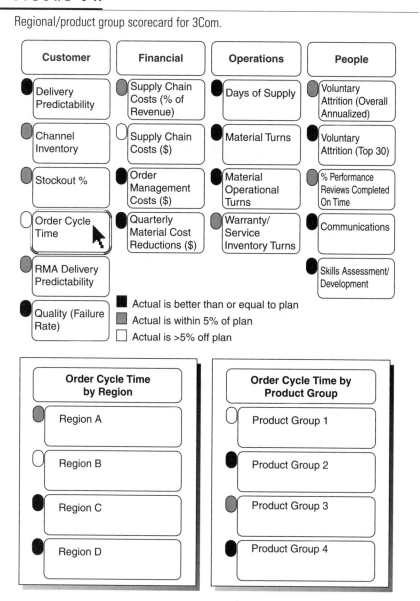

needs to think critically about its immediate performance-management requirements but plan for an integrated solution. Disconnected initiatives managed within specific functions should be avoided at all costs. This integrated CPM approach is wholly consistent with the concept of tightly integrating your end-to-end supply chain with your overall business.

As CPM evolves, we expect to see the following changes:

- Organizations will use consistent supply chain metrics and definitions based on industry standards such as PMG's supply chain scorecard.
- As these standards are embraced, ERP vendors will make performance monitoring and reporting capabilities a basic part of their solutions.
- Companies will develop integrated, enterprisewide performance-management systems. Supply chain, CRM, product life-cycle management, and other functional performance management strategies will be designed within the context of this integrated whole.
- The architecture for business intelligence solutions will be based on a comprehensive approach to corporate performance management, of which supply chain performance management will be a key element.
- Event management systems—which monitor business events in real time and notify users of exceptions and alerts—will become increasingly prevalent, allowing companies to react more quickly to changes in the marketplace.
- Companies will see a growing consensus on how often key metrics should be monitored. Real-time reporting will be reserved for real-time processes.
- "Dashboards" will be replaced by tools with greater functionality. These tools will enable decisions based on current business conditions.

General Motors Profile: Driving Customer Satisfaction

Faced with declining market share and a changing industry, General Motors (GM) launched an ambitious effort that transformed its supply chain and made customer satisfaction a priority.

In the late 1990s, the Internet seemed poised to transform the automobile industry. Consumers armed with information could quickly compare prices, options, quality, and service—and make more informed choices. New business models threatened to squeeze industry margins and disrupt the long-standing original equipment manufacturer (OEM)-dealer relationship. General Motors observed these changes warily.

The world's largest vehicle manufacturer, GM has revenue of $185.5 billion, production facilities in 32 countries, and a workforce of about 325,000. In 2003, the company sold more than 8.6 million cars and trucks—about 15 percent of the global vehicle market. Despite its size and clout, though, GM had seen its global market share erode from 17.7 percent in the early 1990s to 15 percent in 2002 mainly due to declining levels of customer satisfaction and competition from foreign imports. The industry had changed.

In the 1970s and 1980s, GM alone decided what products to make—with little input from dealers or customers. Explains Harold Kutner, group vice president of worldwide purchasing and production control and logistics at the time, "We were an arrogant company. We had an attitude of 'we'll make it, and the customer will take it.'" This attitude typified the "Big Three" automakers at the time. Running plants at full capacity was the name of the game—whether or not the vehicles being made were the ones customers wanted.

THE IMPETUS FOR CHANGE

By the late 1990s the need for change was becoming clear. Consumers were more savvy, powerful, and demanding. Yet GM's responsiveness lagged the industry. Dealers grew increasingly frustrated by the mix of inventory foisted on them. Even in key markets, dealer lots were clogged with over 100 days of supply. To clear out slow-moving products, GM had to offer sales incentives, which squeezed profit margins.

Dealers couldn't get the vehicles they wanted—the vehicles their *customers* wanted. Desirable options such as aluminum wheels, leather interiors, and V8 engines often were not available in adequate quantities. Unavailable options, or *constraints,* were high at GM dealerships relative to the industry as a whole, averaging tens of thousands of orders affected at any given time over the range of GM products. This meant that customers could rarely get their first-choice vehicle. As a result, they often settled for more basic, lower-margin models, which ultimately hurt GM's bottom line.

Customers who chose to special-order a vehicle had to wait as long as 70 to 80 days for it to arrive. Furthermore, GM was uncertain of its delivery-date reliability because delivery-date promises were not tracked at the time, and neither dealers nor customers had any way of checking on the status of their orders—there was no visibility into GM's order-fulfillment process.

At the same time, the company's supply chain costs were growing. High levels of raw materials and work-in-progress inventory, inefficient processes, outdated information-technology systems, and bloated overhead resulted in a costly, sluggish organization—at a time when streamlined operations were becoming more and more critical. Now, with market share down and Internet-driven change on the horizon, GM knew that it could no longer operate as it once had if it hoped to remain a market leader.

Change at the mammoth company wouldn't be easy. After all, GM makes over 30,000 vehicles every day, using over 160,000 parts from a vast network of global suppliers—a staggeringly complex undertaking. Brad Ross, head of GM's global order-to-delivery (OTD) organization, describes the process as a "tremendously orchestrated set of events that integrates orders across sales, manufacturing, and logistics, resulting in what we refer to as the daily miracle of production."

GM's OTD process encompasses four of the Supply-Chain Operations Reference-model's key supply chain processes—*plan, source, make,* and *deliver.* Given this complexity, transforming OTD would be like "turning the *Titanic* around on the Flint River," notes Kutner. Yet that's what GM set out to do. The goal? To ship customer orders in less time, with less inventory, at a lower cost—and to satisfy customers better than anyone else in the industry.

THE NEW MANDATE: SENSE AND RESPOND

GM's ambitious undertaking meant moving from a make-and-sell to a sense-and-respond organization. First, the company had to start tuning into what customers wanted by sensing the marketplace better. GM had been making the wrong products. Its declining market share and the glut of inventory at the dealer lots were proof of that. Notes Ross, "In this business, product is everything. The supporting processes are important, but without the right product in the right place at the right time, you're not even in the game."

Second, GM had to put in place an organization that could respond more quickly and effectively to customer demand—and provide better service quality. This meant rethinking key processes and replacing the functional mind-set with a more cross-functional, collaborative approach.

The Internet became a critical tool for sensing consumer preferences and market trends. In collaboration with dealers, GM developed BuyPower, an online portal that lets potential customers get detailed product and dealer information. By monitoring the "click streams" of online shoppers doing vehicle research, GM now gains a wealth of information that helps with product development, production planning, and sales forecasting. The company also set up dealer councils, regular forums for getting dealer input on consumer trends and better ways to sell.

To align real demand with production schedules—and provide visibility into the OTD process—GM upgraded its vehicle order management (VOM) system to allow dealers access through the Internet. Previously, customer-specified orders went to the end of the manufacturing queue, which is why lead times were so long. Dealers were unable to specify the mix of inventory they wanted. Instead, GM "pushed" inventory to the dealers. With the new VOM system, dealers place orders for the vehicles they want on a weekly and daily basis and can see the status of those orders as they move through the order-fulfillment process.

Using the new system, dealer orders are automatically compared with the current manufacturing schedule. In the past, GM often built the "right" vehicles but sent them to the "wrong" dealers because there was no mechanism in place for matching production with demand. Now GM does its best to make sure that dealers get the vehicles they want. To speed order delivery, the new process looks for the fastest way to fill orders. Is a desired vehicle already in production? Scheduled for assembly? Available at another dealer's lot? Close enough to a vehicle currently in production that a few adjustments will seal the deal? Orders are viewed daily, and assembly schedules are adjusted accordingly.

When desired options are constrained by parts availability, those constraints are systematically flagged, analyzed, and minimized through a new constraint-elimination process. Strategic parts buffering has been a useful new approach to minimizing parts shortages (and order constraints); a new tool has been implemented that enables GM to stock up on select parts and materials that are potential bottlenecks. Getting the right part to the right operator in the plant at the right time is critical. With better supply chain visibility and a focus on strategic parts buffering, GM has been able to improve parts availability overall, boosting quality and cutting costs.

Although demand forecasts still drive production—long lead times for certain materials make this the most practical approach—GM now balances its traditional build-to-stock model with more build to order to lower inventory levels throughout the distribution chain and better respond to customer needs. The company now accepts new orders on a daily basis and can schedule them for the assembly plant the same day and have them come off the line in the same week.

As a result of these changes, lead times for special orders and dealer-replenishment orders have improved by 60 percent, and customer surveys show that GM customers receive their vehicles eight days faster than vehicles from competitors. Delivery reliability also has improved dramatically. Today, GM meets its delivery date commitments 90 percent of the time. Now recognized as one of the most reliable suppliers to the commercial fleet market, GM recently received *Fleet Magazine's* Best Order to Delivery Fleet Company award for the second consecutive year.

And since production better matches demand, customers have a greater probability of receiving their first-choice vehicle. Orders affected by constraints have been reduced by over 90 percent. GM received its best-ever National Automobile Dealers Association (NADA) survey results for OTD/distribution elements for allocation system, product availability, and timeliness of delivery. And it's realizing higher margins on vehicles that are built to customer order.

A NEW ORGANIZATION

One of the greatest obstacles to transforming GM's OTD organization into one that would be customer driven was the company's functional "silos." Too often different groups worked at cross-purposes rather than together. This led to finger pointing and an added layer of complexity while boosting schedule changes and increasing parts shortages, causing unnecessarily high inventory levels and carrying costs.

GM created a global cross-functional OTD organization to ensure that operating objectives were aligned and to eliminate competition for resources. It is organized around GM's three core supply chain subprocesses: supply operations, order fulfillment, and logistics. Order fulfillment deals with dealer-facing and planning activities; supply operations manages materials, internal plant activities, and supplier interaction, and logistics coordinates the movement of parts inbound from the suppliers to the assembly plant and outbound transportation of vehicles to the dealer. Each of these subprocesses is run by a global leader. Together, the three leaders formed a global leadership team that drove the OTD transformation.

The new organization colocates the people who support each other and depend on each other for information. Supply operations was aligned within manufacturing, for instance. Likewise, order fulfillment was embedded within sales and marketing. Outbound logistics was colocated with order fulfillment and inbound logistics with supply operations.

In the old organization, GM had two order-management groups. Vehicle order management reported to sales and marketing, production order management reported to production control and logistics. The OTD team realized that only one order-management process was needed. Accordingly, both processes were combined under OTD within sales and marketing. (See Chapter 3 for more detail on designing processes first and then realigning organizational structure to empower the processes.)

When the dust had settled, GM was able to cut back on the number of people needed to run the global OTD organization by nearly 30 percent, achieving far greater efficiency and a major reduction in costs.

RETHINKING LOGISTICS

In seeking ways to further streamline the OTD organization and cut costs, GM realized that logistics were a weak link. The company had long outsourced inbound and outbound logistics activities to a network of third-party service providers at a high cost. However, a lack of communication and coordination among the providers led to inconsistent performance and long lead times.

To reduce costs and improve efficiency, GM partnered with a global logistics company to create the joint venture Vector SCM. Today, Vector centrally manages GM's large, complex logistics network through a series of command centers equipped with the technology needed to track GM's assets and carriers. To further improve performance and visibility, Vector created one integrated information system for the third-party service providers. By improving logistics, GM's goal was to reduce costs by 20 percent in five years. By year three, GM had already achieved cost savings of 17 percent.

The logistics team also sought to further cut costs by minimizing in-transit damage. Vehicles are treated as "jewels" in the auto industry, and consumers want their jewels delivered unscratched, undented, and "polished." By streamlining the route from assembly plant to dealer and minimizing vehicle handling, GM has reduced vehicle damage incidents by 35 percent.

A FOCUS ON BUSINESS RESULTS

Throughout the OTD transformation, GM maintained a rigorous focus on business results. Because the initiative was so ambitious—with so many improvement opportunities—the company risked losing sight of the big picture while chasing down avenues with limited value-add. GM chose four key metrics to guide the transformation: quality, net income, cash conservation, and market share. Every initiative and every decision had to support one or more of these metrics.

The primary drivers of quality are fewer vehicle damage incidents and providing parts to the assembly line on time to support the build plan. Lower costs and fewer constraints boost net income. Lower inventory levels help to conserve cash. The OTD initiative systematically addressed each of these areas.

The final metric—market share—was selected as the way in which customer satisfaction improvements could be translated into improved company performance. The drivers of customer satisfaction that OTD can influence are order lead time, delivery-date promise reliability, and vehicle-of-choice availability. By improving these drivers, GM would boost customer satisfaction. This would be good for business because satisfied customers buy more products.

These four business-focused metrics were a focal point for the transformation, driving the change forward by forcing the organization to keep its eyes on the road. Notes Ross, "We were always able to map the improvement initiatives to these objectives."

THE INFORMATION TECHNOLOGY CHALLENGE

Although the primary focus of GM's transformation effort in the early stages was on redesigning the key processes and organization, GM couldn't have transformed its OTD capability without addressing the company's underlying information systems. Like most large, complex organizations, GM had a tangle of legacy systems—many redundant—and a lack of integration across functions, business units, and geographies. Since most off-the-shelf software requires significant customization, many of the legacy systems and applications were developed by or for GM and were specifically designed to manage the company's high degree of product and process complexity. GM is in the process of moving many of its legacy systems to the Internet, but a high-performance, wholly integrated IT environment remains a vision that will take many years to achieve.

In the meantime, GM is working with what it has. Given the scope of the effort, the OTD team had to prioritize the needed capabilities and then find technology solutions that didn't cost too much or take too long to implement. The team's strategy has been to enhance key legacy systems with Web-enabled tools and integration, incorporating new tools selectively.

Bill Kala, director of North American manufacturing supply operations and part of the original OTD leadership team, credits GM's global materials scheduling system—a legacy system dating back to the 1980s—with driving many of the savings in supply operations. Kala realized early on, however, that he had to rein in enhancement and maintenance costs. As he explains, "Everyone wanted to make frequent changes to the system, and those changes were contributing to a $70 million annual spend." To gain control, Kala stipulated that any changes be clearly explained and justified. Moreover, changes had to benefit at least two geographic regions. Any request for a new stand-alone system was scrutinized carefully. The result? Kala's group cut the annual cost of the system by almost 30 percent.

In some areas, GM had to push IT changes faster than planned to improve partner collaboration. GM's Information Systems Group supported a move to better integrate the company's processes and systems with those of GM's dealers at the point of sale. Until then, integration had been limited to the basics—parts ordering or submission of warranty claims and financial reports. GM is also piloting a program that deploys one personal computer (PC) for every two service bays at dealer locations to support integration between service and parts and GM. Early tests at Saturn have shown that GM can centrally manage parts inventory at the store level with this system, increasing inventory turns and first-time fill rates and lowering retail inventory levels.

GM's IT strategy is working. The company has taken an additional $1 billion out of IT expenses related to the supply chain since the OTD initiative was launched. The focus on process first and technology second has had a bonus effect. Explains John Whitcomb, GM director of sales and retail process technology, "Once people have a common understanding of business process, which is manifested by the workflow, the discussion about legacy components becomes much more fact-based. You remove the emotional arguments about keeping those systems which people have grown comfortable with."

THE NEXT FRONTIER

What's next for GM's OTD transformation? Reduced cycle times and lead times. More personalized vehicles with special accessories and features. Better integration with dealers, who have already embraced the VOM system and several other Web-based tools that are being built into an integrated "workbench." GM is also looking at more build to order through the dealer channel, which is valuable for its high-touch, high-tech capabilities, and a more flexible supply base. It's looking at more commonality among global systems and processes. "There really is no end point to an initiative like this," says Ross. "We expect to continue on this improvement trajectory for the next several years, providing more competitive advantage for GM—and setting new standards for customer satisfaction."

**GM SERVICE AND PARTS OPERATIONS—
A TRANSFORMATION OF ITS OWN**

The story of GM's supply chain transformation would not be complete without a discussion of another, parallel effort to transform the supply chain of GM Service and Parts Operations (SPO), another key factor in customer satisfaction.

The SPO supply chain is complex: 400,000 order lines every day, generating requirements for 600,000 part numbers from 4,100 suppliers. In the mid-1990s, GM SPO lagged the service parts operations of OEM competitors in several measures by a wide margin. Costs, inventory levels, and response times were all out of line with the competition. To make matters worse, GM's dealers' service parts business was hurting. Faced with new competition from quick service chains, dealers with slow response times were having trouble holding onto customers beyond the warranty period. Today, however, the organization is focused on closing the gap with the competition, and GM SPO is setting its sights for top performance in the industry.

By focusing on five common objectives, SPO has been able to align all of its people and energy behind a common strategy. According to Dennis Mishler, GM SPO's director for logistics and supply chain management, "We focus everyone on better serving the customer through improvements in *order response time, material availability, inventory management, value creation in logistics,* and *new-launch support.* We learned quickly that change cannot come from spreading ourselves too thin. We say, 'The main thing is to keep the main thing the main thing.'"

FOCUSING ON THE CUSTOMER

The "main thing" for SPO is the customer. The group recognized that its supply chain was defined by the needs of its customers, and therefore, the most important guiding principle for the transformation effort should be to "make it easier for SPO's customers to service the end customer." In fact, SPO realized that it was serving multiple supply chains, each with varying requirements. There are three separate brands and multiple product-line businesses covering collision, powertrain, maintenance, and repair, as well as accessories.

IMPROVING ORDER RESPONSE TIME

To provide dealers and retailers with better service, SPO had to improve order response times and delivery reliability. So it implemented a one-day delivery policy for most customers, shipping overnight or in some cases the same day. Meeting the new delivery policy while continuing to lower costs required some key changes in inventory deployment. SPO revaluated which inventories would be stored in the field and which would be held in central locations, leading to a more centralized deployment approach overall.

IMPROVING MATERIAL AVAILABILITY THROUGH FORECASTING

The service parts business is one characterized by seemingly random patterns of demand spread across a wide range of products for a wide range of customers. According to Mishler, approximately 10,000 of the 600,000 parts are considered fast movers, requiring little in the way of advanced planning and forecasting. The other 590,000 parts are slow movers, requiring much more sophistication in forecasting and inventory planning. SPO restructured its overall approach to forecasting: Parts were grouped by business (collision, maintenance and repair, etc.) with similar life-cycle demand curves, and SPO forecasters were trained to understand characteristics, trends, and events related to demand across the life cycle. SPO also implemented world-class forecasting tools that allowed its experts to easily test different forecasting models and implications. For example, patterns related to seasonality, demand spikes, or supply chain events could be "clicked and dragged" into the models to test the overall impact on the forecast. While there is still room for improvement, the results to date have already been striking: SPO has reduced inventory by over 25 percent due to improved forecasting capabilities.

IMPROVING INVENTORY MANAGEMENT AND VISIBILITY

Improving inventory management required GM to greatly enhance its ability to see and manage demand, supply, and inventory information at another level of detail. By developing forecasts and schedules at the level of each PDC (product distribution center), SPO is now moving into a more deterministic, data-driven environment that is enabling significant new reductions in inventory. SPO also has established the capability to see inventory availability across its network, which will soon be extended to include dealer parts departments.

CREATING VALUE IN LOGISTICS

SPO faced a significant gap in the competitiveness of its warehousing and logistics operations. The management team is addressing the challenge in partnership with a third-party logistics provider, systematically implementing principles of lean manufacturing. Over time, this consistent focus has enabled SPO's people to "lean out" material flows one at a time, implementing standardized work processes along the way. Says Mishler, "We have improved our productivity [in the distribution centers] by over 50 percent."

CREATING A BALANCED PARTNERSHIP WITH SUPPLIERS

SPO acknowledges that much of its improved supply chain performance has been due to its improved relationships with its suppliers, including its logistics providers. In conjunction with other GM organizations, it has implemented a rigorous process of supplier collaboration, whereby performance is reviewed and ideas for reducing waste in the supply chain are exchanged on a quarterly basis.

EMPOWERING THE "OAKS"

People also play a powerful role. As Mishler explains, they're the "oaks" that hold up the organization. The SPO is now organized around business lines, reinforcing the focus on customers in each brand/product business. Each business line is supported by a cross-functional team that is held accountable for supply chain performance. The teams include "oaks" from key functions—people who know the processes and have been around the business for years and are continuously trained in skills that will help them eventually optimize each of their supply chains.

Future plans include an aggressive "digital supply chain" initiative that will incorporate virtual warehousing, enhanced supplier collaboration, event management, advanced planning/optimization, and other new capabilities. "It's really a journey," says Mishler. "Once you get the entire organization focused on what is really important, you can really make progress."

6

A Roadmap to Change

While the five core disciplines provide the foundation for supply chain excellence, none is sufficient on its own. Supply chain performance is all about integration—integration of strategy, processes, organization, and information systems. Moreover, making sure that this integration happens—given the complexity of the supply chain and the hundreds of potential practices and competing priorities—requires a multidimensional plan. We call this plan the *roadmap to change.*

An effective roadmap is developed and managed as an iterative and ongoing activity. Unlike a plan that focuses on a single project, a roadmap describes each of the major initiatives to be executed over a given time period—typically one to three budget cycles. It shows the links between the different initiatives and the expected performance improvements at meaningful intervals. Progress toward objectives is monitored as part of regular business or operations reviews.

Creating and managing a roadmap to change (see Figure 6-1) is a cross-functional effort with ongoing collaboration among the supply chain organization, the information technology organization, and other functions, such as marketing, sales, finance, and engineering. Working together, thought leaders from these groups ensure that each initiative is clearly defined, launched, and executed in a manner consistent with the overall business strategy.

F I G U R E   6–1

Creating the roadmap to change.

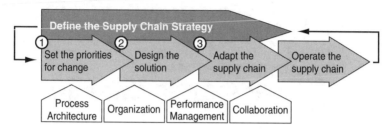

Developing and executing the roadmap can be time-consuming and resource-intensive but is the key to supply chain maturity and is well worth the effort. A highly mature supply chain is one that has achieved advanced capability across each of the core disciplines (see Figure 6-2). Research by PRTM's benchmarking subsidiary, The Performance Measurement Group, LLC (PMG), finds that there is a strong correlation between supply chain maturity and superior performance. Companies with mature supply chains experience

- ◆ A 40 percent profitability advantage, where profitability is expressed as earnings before income and tax as a percentage of revenue
- ◆ Average total supply chain costs just above 8 percent of revenue, versus 10 percent for companies with less mature supply chain practices
- ◆ Superior customer service, with 25 percent less inventory investment

ADVANCED SYSTEMS AREN'T ENOUGH

> There is a strong correlation between supply chain maturity and superior performance.

Advancing your company's supply chain performance means moving from where you are today to a future state that includes next-generation processes and infrastructure, including information systems. Technology is only one part of the story—and it isn't the first chapter. Throughout this book we have noted where the five core disciplines can and should be enabled by effec-

F I G U R E   6–2

Stages of supply chain process maturity.

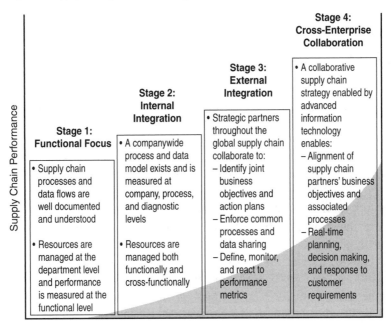

tive information systems, but we've deliberately avoided structuring them around systems. Why? Clearly, a high-performance supply chain depends on integrating processes and data both inside the enterprise and with trading partners. Yet many companies are ill-prepared to take advantage of the power of the tools that enable integration—because their strategy is unclear, their processes are weak, their organization lacks required skills and capabilities, or the companies they want to partner with aren't ready to do so. Positioning a company to excel in the next generation requires addressing these issues.

In addition, while much of today's technology has existed for several years, it hasn't evolved enough to support the way supply chains actually operate. Many of the information systems that came into being at the height of the Internet bubble were like solutions looking for problems to solve. Those that were focused too narrowly or attempted to create a market where none existed disappeared when the bubble burst. The "survivors" are now being refined to address the way companies really work,

In the next generation, applications will be far better aligned with what companies want and need.

as opposed to a technologist's opinion as to how they *should* operate.[1] In the next generation, we believe applications will be far better aligned with what companies want and need.

To understand the appropriate role of systems in creating your roadmap, think of creating a ladder that will allow you to climb from where you are today to the next generation. If the core disciplines form the sides of the ladder, then the supporting systems are the rungs that allow you to climb. Although it is possible to ascend a ladder with no rungs, you would have to pull yourself along with great effort to do so. Now imagine the rungs with no supporting sides—there is no way to climb at all! This is what happens when companies attempt to achieve the characteristics of the next-generation supply chain without focusing on the core disciplines first.

Perhaps the most interesting finding of our research is the benefit of the synergy that results from integration of best practices *and* effective information systems. It's not surprising that mature processes, combined with advanced technologies, lead to better performance. What is surprising, however, is that companies that implement sophisticated technology—such as an advanced planning system—without the same level of attention paid to their processes and organization actually perform worse than those that make no use of advanced technology at all.[2]

CHARACTERISTICS OF THE NEXT GENERATION

An effective roadmap will take you to the next generation—but what will the next generation look like, and how will it be different from today? Few would argue about the benefits of the extended supply chain and the idea that in order to optimize value, you need to look beyond your own organization and your immediate customers and suppliers.

In practice, this means achieving

- *Enterprise connectivity*—business and transactional systems that are linked, allowing data to be seen and transported to different entities within the supply chain
- *Distributed decision making*—bidirectional information flow and defined business rules used to manage ongoing changes in demand and supply

- *Real-time performance management*—real-time, accurate information available to enable rapid and informed decision making

While reacting immediately to events within the extended supply chain and establishing seamless collaborative processes are objectives for many companies, in actuality, very few can do them effectively. This is so because today, process and data standards, as well as information-system architectures, can be major inhibitors to the various collaboration approaches discussed in Chapter 4. Many systems in use today still rely on point-to-point or hub-and-spoke architectures. Their primary utility is to move materials more quickly and efficiently. And today's supply chain strategies and processes reflect the limitations of these tools.

Next-generation supply chain tools will emphasize collaboration and information availability more than speed and efficiency and support three fundamental characteristics: *transparency, flexibility,* and *simultaneity.* As these technologies continue to evolve and supply chain practitioners become more comfortable with their effectiveness, strategies, processes, and organizational capabilities will evolve in parallel. Figure 6-3 shows some specific applications that you may consider using to enable these next-generation characteristics as you develop and manage your roadmap to change.

Transparency

Transparency enables visibility into the end-to-end supply chain. Companies that can see the status of their supply chain resources and transactions—both internal and external—can make more timely decisions. Transparency can create value in numerous ways. If you know the status of key resources, you can make better use of them and optimize the ongoing balance between demand and supply, boosting efficiency and productivity and lowering costs. End-to-end visibility also can provide early warning of potential problems and facilitate root-cause analysis when something goes wrong.

Flexibility

Flexibility is the modern-day hedge against uncertainty. As supply chains become increasingly lean, cushions of inventory and backup resources used to meet unexpected demand surges or supply constraints are being called into question and scrutinized carefully—they're too costly to serve as buffers. Thus companies will find new ways to be flexible without the

FIGURE 6–3

Enablers of next-generation systems capability.

Next Generation Characteristic	Examples of Information System Solutions	Description
Transparency	Enterprise Resource Planning (ERP)	Provides a foundation for visibility of information, such as inventory levels by location
	Supply Chain Analytics	Enables extracting, processing, and pushing data toward decision makers
	Supply Chain Event Management (SCEM)	Alerts designated recipients to exceptions to preset boundary conditions so that corrective actions can be taken as needed
	Radio Frequency Identification (RFID)	Wireless, radio-wave-based technology that allows companies to track tagged items without contact or line-of-sight scanning
Flexibility	Portals	Enables shared information on orders, forecasts, inventory status, and stockouts
	Private Networks	Enables shared information on orders, forecasts, inventory status, and stockouts
	Advanced Planning and Scheduling (APS)	Optimizes use of supply chain resources, including capacity, materials, and labor, while enabling execution in accordance with company-defined priorities
	Collaborative Supply Chain Planning Tools	Allows companies and their key customers and suppliers to integrate the requirements and constraints of each collaboration partner in co-developing forward supply plans
Simultaneity	Enterprise Application Integration (EAI)	Integrates the workflows needed for simultaneity
	Business Process Automation (BPA)	Defines business rules and associates them with business processes so that companies can create expert systems that monitor the supply chain

asset "cushions" of the past. They'll use a combination of internal flexibility (e.g., highly configurable products and effective use of postponement strategies), supplier flexibility, and the ability to substitute highly accurate information for physical inventory.

Simultaneity

Simultaneity refers to the execution of supply chain activities in parallel rather than sequentially. It results in start-to-finish transactions that can be completed quickly without further inputs, allowing greater customer responsiveness and lower transaction costs. This means that each participant has all the information needed to make decisions at the moment an event—such as a new customer order or replenishment signal—occurs. Within the extended supply chain, this information is available both within an enterprise and, for collaborative practices, between the organization and its trading partners.

A supply chain that is transparent, flexible, and simultaneous can substitute execution based on real-time requirements for the frequent planning and replanning that characterize most supply chains today, enabling increased manufacturing responsiveness and automatic sequencing and fulfillment of customer requirements.

Why are these elements so important? For one thing, the supply chain is fast becoming a critical driver of both shareholder value and competitive differentiation. The pressures of global competition that exist today will increase in the years to come, making a focus on efficiency and ongoing cost reduction essential for staying power. In addition, supply chain performance will grow in importance as a competitive differentiator as companies become better at adapting their supply chain strategies and capabilities in accordance with changing market requirements. Solid processes will be the price of entry; superior processes will set companies apart.

We've noted that the next generation is all about integration—and the innovation results in a highly integrated supply chain that can have an impact on both revenue and profitability. This means that you need to build your roadmap with a vision of the future in mind—and the innovative practices and tools that will enable this vision to become a reality. While every industry is different, we see several trends that should be incorporated in any company's vision of the future.

As the supply chain becomes a larger contributor to both the top and the bottom lines, activities that occur before and after a product ships will become increasingly important. In the next generation, the supply chain will be used as a way to increase sales opportunities and enhance customer relationships before, during, and after the sale. This means that you'll need to pay close attention to the front end of the supply chain—the activities associated with demand creation—and the increasing impact of the Internet, online marketplaces, and collaborative relationships. And as customers focus increasingly on their total cost of ownership, they will look for suppliers who can extend superior supply chain execution to their service offerings. Thus your roadmap also needs to include a focus on the service supply chain.

We expect that today's trend toward outsourcing will continue to gather steam and that, in the future, companies will outsource even more heavily in an attempt to transition as many fixed costs to variable costs as possible. This means that effective collaboration will be even more critical to success. Companies will need to be highly skilled at evaluating their prospective partners and identifying those with whom a relationship will result in the maximum economic value for each party. Logistics service providers and manufacturing outsourcers will expand their skill sets, helping their customers increase efficiencies while reducing labor requirements.

As technologies such as Web-enabled planning and optimization tools continue to advance, more data will be available, and integration with suppliers and customers will become more straightforward. At the same time, the functionality enabled by these technologies will become more modular, "commoditized," and widely available. This means that information systems aren't likely to provide the level of competitive advantage they imparted in the past; as with robust processes, they simply will be the price of entry.

DEVELOPING A ROADMAP

To understand how to develop your roadmap for an integrated, extended supply chain, then, let's revisit the steps shown in Figure 6-1 one by one.

Step 1: Set the Priorities for Change

The complexity of the supply chain—which touches numerous corporate functions, including product design, procurement, manufacturing, distribution, and postsales support, as well as diverse, often global sales channels and external partners—makes pinpointing the right focus for improvement efforts a challenge. Your supply chain strategy is the right place to start.

Note that developing and executing to your roadmap and addressing the core disciplines may be somewhat iterative. As an example, the approach you take to a certain roadmap initiative may require that you make changes to the organization or redefine performance targets. However, your strategy always should drive your roadmap, not the other way around.

> Your strategy always should drive your roadmap, not the other way around.

Chapter 1 provides a detailed approach to developing your supply chain strategy; use the strategy to evaluate your current capabilities and determine any structural supply chain changes that are required to execute it. Clearly, if any basics are broken, you'll need to fix them. Perhaps you are experiencing specific performance problems. Or if you've bought or sold a business recently, you may have to adapt your supply chain accordingly.

To set the priorities for change, use the following principles as a guide:

* Use a business-driven approach.
* Identify the type of change required.
* Understand the interrelationships among initiatives.
* Consider your culture and environment.

Use a Business-Driven Approach

You need to ensure that each improvement initiative will deliver real business value. Almost invariably, a portfolio of prospective initiatives will have total resource requirements far in excess of the resources actually available to support them—and varying opinions about what needs to be done first.

To overcome these obstacles, define the performance objectives for key supply chain metrics, such as on-time delivery, inventory days of supply, or total supply chain management costs. As described in Chapter 5, you'll need to look at these metrics as an interdependent set and make any necessary trade-offs. Base these trade-offs on the primary basis of competition that forms the foundation of your strategy—innovation, cost, service, or quality. Then decide on appropriate targets and performance priorities.

Next, quantify the value of reaching these targets—this may be a cost saving or an improvement in customer service that will result in increased revenue. Then, when you have determined the resource level required to make the changes that will result in these benefits, you will be prepared to calculate the overall return for a specific set of initiatives. This will give you an objective way to make the trade-offs necessary to maximize the overall benefit to your business.

As an example, let's look at Company X, a consumer-electronics company that has chosen superior customer service as its primary basis of competition. For Company X, on-time delivery or fast-order fulfillment will be a high priority. This means that the management team should establish quantitative, time-phased targets for ongoing performance improvement in areas such as "improve on-time delivery to commit performance by x percent every six months." They'll need to tie these objectives to specific initiatives designed to enhance performance. They'll also need to quantify the value of achieving these targets and balance this value against the investment required to achieve it.

Identify the Type of Change Required
Before even considering specific initiatives for your roadmap, it's important to have a view of the order of magnitude of change required to realize the value of the performance objectives. Although large investments in new processes, skill sets, or information systems may seem like prerequisites for significant performance improvement, they may not be the right place to start.

> You need to fix what isn't working today before you can focus on taking major steps toward next-generation performance.

You need to fix what isn't working today before you can focus on taking major steps toward next-generation performance. For example, many companies own enterprise resources planning (ERP) systems that provide them with standard material requirements planning (MRP) functionality but manage material requirements planning offline. These same companies may look to sophisticated applications, such as advanced planning and scheduling (APS) applications, as the solution to the issues they experience as a result of not having centralized planning data. While using MRP isn't necessarily a prerequisite to a successful APS implementation, the discipline, control, and data integrity inherent in a stable planning process are. This means that these companies will need to focus first on resolving any data-quality and process-compliance issues. Layering a sophisticated information system on top of a weak process is likely to make things worse, not better.

As noted earlier, on-time delivery or fast-order fulfillment is critical for organizations such as Company X which compete based on superior customer service. These companies may seek technology-based solutions designed to improve performance in these areas, such as a Web-based order-entry portal for customers or real-time radio frequency identification (RFID)–based tracking of products that are in transit to the customer. If customers are unwilling to use a portal, or if orders are constantly bogged down by internal inefficiencies or product shortages, however, these solutions won't improve performance in the short term. These operational problems need to be addressed first, with the technological solution being part of the longer-term roadmap.

Figure 6-4 shows the categories of change, which range from fixing the basics, to extracting additional value from existing processes and information systems, to investments in wholly new processes and technology.

Companies that begin their roadmap development after achieving a high level of process maturity may need to consider more significant investments in processes, organization, and information systems to reach the next level of performance.

Understand the Interrelationships among Initiatives
The General Motors (GM) profile highlights the importance of evaluating prospective supply chain initiatives as an integrated effort. Rather than

FIGURE 6–4

Categories of change.

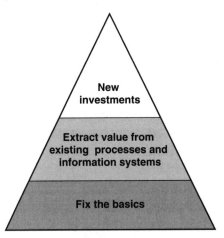

focusing on the return on investment of individual supply chain initiatives, GM looks closely at how different initiatives can work together to support its overall supply chain goals and analyzes which need to precede others. This sort of approach is critical in creating a path to next-generation performance.

Consider, for instance, the interrelationship between structural-simplification and process-change initiatives. Should the physical distribution network be simplified before inventory management practices are changed? Should SKU proliferation be addressed before embarking on a new approach to supply chain planning? Identifying dependencies may reveal that initiatives previously thought to be unrelated are, in fact, on the critical path to the success of the overall effort. You also may find that a proposed initiative is likely to have an impact on the return of one or more existing projects, which may lead to reprioritizing or even canceling an in-process effort.

Continuing our example of Company X, the management team will need to consider a number of factors that affect delivery performance. These may include

- Issues with the core planning processes that result in ongoing imbalances between demand and supply
- Internal policies that cause orders to get caught in an extensive credit-verification process
- Aggressive inventory targets that cause business units to operate with overly conservative inventory levels
- Skill gaps inside the organization that limit overall effectiveness
- Conflicting performance targets that drive suboptimal behavior
- Inconsistent performance by key partners, such as material suppliers or logistics service providers

Addressing these issues requires a clear understanding of the interdependencies of the major activities being considered. Will a redesign of the planning process have the necessary impact if supplier delivery performance remains below acceptable levels? Do the responsible individuals have the experience and skills to define and execute the required process changes? Are the new processes dependent on new systems capabilities? These are just a few of the questions that need to be answered as part of developing the roadmap.

Consider Your Culture and Environment

Including an initiative in your roadmap requires that you look beyond any technical solutions and consider the "softer" factors of your culture and environment. How does your organization deal with change? At some companies, transformation efforts are embraced. At others, past experience has created a strong mistrust of large-scale initiatives, and only small steps are acceptable.

> Look beyond any technical solutions and consider the "softer" factors of your culture and environment.

Also consider your business environment. How important is improving supply chain performance relative to other business priorities? Can the right resources be made available? Although current performance may be well below what is dictated by your supply chain strategy, the reality of how your company operates may override what you view as a critical initiative, and other business imperatives may claim the resources necessary to execute the roadmap. If this happens, you'll need to adjust your ambitions accordingly.

Finally, take the stability of your organization's management team into account, particularly at the most senior level. Next-generation supply chain practices have a major impact on decision making; as such, any new initiative will be shaped by the management team's vision of how decisions should be made. A lack of continuity at the executive level, especially during the more difficult, early phases of implementation, may destroy an initiative's momentum. If this is a concern, consider delaying the start of the roadmap execution until you are confident that you will have the ongoing support you need.

Test your readiness to establish and manage the priorities for change by making sure that you can answer the following questions:

- What are your value objectives and priorities?
- What type of change is needed to create the value?
- Are ongoing supply chain initiatives still appropriate, or do you need to stop or redirect initiatives?
- Given your environment (resources, other business priorities, potential management team turnover), what type of change is feasible?
- Given your culture, what approach (big bang, small steps, etc.) is most appropriate?

Step 2: Design the Solution

Once you have consensus on your priorities, the next step is to identify the changes needed to support your value objectives. To do this effectively, you'll need to be familiar with each of the remaining core disciplines—and know how you plan to approach creation of your supply chain process architecture, organizational structure, a plan for collaborating with selected supply chain partners, and appropriate metrics.

Your solution design should focus on streamlining business processes and increasing the velocity of product and information flow. The overall objective: delivering the business value you used to set the priorities.

Understand What's Already There

In essence, the solution design describes how work will be performed in the future. In order to get this right, you'll need a clear understanding of how things work today. Start by analyzing the major supply chain processes that drive the critical metrics and understand the sequences of processes and events. As necessary, decompose these processes into smaller activities. You are looking for causes of errors, non-value-added activity, redundancy, queuing, and any other factors that have an impact on process efficiency and effectiveness.

Let's return to Company X, where the management team is planning an initiative focused on implementing improvements to the overall order-fulfillment process. As we saw in Chapter 5, from the customer's perspective, this process starts when a sales order is generated and stops when the product is received. Analysis of the current process needs to be consistent with the customer's viewpoint.

Company X should start by analyzing current performance and what metrics are being used, how they are defined, and the data sources. What is the average order-fulfillment cycle time? What does the distribution of the data look like? Do some orders take much longer than others? How good is the company at making and meeting commitments? Is there a good understanding of the causes of delays or missed commitments? Are clear targets and accountabilities in place?

Next, the company needs to document the path orders take once they are generated by the customer and understand exactly what happens to them. Some of the questions to consider are: In what order are activities done? Where and why does an order get "stuck"? How many people handle each order? Who can modify orders? Who is responsible for scheduling delivery and communicating with the customer? Are there any areas of rework or backtracking? Is the same activity performed more than once? How long does each activity take? Where is value added? Of critical importance: For each of these questions, Company X must know *why* the activity is performed the way it is.

This effort is likely to uncover some issues initially thought of as only tangentially related to delivery performance. If product-availability issues are causing a large percentage of problems, attention needs to shift to the planning process. What is causing the stockouts? Is there a problem with the forecasting or demand-management process? Are suppliers failing to deliver? Is the factory having yield issues? Are the system tools being used to balance demand and supply working properly? Is their output being interpreted correctly, and are the right actions being taken?

As it reviews the process, Company X also will look at the associated organization and the specific roles and responsibilities within it. Where are the handoffs between functional areas? Do people understand what they need to do? Are they well trained? Can they think analytically about how the process can be improved?

Company X also will need to look critically at the systems that support the process and determine if there are any issues with current functionality. A word of caution here: In our experience, there is a common tendency to look at systems as the cause of many process problems. Quite often the real problem is how the systems are being used—or misused—rather than an issue with existing functionality. Or the functionality is well suited to the business requirements, but data-integrity issues are causing people to mistrust the system's recommendations.

Develop a Vision of Where You Want to Go

Your supply chain design should incorporate the next-generation characteristics of transparency, flexibility, and simultaneity. Depending on your starting point, this may require major change or only minor updates to what you are already doing. Your roadmap to change doesn't have to be a massive undertaking.

As you design your future supply chain, ensure that it satisfies the four tests of supply chain architecture discussed in Chapter 2: strategic fit, end-to-end focus, simplicity, and integrity. Once your process design is complete, you can define the organizational structure required to ensure that it can be executed effectively and efficiently. You also can identify the information systems that will be needed to support the process and make the necessary data available.

> Your supply chain design should incorporate the next-generation characteristics of transparency, flexibility, and simultaneity.

Test the strength of your solution by answering the following questions:

- Is the future process clearly defined?
- How does the new process affect the existing process architecture, organization, physical infrastructure, and IT?
- Do business and IT managers agree on the nature and scope of required changes?
- Does the initiative meet all evaluation criteria—return on investment, strategic alignment, business risk, and supply chain architecture rules?
- Are the proposed changes ambitious but achievable?
- How will you measure success?

Step 3: Adapt the Supply Chain

The final step in managing the roadmap to change is all about implementation—and ensuring that the solution is implemented in a way that achieves your value objectives. How you adapt your supply chain will depend on the types of initiatives you include in your roadmap, but the core disciplines provide an excellent framework for guiding your efforts.

The most successful roadmap implementations use a phased approach, which minimizes risk and maximizes the likelihood of success. The phases generally include detailed design, prototyping or proof-of-concept, a controlled pilot, refinement based on the results from the pilot, and rollout. A number of work streams are needed to support these phases, including program management, change management, and value management. While it is not our intent to provide a primer on effective program-management methodologies in this book, we note that successful implementation requires understanding and mastering these challenges. We will touch on each briefly, focusing on specific challenges associated with increasing focus on collaboration and information availability.

Value Management

The next-generation supply chain emphasizes the value of information and the ability to make real-time decisions far more than in the past. This means that many of the changes you put in place will focus less on tangible physical assets making it more difficult to measure and manage the value of your efforts. As an example, the value of reducing inventory days of supply from 150 to 100 days is relatively easy to measure. However, the value of increasing on-time delivery to commit from 70 to 90 percent is much more difficult.

Since you'll need to monitor performance improvements at critical milestones, make sure that you have agreement up front on the specific metrics definitions and on the value created by hitting certain targets. Perhaps for every percentage point in improved delivery performance you can expect a 5 percent increase in the customer revenue stream for the life of the product. Or for every day you reduce your average order-fulfillment cycle time you will realize a one-time release of cash equal to one day's revenue, which can then be invested at your current cost of capital. Since the value of performance improvements will be different for every organization, there is no set formula to follow—so make sure that you have agreement up front.

Use the operational metrics you chose while designing the solution to measure progress toward your overall business objectives, and systematically audit value achievement after significant milestones are reached to assess whether the solution needs fine-tuning.

Program Management
Although all core elements of program management—issue management, resource management, scope management, risk management, action-item management, status reporting, budgeting, and planning—are important in implementing the roadmap to change, our experience is that managing the overall scope of effort can be the most challenging.

Changes affecting physical assets or human resources are relatively easy to "see," but the inherent complexity of the next-generation supply chain and its focus on information and decision making mean that the scope of effort will go far beyond changes to tangible resources. And because the technologies that enable next-generation characteristics are still not widely adopted, many companies don't fully understand the challenge of collecting, manipulating, and maintaining information across the supply chain. This can lead to initiatives with unrealistic expectations and high rates of failure.

You can minimize "scope creep" by actively involving your supply chain architects—your business-process and IT experts who are in the best position to understand the details of your process and applications architecture—during implementation.[3] Moreover, regular program reviews help to maintain a focus on scope management and ensure that the executive management team approves any major scope changes.

Change Management

Since your supply chain should be evolving constantly, you need to ensure that the culture within your organization is one that embraces frequent change. This means that you need to understand and use basic change-management principles: managing expectations, communicating frequently, involving key stakeholders, identifying and managing resistance to change, and monitoring and reporting on progress. You'll also need to ensure that this culture extends to your supply chain partners. Involve them early and often—in team-building exercises, training programs, and progress reporting.

> **Poor communication is often the culprit when roadmap initiatives don't progress according to plan.**

Poor communication is often the culprit when roadmap initiatives don't progress according to plan, but the next-generation supply chain also requires new skills. As discussed in Chapter 3, next-generation practices have a major impact on the organization, creating new roles and required capabilities. These include the ability to manage collaborative relationships and supply chain performance and to ensure tighter integration between the supply chain and other core processes, such as technology and product and service development.

Achieving these new capabilities is a key success factor, and progress should be assessed on a regular basis. We recommend placing managers in their new roles even before a new supply chain solution has been rolled out. And whenever possible, managers who will be taking on new roles also should be involved even earlier in defining the parts of the solution that relate to those roles. (See the Owens-Corning profile for an example of role reengineering.)

IN CONCLUSION

As you develop and manage your roadmap, make performance a priority. As we noted at the beginning of this chapter, companies with more mature supply chain practices already have a significant performance advantage. As these more advanced companies adopt next-generation practices, the performance gap between leaders and laggards will grow—and those with less mature supply chains likely will experience declining profitability.

The five disciplines provide the foundation for supply chain excellence and are the levers that allow your supply chain to increasingly contribute directly to the growth of both revenue and profit. Many companies have already made significant progress in putting these disciplines in place—and are reaping major benefits as a result.

Our consulting experience and our in-depth discussions with the companies profiled in this book show clearly that process work has to precede technology enablement. The two can then work, hand in glove, to make both quantum and incremental improvements in performance. By focusing on improving the five core disciplines of strategic supply chain management, you'll be prepared for the increased competitiveness, speed, and agility of next-generation supply chain management.

Seagate

Seagate Technology Profile: Real-Time Response to Demand

Driven by a vision of multitiered visibility and real-time demand fulfill-ment, Seagate Technology is investing heavily in technology and process improvements and an electronically linked end-to-end supply chain.

Founded in 1979, Seagate helped fuel the information age by building the personal computer (PC) disc drives needed to store vast sums of data. Today, data-storage technology has evolved far beyond the PC. And as our appetite for storage keeps on growing—driven by the Internet, consumer electronics, and our desire for anytime, anywhere access to information—so does the need for increasingly sophisticated disc drives.

What few people realize is just how complex these products are. Seagate notes on its Web site that building disc drives is considered the "extreme sport" of the high-tech industry, involving expertise in physics, aerodynamics, fluid mechanics, information theory, magnetics, process technology, and many other disciplines. The company constantly strives to boost storage capacity and set new records for disc-drive performance. Besides staying ahead of the technology curve, Seagate faces a number of unique business challenges that drive its supply chain strategy.

KEY BUSINESS CHALLENGES

Seagate's products use components that are so complex to manufacture that lead times can range from one month to an entire quarter. Then there's the geographic challenge. The component manufacturing plants are often far removed from the subassembly and drive manufacturing plants. Explains Karl Chicca, senior vice president of global materials, "Every disc drive has several hundred of these very complex parts, each of which

Seagate produces 15 to 20 million disc drives a quarter using 65 million components a *day*.

has process technologies that are literally bleeding edge, coming together from all corners of the world, in massive quantities—we produce 15 to 20 million disc drives a quarter." This translates into about 65 million components a day—many purchased from outside suppliers—that go into disc drives that are increasingly customized to specific customer needs. Customers range from Sony and Microsoft which use Seagate's drives for consumer applications, to companies with high-end storage systems, such as EMC.

For every customer, Seagate maintains one or more just-in-time (JIT) hubs—inventory warehouses operated by a third-party logistics provider. These vendor-managed inventory (VMI) arrangements are the industry norm. Each hub is stocked with anywhere from one or two to dozens of different types of disc drives, depending on how broad a range of products the customer sells. Some of Seagate's customers have 15 to 20 locations—and just as many JIT hubs—but they don't pay for the inventory stocked in their hubs until they use it.

Seagate's ambitious goal is to ship to real-time changes in demand—not to plans or forecasts.

Now add the complexity of unpredictable demand. In this business, customer demand is infinitely dynamic, and Seagate's ambitious goal is to ship to real-time changes in demand—not to plans or forecasts. This means that the company has to monitor the economy, the high-tech industry, and the information-technology subset of the industry to get a sense of which way demand is flowing.

In the early days, a plan would hold for six months. No more. Notes Richard Becks, vice president of e-business and supply chain, "Looking back on almost 25 years in this business, the biggest change has been the demand dynamic. It can't be predicted anymore. We've had to migrate from a mind-set of plan-based stability to a model of infinite flexibility and building to pure customer demand."

Extreme product complexity, lengthy component lead times, global operations, high volume, dynamic demand, customized products—Seagate has to meet these challenges as well or better than its competitors to sustain and build on its leadership position. The company's supply chain plays a critical, strategic role.

REAL-TIME DEMAND FULFILLMENT

Earlier in its history, Seagate focused on low-cost manufacturing and operating to plan. But the company has evolved. Today, the focus is on being a technology leader, getting more innovative products to market more quickly, and building speed and flexibility into the organization for greater agility—all while maintaining a sharp focus on customer satisfaction. Notes Chicca, "Everything we do has the fundamental premise that it has to benefit the customer."

Seagate's supply chain has evolved accordingly. A cornerstone of the company's supply chain strategy is meeting customer demand in real time—literally responding to customer orders as they arise. To do this successfully and cost-effectively, Seagate has to maintain a greater degree of flexibility in its factories and lower levels of inventory overall. The key is information flow, and that's been a critical focus of the company's supply chain efforts.

Seagate acquired a jumble of dissimilar processes and information systems in its early years as it grew through acquisition. For the last five years, making processes, systems, applications, and databases consistent throughout the company has been a top priority. For example, the company had several engineering-change control tools to manage product configurations. Now Seagate has just one worldwide system—Metaphase from EDS. The company also consolidated nine enterprise resources planning (ERP) systems from Oracle into two worldwide systems and eventually will move to a single system. This effort to consolidate and standardize is paying dividends now. Information is flowing more freely throughout the supply chain because it no longer has to be reworked or reentered manually. And integrated systems give the company a clear view into every aspect of operations—a must for real-time demand fulfillment.

"Electronic connectivity gives us visibility up and down the supply chain, so we don't have to generate new capacity every time there's a request for more product," says Chicca. "We understand what our capability to flex really is, and we can commit to the customer very quickly." Responding to customer requests used to take a week or longer. Now it takes about a day to inform customers if and when they'll get product. Seagate's goal is to commit on the spot.

END-TO-END CONNECTIVITY

Seagate's customers and suppliers are linked electronically to its internal network.

> Responding to customer requests used to take about a week. Now it takes about a day.

When a customer pulls a drive from the JIT hub, that pull sends a signal back to the factory and triggers two things: an automatic shipment request to replenish the drive or drives that have been pulled and an automatic order to the manufacturing line to start additional drives to backfill the ones used. Seagate's automatic response to real demand allows the company to maintain lower levels of inventory, while industry competitors still shoulder the cost of loading up the JIT hubs. Seagate's annual inventory turns have nearly doubled, going from 8 per year to 15.

But it doesn't stop there. Those pull signals are also conveyed upstream to Seagate's internal subassembly and component manufacturing plants and to external suppliers. Seagate's internal subassembly plants use the same JIT hub processes that are required of external suppliers and stock inventory ahead of the downstream factories that use the inventory. These internal hubs are continually resized to accommodate actual customer demand.

By integrating electronically with its factories and suppliers, Seagate eliminates the touch points that slow things down and lead to errors. Over 160 suppliers are connected, with a direct view to Seagate's daily consumption rates. The suppliers can track changes in demand over time, analyze consumption rates, and start to make better use of their own capacity. To make this work, Seagate partnered with e2open to set up a business-to-business (B2B) supply chain hub to communicate real-time demand and immediate supplier acknowledgment. e2open worked with suppliers that already used electronic data interchange (EDI) to translate their feedback into the RosettaNet signals that Seagate uses. During this transition, Seagate became one of the world's largest RosettaNet implementations, sending supply and demand information to all its direct materials suppliers.

Unlike a few years ago when EDI put this level of connectivity out of reach for many suppliers, the Internet has leveled the playing field—everyone can access the World Wide Web. e2open provided an Internet-based application that any supplier with a Web browser can use. This allowed even small suppliers with limited information technology capabilities to have the same visibility as larger, more sophisticated suppliers.

The suppliers that adopted the Web-based system are very pleased with the results. Now they're looking for the next level of integration, where the unfiltered demand goes directly into their planning systems so that they can respond even more quickly to Seagate's needs. To this end, e2open is developing a low-cost B2B server appliance with integration software premapped and loaded for most of the popular ERP systems in use today. This server appliance will sit behind a supplier's firewall.

Seagate sees this as a major opportunity to cut costs both internally and externally while increasing the speed and accuracy of information flowing up and down the supply chain.

Linking with suppliers also gives Seagate a better idea of where its orders are in the queue. This information is especially critical when suppliers have long lead times, such as semiconductor manufacturers. Seagate can get a better view into their processes and immediate updates on order status.

VISIBILITY—THE HOLY GRAIL

This multitiered visibility—the ability to see up and down the supply chain—is a critical component of Seagate's supply chain strategy. It's also the "Holy Grail" for many of Seagate's customers that have outsourced production to contract manufacturers. These customers have less control over their supply chain as a result and fear that scarce components may go to their competitors.

Seagate is extending the concept of multitiered visibility beyond its immediate suppliers, as reflected in its dealings with providers of application-specific integrated circuit (ASIC) semiconductors, for instance. Once vertically integrated, ASIC suppliers could no longer afford to maintain their manufacturing facilities, so the companies sold their plants and outsourced production to major subcontractors. Seagate is now in the position of placing orders and forecast demands with suppliers that aren't actually manufacturing the parts—and through multiple levels of subcontractors. The wafers may be built in Taiwan, for instance, sent to Korea for testing, and then shipped to Singapore for packaging and final testing before going back to the original semiconductor company for shipment to Seagate.

To deal with this added layer of complexity, Seagate is working on a process for gaining visibility into these subcontractors. The company is piloting a project that dives deep into a supplier's supply chain. And then it is tying that process all the way through to one of Seagate's end customers for true end-to-end multitiered visibility. The bottom line of multitiered visibility, both upstream and downstream, is better capacity utilization throughout the supply chain.

VERTICAL INTEGRATION

Gaining visibility into subcontractors is one way that Seagate manages the risks inherent in an extended supply chain. But the company also maintains

control through vertical integration—a maverick approach among industry players.

The industry trend has been to disaggregate, outsource, and get lean.
Bucking that trend, Seagate adopted a vertically integrated model, which
many observers thought was unwise. The benefits of breadth, control, and
flexibility seem to work to Seagate's advantage. The company's competitors can't always be sure they'll get the critical components they need
when they need them, and any change order triggers a negotiation process
and a series of requests that has to trickle down through many layers. By
contrast, Seagate can move more quickly on behalf of the customer and
believes that developing component technology in-house gives the company an edge, given the technical complexity of its products. Seagate can
codevelop and codesign each component and the respective process technologies instead of buying components from a variety of vendors and cob-
bling them together. Today, Seagate manufactures many of its high-cost/
high-complexity components in-house.

Vertical integration doesn't come cheap, though. The barriers to
entry are huge, given the capital needed for technology development and
to produce components and drives. Seagate spends $700 million a year
on research and development and $600 million in capital—far more than
its non-vertically-integrated competitors. This investment pays hand-
some dividends. Customers are willing to pay a premium for Seagate's
high-performance disc drives while the company's competitors race to
catch up.

CHANGE-MANAGEMENT CHALLENGES

Although Seagate's supply chain efforts have delivered substantial benefits, managing change has been a challenge, both internally and externally.
Altering decades-old attitudes takes time and effort. Not surprisingly, customers and suppliers didn't embrace the changes Seagate introduced
immediately. Customers were used to the security of a fully stocked JIT
hub, even if it was a false sense of security. The drives in stock weren't
necessarily the drives they'd need. And those safety cushions of inventory
were driving up costs throughout the supply chain.

Seagate's value proposition was a strong one: Let us cut the inventory levels of your JIT hubs, and we'll actually be more responsive to
changes in your demand—we'll have the capacity in reserve to meet your
needs as they arise. To further support this effort, Seagate has invested
heavily in a "factory of the future" alliance—fully automated drive assem-

bly lines that also are so flexible that any drive can be built on any line at any time.

The education process is ongoing. Some customers get it. Others just won't hear of it, especially those with conflicting incentive systems. If a customer's procurement people aren't measured against excess inventory or total cost of ownership—even in a VMI/JIT system—they'll want as much inventory as they can get. Today, even Seagate's most hardened critics acknowledge a night-and-day difference between current service and that of five years ago. "They'd much rather have today's supply chain servicing them than yesterday's," notes Becks.

Suppliers also were reluctant to change their old ways of operating. Before coming on board, they suspected that Seagate was just passing costs on to them. In the late 1990s, VMI had begun to spread throughout the industry, and the suppliers were getting pressure from all sides. Their first reaction was that it would not be good for their business. But Seagate's value proposition was that if suppliers would agree to link up electronically and share information on order status, Seagate would be completely open with them on consumption. This is critical information for suppliers, especially in times of constraint, when many buyers start to double-book. Explains Becks, "I can look those suppliers in the eye and say, 'Look, I don't have the ability to waste your capacity by double-booking you— you've got online visibility in real time to what we're actually consuming.' The suppliers love this."

Industry observers have commented on the "new" discipline in the electronics industry today, notes Becks, but it's not really more discipline— it's more visibility. He explains, "When everyone switched to VMI, suppliers got a better sense of consumption, of what the customer was really using, as opposed to just delivering pallets of parts—only to be surprised by unexpected demand once those pallets ran out."

NEW REWARD SYSTEM

Changing internal attitudes and behaviors has been equally challenging. Seagate is in the process of putting in place new reward systems that better align with its new ways of working. The company's old "build to forecast" incentives rewarded plant managers for using capacity to its fullest extent. Now Seagate realizes that running capital equipment or a plant "full out" actually wastes capacity if the product it's building isn't what the customer really needs. The result is high levels of inventory waiting for customer demand. This hurts Seagate in two ways. First, an oversupply of finished goods inventory can quickly cause price erosion. And second, if a customer comes along with a real order and capacity is unavailable, then there's the opportunity cost of wasted capacity.

At Seagate today, success is more often defined as changing the manufacturing line many times and getting lower scores on capacity utilization—but better scores on meeting customer demand and reducing inventory levels. The key is to balance immediate customer demand with forecasted demand that's expected, validated, and underpinned with a sales commitment but hasn't yet arrived. It's a trade-off. Sometimes it makes sense to prepare for expected spikes in demand; other times it makes sense to wait to see the demand first.

Seagate knows that it can't truly anticipate changes in demand or build to plan. Instead, by electronically linking to its customers and suppliers, the company can sense and respond to real demand based on actual pull rates and tee up suppliers to restock inventory based on actual consumption. This makes Seagate's supply chain very opportunistic and nimble.

AN EVOLVING SUPPLY CHAIN

To make sure that Seagate's supply chain strategy stays aligned with the company's business strategy, Becks's team chairs a monthly meeting of senior-level supply chain sponsors and project team members. Meeting participants review the status of all supply chain projects that are underway and recalibrate those efforts as needed to align them with changes in business direction or new customer requests. Seagate has already invested about $5 million in supply chain improvements—a reflection of the company's commitment to supply chain excellence.

The company typically tracks about 30 supply chain projects at any given time. One major new initiative is enterprise planning, which will improve data accuracy and integration among functions and processes, eliminating data silos and separate functional plans. The goal is that when a customer calls and wants to double its order on one disc model and cut another order in half, the order-management group will be able to commit to the order immediately but also calculate the impact on revenue, margin, and capacity utilization throughout the company.

Seagate often puts in place one building block of its supply chain architecture and then monitors how well it works out. If a better solution comes along that delivers more flexibility, responsiveness, or value, the company doesn't hesitate to rethink its first approach and deploy the new solution.

Like its business, Seagate's supply chain is flexible, agile, and evolving constantly. What doesn't change, though, is the company's view of its supply chain as a key source of competitive advantage—one well worth the ongoing investment.

APPENDIX

Source and Methodology for Benchmarking Data

The benchmarking data presented in this book are sourced from The Performance Measurement Group, LLC (PMG), a subsidiary of PRTM.

PMG maintains a repository of company-confidential supply-chain information dating back to 1995. Companies that access this database are required to complete extensive surveys of their supply chain performance, practices, and information-technology (IT) usage. They can then compare their performance against benchmarks derived from the performance of a selected population of companies in the database. This provides them with a basis in fact for assessment, highlights differences in practices, and helps them to understand which practices will help them improve performance.

PMG conducts analysis on an ongoing basis to determine trends in dominant and emerging practices, supply chain strategy, and performance levels for key supply chain metrics.

The metrics used in this book were chosen because they show the level of performance gains that can be obtained from better practices and systems and what supply chain performance is considered significantly better than average, as well as what is considered best overall. To accomplish these objectives, PMG explored the link between supply chain practices and financial performance, developed an aggregate measure of supply chain performance, and evaluated various segments of the population according to this measure. PMG calculated customer-facing and internal benchmarks of supply chain performance across populations of companies in similar industries; these are referenced throughout this book.

THE DATABASE POPULATION

A small subset of PMG's overall database was selected for analysis based on surveys submitted during 2001 and 2002, except where historical data are used to show a trend or where single-calendar-year data are used to show even more current performance levels. In most cases, broad cuts of the database—for example, groups of industries—are used. The benchmarks provided throughout the book are based on a robust set of companies that have similar demographics and business characteristics (e.g., industry segment, company size, etc.), allowing for a highly reliable data source.

PMG focused on the high-level findings (e.g., SCOR level 1 metrics or practice elements) and aggregated analysis rather than on more detailed analysis, which is valuable but better suited for supply chain topics more narrow than those addressed in this book.

WHAT'S BEST IN CLASS?

Best in class (BIC) denotes a superior level of performance in a particular area. PMG defines BIC as the average of the top quintile of a population. For example, in a population of 20 survey responses on *inventory levels*, the BIC level is defined as the average of the four *lowest* numbers; for *inventory turns,* on the other hand, it would be the four highest numbers. For a normal distribution, where about two-thirds of the population falls within one standard deviation, this means that more than 90 percent of the responses fall below the BIC performance level.

This definition can be applied to the majority of quantitative and many qualitative practice-assessment questions, where a certain practice is recognized as superior to others. In addition to the simple example just given, best-in-class analysis can be used to provide insight into the range of operational performance levels associated with a particular strategy, practice, or financial result. For example, in an industry population of companies that have BIC *delivery performance*, we can see which manufacturing strategy and IT-enabled delivery practices are dominant. For companies that have BIC performance across a set of metrics, we can see what *profit margin* is achieved relative to other companies in their industry.

There are many survey questions where the BIC definition cannot be applied. Some examples include those related to demographics (e.g., number of locations) or business characteristics (e.g., percentage of sales by region) that do not represent relative performance and for which BIC is not applicable.

While the BIC performance level provides a useful measure of the top level of performance represented by the best 20 percent of respondents for a given metric, the BIC levels across a set of metrics do not represent the performance of any one set of companies. For example, for a population of 20 companies in the chemical industry that primarily use a *make-to-stock* manufacturing strategy, the four companies that have the best delivery performance may not be the same four companies that have the best inventory performance. Because virtually no company is best in all metrics, PMG created an index consisting of several different supply chain metrics. This best-in-class company (BICC) index provides a method for sorting the "high performer" companies from the "typical performer" or "low performer" companies and enables comparisons among subpopulations.

ENSURING "QUALITY" BENCHMARKS

To be effective, a benchmark must have a precise definition that can be applied consistently across companies. For quantitative metrics, this means a clear description of the formula and the data sources. For qualitative practice measures, this means a detailed characterization of practices, including IT-enabled functions, and a rule to clarify how consistently the practice is used in the organization.

Quality benchmarks are rooted in the age-old saying, "An apples to apples comparison." PMG provides support and logical estimation techniques to participants during data collection and validates all survey submissions prior to creating benchmarks. Quality benchmarks are maintained by screening out data that are extreme outliers relative to the population, requiring a certain minimum number of data points, and updating the benchmarks on a regular basis based on the latest survey submissions.

Confidentiality of company-specific data is ensured by disclosing only benchmarks, rather than individual company data, for use in comparisons with the database. The vast majority of companies consider measures of their internal operations and business-unit financial performance to be confidential. Contractual obligations between participating companies and PMG prohibit the disclosure of company-specific survey information, and PMG limits the disclosure of the names of companies in the database to companies that are interested in using the database.

POPULATION DEMOGRAPHICS AND SCOPE OF SURVEY

PMG's supply chain database contains several surveys that address an organization's supply chain activities at various levels, for example, surveys that focus on reverse logistics and repair operations or supply chain planning practices and performance. For both the analysis of BICC and the analysis of supply chain maturity (see Appendix B for a definition of stages of process maturity), we selected companies that had fully completed PMG's supply chain performance scorecard survey during 2002.

This survey assesses quantitative performance based on the calendar year 2001 and dominant (2001) and emerging (projected for 2003) supply chain practices. The population consists of 89 organizations from 65 companies. The industry distribution reflects PMG's participant base, which is largely high tech (44 percent), followed by consumer goods (30 percent), with the remaining from process industries such as chemicals and pharmaceuticals (see Figure A-1). These organizations employ a variety of manufacturing strategies. More than half the companies use *make to stock* as their primary manufacturing strategy, and more than a quarter use *make to order* (see Figure A-2).

FIGURE A–1

Industry distribution.

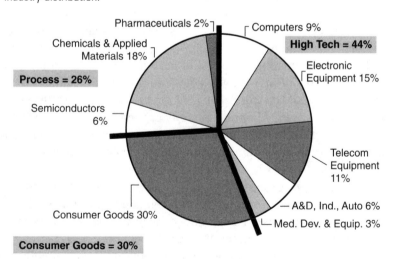

Number of Businesses / Data Sets = 89

FIGURE   A–2

Primary manufacturing strategy.

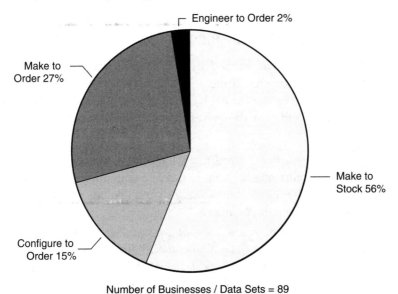

Engineer to Order 2%

Make to
Order 27%

Make to
Stock 56%

Configure to
Order 15%

Number of Businesses / Data Sets = 89

© Copyright 2004 The Performance Measurement Group, LLC

Quantitative performance is assessed using a detailed questionnaire that covers a set of SCOR-compliant metrics, as well as other questions designed to assess supply chain performance. High-level metrics such as *delivery performance* or *cash-to-cash cycle time* (SCOR level 1) are calculated based on responses to more detailed questions. For example, *delivery performance to commit* is calculated based on the number of orders delivered on time to the customer request date divided by the total number of orders delivered. More detailed metrics such as *materials acquisition cost* are collected using detailed definitions that break out all the various components (e.g., inbound freight and duty cost, a SCOR level 3 measure).

The quantitative part of the survey also includes questions that provide further insight into supply chain operations, for example, number of weeks of firm forecast needed in advance of ship date window, as well as questions that assess processing of product returns and repairs.

Qualitative performance is assessed using more than 270 questions that characterize supply chain practices in four areas: *plan, source, make,* and *deliver,* as well as a number of questions that address overall supply chain practices. Participating companies characterize both their dominant and emerging practices. This question set is used to characterize companies by stage of maturity.

CRITERIA FOR SELECTION OF BICCs

The BICC index was developed by selecting a small set of four of SCOR level 1 metrics (see Appendix C and Chapter 2). Based on an evaluation of the rationale for each metric, these metrics were selected to provide a representation of both customer-facing and internal-facing metrics.

+ *Upside production flexibility* was selected based on the assumption that companies with more flexible manufacturing capacity are better able to respond rapidly to and take advantage of changes in market conditions.
+ *Delivery performance to commit date* was selected because companies have more influence over their performance that they commit to than they do over *delivery performance to request*, which varies considerably based on market demand, stability of supply, manufacturing strategy, and demand patterns.
+ *Cash-to-cash cycle time* was selected for its comprehensive view of payables, receivables, and inventory levels.
+ Despite being a component of cash-to-cash, *inventory days of supply* also was selected because it is such a widely used supply chain metric.

These choices are not meant to imply that these are the only metrics appropriate for measuring overall supply chain performance. The traditional and still widely used *net asset turns* metric was not selected because it is influenced by the company's choice of capital structure (i.e., short- and long-term *debt-to-asset ratio*). Similarly, *order-fulfillment lead time* was avoided because a large part of its variation can be attributed to primary manufacturing strategy. *Total supply-chain management cost* was considered, but this also was dropped because the companies with the lowest total supply chain management cost may not reflect the best supply chain performance (e.g., low materials acquisition, order management, and inventory management costs often are the result of spending on supply chain systems or a company's outsourcing strategy). Other level 1 metrics, such as assert turns, were not included because they are considered to be dependent on other metrics.

In order to remove industry bias within the metric values, each of the four components of the index was normalized for each organization over the industry average for the organization. For example, if a specific consumer-goods company's delivery performance is 99 percent, and the consumer goods industry average for delivery performance is 90 percent, then the company's *normalized delivery performance value* = (99/90), or 1.1. The score derived from the sum of the four normalized values produces the BICC index.

The BICC index was used to segment the population into three sub-populations:

* *Best-in-class companies (BICCs).* Top 25 percent of the population, or 22 companies in this case.
* *Median companies (median).* Middle 26 to 75 percent of the population, not the statistical median, or 45 companies.
* *Worst-in-class companies (WICCs).* Bottom 25 percent of the population, or 22 companies.

FIGURE A–3

BICC population by industry segment.

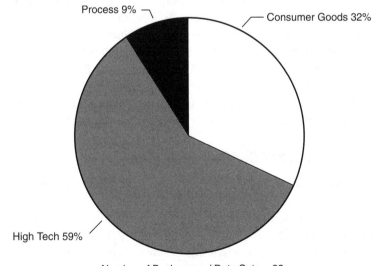

Number of Businesses / Data Sets = 22

© Copyright 2004 The Performance Measurement Group, LLC

Within these three groups we evaluated financial measures of overall business success, such as profitability, supply chain practice maturity, and a variety of measures of supply chain performance. Our hypothesis was that companies with better supply chain performance would have more mature practices and better financial results. While we were not surprised to find this correlation—it has been apparent in analyzing various aspects of the database over the years—the magnitude of the discrepancy among these three populations is compelling.

The bottom line is that the BICCs have better financial results than their industry peers. (See Figure A-3 for the breakdown of BICC population by industry segment.) Operating with more advanced supply chain practices and lower supply chain management costs, these companies have higher profit margins. BICCs have 40 percent higher profits than the median companies in their industry. The lowest-quartile or WICCs had 60 percent lower profits than the median companies. In a high-margin industry segment, this could be a 14 percent profit for BICCs versus a 4 percent profit for WICCs. In a low-margin industry segment, it could mean the difference between making good margin and losing money.

RESULTS FOR SUPPLY CHAIN PRACTICE MATURITY

Evaluation of supply chain practices and IT shows that the BICCs are more closely integrated with suppliers and customers. The overwhelming majority (19 of 22) of BICCs were mature stage 2 or higher, whereas 40 percent of the rest of the population was still trying to figure out how to transition away from the more traditional, functionally focused processes. While the BICCs used a variety of more advanced practices, the differences in practices were most pronounced in the *plan* and *source* areas and in their strategy practices, including overall supply chain strategy, planning strategy, sourcing strategy, and manufacturing strategy (see Figure A-4).

RESULTS FOR SUPPLY CHAIN PERFORMANCE

BICCs were about 10 to 20 percent better than the population median on the majority of all metrics, and WICCs were 15 to 50 percent lower than the median (see Figure A-5).

BICCs schedule a higher percentage of orders to *customer request date* and are more likely to deliver the goods on the committed date. They have slightly higher forecast accuracy, in terms of the number of units required and of the sales price for the units sold (see Figure A-6). Because our selection criteria for BICCs included *inventory days of supply,* it is not surprising that BICCs have lower inventory levels, but it

FIGURE A–4

BICCs' higher levels of external integration.

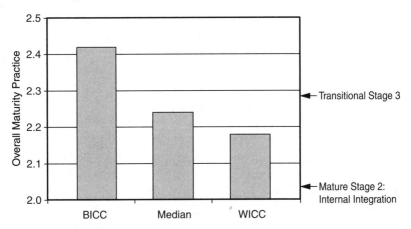

© Copyright 2004 The Performance Measurement Group, LLC

FIGURE A–5

BICCs' performance on customer-facing metrics.

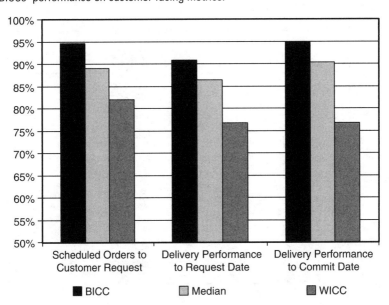

Note: Delivery Performance to Request was 1 of 4 metrics used
to determine the BICC Population

© Copyright 2004 The Performance Measurement Group, LLC

is notable that a greater portion of their inventory is in finished goods, whereas a smaller portion is tied up in raw materials and work in progress (WIP). The BICCs are operating with only about one month of inventory versus two to three months for other companies (see Figure A-7).

BICCs also are able to respond to increases in demand by obtaining labor, materials, or manufacturing capacity needed to react to a 20 percent unforeseen increase in demand within about 3 weeks, compared with about 8 to 10 weeks for the other companies (see Figure A-8).

By definition, significantly lower inventory days of supply are highly correlated with lower cash-to-cash cycle time, which represents the days of inventory plus days of receivables net days of payables. Somewhat shorter cash-collection and accounts-payable cycles translate to about 3 weeks for cash-to-cash cycle time for BICCs versus 9 weeks for median companies and more than 16 weeks for WICCs (see Figure A-9).

In addition to lower inventory financing costs, BICCs showed lower supply chain management costs. While the percentage of revenue spent on supply chain IT assessments and supply chain-related finance and

FIGURE A-6

BICCs' higher forecast accuracy.

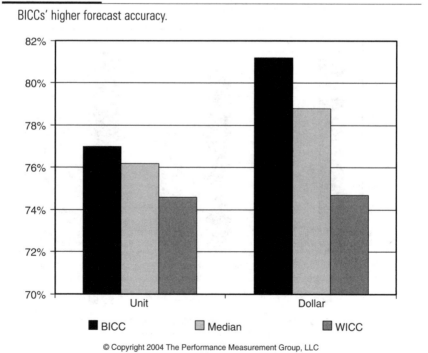

© Copyright 2004 The Performance Measurement Group, LLC

FIGURE A-7

BICCs' performance on days of supply.

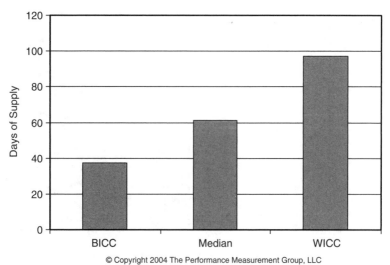

FIGURE A-8

BICCs' performance on upside production flexibility.

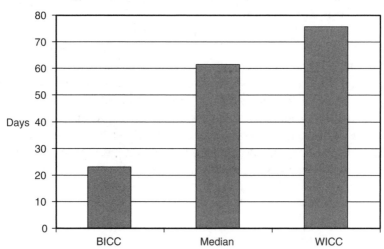

Note: Upside production flexibility was 1 of 4 metrics used
to determine the BICC population

FIGURE A–9

BICCs' cash-to-cash cycle time.

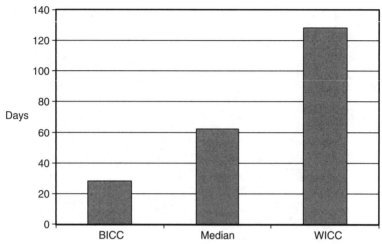

Note: Cash-to-Cash cycle time was 1 of 4 metrics used
to determine the BICC population

© Copyright 2004 The Performance Measurement Group, LLC

planning costs is only slightly lower for BICCs than for other companies, spending on order management, materials acquisition, and inventory management is significantly lower.

Overall supply chain management costs are 9 to 11 percent for most companies, whereas for the BICCs the range is 8 to 10 percent (see Figure A-10). These companies demonstrate better asset turnover, with BICCs at better than 4 net asset turns compared with 3 for the median companies and less than 2.5 for the WICCs. While there could be some industry-specific drivers or more systematic reasons for this result (e.g., inventory levels are a component of assets), it is notable that BICCs with good delivery performance and upside production flexibility also generated a higher level of sales on net assets (see Figure A-11).

FIGURE   A–10

BICCs' supply chain management cost.

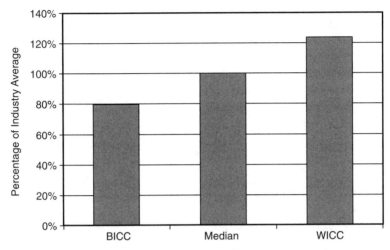

© Copyright 2004 The Performance Measurement Group, LLC

FIGURE   A–11

BICCs' net asset turns.

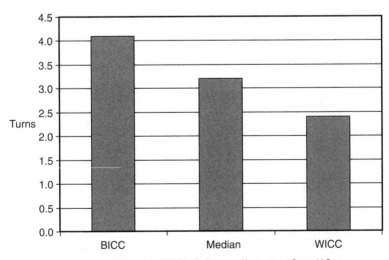

© Copyright 2004 The Performance Measurement Group, LLC

B

APPENDIX

The Supply Chain
Maturity Model

Using knowledge gained from more than a decade of supply chain bench-marking experience and field knowledge of current and emerging practices across both process and discrete industries, The Performance Measurement Group (PMG) and PRTM jointly conducted the supply chain practice and information technology (IT) assessment that formed the basis for development of the Supply Chain Maturity Model in 2000. The model is used to assess the stage of capability for each of four processes defined by the Supply-Chain Operations Reference-model (SCOR)—*plan, source, make, and deliver*—and for what we classify as "overall" supply chain management practices that govern the strategy and link the processes together. The model also evaluates the extent to which IT enables richer practices and cross-enterprise collaboration in supply chain management.

PMG conducts analyses of practices by industry segment, correlations between practice and performance, and distribution of changes in practices over time each year. The findings from the first analysis, conducted in late 2001, showed that process maturity was positively correlated with supply chain performance, profitability, and sales growth. In 2002, the questions in the assessment were refined and expanded.

This book draws on the results derived over the last three years, and results referenced in Chapter 6 are derived from the same population cited in the best-in-class company (BICC) research cited in Appendix A.

DEFINITION OF THE MODEL

Stage of maturity is derived from a qualitative practice assessment that uses more than 270 questions that characterize supply chain practices in four areas—*plan, source, make, and deliver*—as well as a number of questions that address overall supply chain practices. These areas are further broken down with specific questions and multiple-choice answers to cover the following scope: planning strategy; demand planning; supply planning; demand-supply balancing and decision making; sourcing strategy; sourcing processes; supplier development/management; sourcing organization and infrastructure; manufacturing strategy; production scheduling; materials issue, movement, and tracking; manufacturing process control; delivery enablement; order entry and scheduling; warehousing, transportation, and delivery; invoicing and cash collection; overall supply chain strategy; overall supply chain performance management; overall supply chain processes; and overall supply chain organization.

Each answer choice is organized to denote that the practice is associated with a specific stage of capability. Participating companies characterize both their dominant and their emerging practices. Dominant practices are those which are well established and are used across at least 75 percent of the organization. Emerging or *future practices* are those which were defined but not fully implemented during 2001 but were anticipated to be dominant by 2003.

Based on the company's response in each of the 20 areas listed above, PMG calculates its *stage of process maturity*. In order for a company to be considered mature for a given stage, it must be effectively using a majority of its practices from that stage. For example, a company with average process maturity ranging from 1.5 to 1.9 is categorized as transitional stage 2 due to a mix of stage 1 and stage 2 practices. A company in this group has most of its practices fully established at stage 1 and also has implemented some practices associated with internal integration, or stage 2.

Stage 1: Functional Focus

Functional departments within an organization focus on improving their own process steps and use of resources. Managers typically focus on their individual department's costs and functional performance. Processes that cut across multiple functions or divisions are not well understood, resulting in limited effectiveness of complex supply chain processes.

Stage 2: Internal Integration

Division- or companywide processes are now defined, allowing individual functions to understand their roles in complex supply chain processes. Cross-functional performance measures are clearly defined, and individual functions are held accountable for their contributions to overall operational performance. Resource requirements typically are balanced across the organization. A well-defined demand-supply balancing process that combines forecasting and planning with sourcing and manufacturing is evident at this stage.

Stage 3: External Integration

Stage 2 practices are now extended to the points of interface with customers and suppliers. The company has identified strategic customers and suppliers, as well as the key information it needs from them in order to support its business processes. Joint service agreements (JSAs) and scorecard practices are used, and corrective actions are taken when performance falls below expectations.

Stage 4: Cross-Enterprise Collaboration

Customers and suppliers work to define a mutually beneficial strategy and set real-time performance targets. IT now automates the integration of the business processes across these enterprises in support of an explicit supply chain strategy.

See Figure B-1 for a list of the practices for *plan, source, make, and deliver* under the four stages.

SELECTED RESULTS OF SUPPLY CHAIN MATURITY ANALYSIS

PMG's analysis found that the study population defined in Appendix 1 was distributed largely between transitional stage 2 and stage 3. More than a third (36.6 percent) had dominant practices associated with mature stage 2, internal integration, showing an average stage of 2.3. Another third (34.1 percent) was in the process of transitioning to stage 3 and beyond.

Subprocess components of Supply Chain Maturity Model.

	Stage 1: Functional Focus	Stage 2: Internal Integration	Stage 3: External Integration	Stage 4: Cross-Enterprise Collaboration
PLAN	Demand/supply planning is done internally, with no integrated processes and tools across plants.	Global demand/supply planning is consistently aggregated across the firm, focused on functional accountability, and continuously improved by comparisons to historical performance.	Strategic partnerships with customers and suppliers is facilitated by direct, collaborative, electronic data exchange, and governed by formal supply chain performance agreements.	Dynamic global demand forecasting and capacity utilization calculations feed demand/supply decision-making mechanisms. Joint demand/supply decision-making bodies leverage and share data globally.
SOURCE	Supplier partnerships are poorly defined; processes are informal; there is no integrated set of tools to allow common access to procurement data.	Cross-functional commodity management teams and supplier partnerships are in place. Common ERP systems are used effectively.	Strategic commodity/supplier partners participate in collaborative product development, process/TCO improvement programs, and consortia buying, and have access to select online data.	Integrated supply network uses e-enabled systems to automate/optimize all commodity and supplier transactions.
MAKE	Manual material and production control activities are driven by rudimentary implementation of MRP/MPS tools.	Material and production control data are tracked electronically to optimize internal scheduling and inventory management.	Customer-driven, APS (linked to suppliers) *kanban* demand pull manufacturing; real-time inventory control; automated product quality control; and total life-cycle product data management are dominant.	Fully-enabled, electronically-captured APS; product configuration specification; demand pull; inventory backflushing; product history; and quality-control systems allow instantaneous product changes and drive continuous improvement.
DELIVER	No formal, standardized processes or tools are in place for order management, channel rules, product delivery, or invoicing.	Formal outbound logistics processes, automated order management systems, specific channel rules (terms and conditions), delivery quality standards, and automatic invoicing exist. Variability exists in order entry and scheduling across product divisions.	Product and delivery process data maintenance systems function simultaneously throughout the supply chain, and are accurate and visible to all supply chain partners via e-commerce systems. Differentiated service levels and performance agreements are formalized.	Comprehensive e-commerce linkages throughout supply chain optimize warehousing (outsourced but integrated), tracking, transportation and delivery, and automated invoicing. Differentiated channel rules and order/service levels, including real-time commitments.

As shown in Figure B-2, most companies in the population expect to move forward with their practices and achieve a half-stage advancement to transitional stage 3 with an average stage of 2.9.

The most mature companies expect to achieve fully mature stage 3 (32.1 percent) and begin to transition to stage 4, cross-enterprise collaboration. Stage of maturity varies by industry, with the consumer goods, semiconductor, and high-tech industries demonstrating more advanced practices than other industries.

The relation between practice and performance was evaluated by dividing the population into two groups based on the overall average score of the population's dominant maturity: stage 2.3. Those with more mature practices (>stage 2.3) represented 44 percent of the population, and those with less mature (<stage 2.3) represented the remaining 56 percent. We analyzed the relative performance of the two groups across the complete set of SCOR level 1 metrics, as well as a variety of supporting level 2 and level 3 component metrics. Our premise was that more advanced practices result in better quantitative performance, and this correlation was true across the majority of metrics. The results are shown in Figure B-3, along with selected results cited in Chapters 2 and 5.

FIGURE B–2

Average stage for dominant and emerging practices.

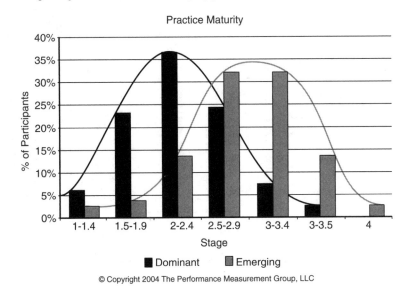

© Copyright 2004 The Performance Measurement Group, LLC

Summary results of population comparisons.

Metric	Population Characteristic: Higher SC Maturity	More Advanced Planning Practices	Best-in-Class Companies
On-Time Delivery Performance to Request	↑	↑	↑
On-Time Delivery Performance to Committed Date	↑	↑	↑
Scheduled to Custom Request Date	↑	—	↑
Fill Rate % by Order (MTS Only)	—	↑	—
Order Fulfillment Lead Time	↑	↑	X
Forecast Accuracy – Unit	↑	—	↑
Forecast Accuracy – Dollar	↑	—	↑
Upside Production Flexibility	X	—	↑
Total Supply Chain Management Costs	↑	↑	↑
Inventory Carrying Cost	↑	↑	↑
Inventory Days of Supply	↑	↑	↑
Cash-to-Cash Cycle Time	↑	↑	↑
Net Asset Turns	X	X	↑
Revenue Growth	inconclusive	—	inconclusive
Profitability	↑	↑	↑

Key ↑ : Indicates that the subpopulation of companies with higher SC maturity, more advanced planning practices, or BIC performance, showed better performance in the metric cited
—: Indicates data not available because question was not asked in this survey
X: Indicates that the subpopulation of companies with higher SC maturity, more advanced planning practices, or BIC performance, showed no better performance in the metric cited

C

A P P E N D I X

Comparison of Characteristics for Levels 2 and 3 SCOR Metrics

The metrics contained within the Supply-Chain Operations Reference-model (SCOR) are hierarchical, just as the process elements are hierarchical. Level 1 metrics are high-level measures that may cross multiple SCOR processes; they do not necessarily relate to a specific SCOR level 1 process (*plan, source, make, deliver,* and *return*). Each of the 13 level 1 metrics is associated with one of five specific performance attributes—supply chain reliability, supply chain responsiveness, supply chain flexibility, supply chain costs, and supply chain asset management. The performance attributes are the characteristics of the supply chain that enable evaluation against other supply chains with competing strategies. For example, without these characteristics, it would be extremely difficult to compare an organization that chooses to be the low-cost provider against an organization that chooses to compete on reliability and performance. Figure C-1 shows this alignment.

Level 1 metrics are typically "assigned" to the *plan supply chain* process category and then decomposed into lower-level metrics. Level 2 metrics are associated with a narrower subset of processes. Level 3 metrics (also called *diagnostic metrics*) are used to identify variations in performance against plan. Each level 2 and level 3 metric is also associated with one of the five performance attributes.

FIGURE C–1

Performance Attributes of SCOR Level 1 Metrics.

Performance Attribute	Performance Attribute Definition	Level 1 Metric
Supply Chain Delivery Reliability	The performance of the supply chain in delivering: the correct product, to the correct place, at the correct time, in the correct condition and packaging, in the correct quantity, with the correct documentation, to the correct customer.	• Delivery Performance • Fill Rates • Perfect Order Fulfillment
Supply Chain Responsiveness	The velocity at which a supply chain provides products to the customer.	• Order Fulfillment Lead Times
Supply Chain Flexibility	The agility of a supply chain in responding to marketplace changes to gain or maintain competitive advantage.	• Supply Chain Response Time • Production Flexibility
Supply Chain Costs	The costs associated with operating the supply chain.	• Cost of Goods Sold • Total Supply Chain Management Costs • Value-Added Productivity • Warranty/Returns Processing Costs
Supply Chain Asset Management Efficiency	The effectiveness of an organization in managing assets to support demand satisfaction. This includes the management of all assets: fixed and working capital.	• Cash-to-Cash Cycle Time • Inventory Days of Supply • Asset Turns

As discussed in Chapter 5, every organization should select and use a portfolio of metrics that supports its overall business strategy and drives desired behavior. In order to provide the reader with a starting point, we have included the complete list of SCOR level 2 and level 3 metrics in this appendix (see Figures C-2 through C-14). To facilitate use of this list, we note which level 2 process category is associated with each level 3 metric. Further detail, including association of each metric with a specific performance attribute and standard definitions for each metric, is contained within SCOR, version 6.0, available through the Supply-Chain Council (*www.supplychain.org*).

F I G U R E   C–2

SCOR metrics—*Plan* level 2.

Plan Level 2	Supply Chain	Source	Make	Deliver	Return
Ability to Augment Return Capacity Rapidly					X
Capacity Utilization	X				
Cash-to-Cash Cycle Time	X				
Make Cycle Time			X		
Source Cycle Time		X			
Cumulative Source/Make Cycle Time	X				
Delivery Performance to Customer Request Date	X			X	
Demand/Supply Planning Costs	X				
Fill Rate	X			X	
Finished Goods Inventory Days of Supply				X	
Forecast Accuracy	X			X	
Inventory Days of Supply	X				
Order Management Cycle Time				X	
Production Plan Adherence			X		
Re-Plan Cycle Time	X				
Return Assets Utilization					X
Return on Assets	X				
Return Product Velocity					X
Sales per Employee	X				
Source Flexibility		X			
Supplier On-Time Delivery Performance		X			
Supplier Fill Rate		X			
Total Deliver Costs					
Total Supply Chain Cost				X	
WIP Inventory Days of Supply			X		

FIGURE C–3

SCOR metrics—*Plan* level 3.

Plan Level 3	Supply Chain	Source	Make	Deliver	Return
Asset Turns	X				
Cash-to-Cash Cycle Time	X				
Cumulative Make Cycle Time			X		
Cumulative Source/Make Cycle Time	X				
Delivery Performance to Customer Request Date	X			X	
Fill Rate	X			X	
Finished Goods Inventory Days of Supply				X	
Forecast Accuracy	X	X	X	X	
Forecasting and Demand MIS Costs	X				
In-Stock Position (Inventory)				X	
Intra-Manufacturing Replan Cycle Time	X				
Inventory Carrying Costs	X				
Inventory Days of Supply	X				
Inventory Turns	X				
Material Planning Costs		X			
On-Time Delivery	X				
Order Fulfillment Lead Time	X				
Order Management Cycle Time				X	
% Overtime Labor				X	
Perfect Order Fulfillment	X				
Planning Costs as a % of Total Supply Chain Costs	X				
Product Data (MIS) Management Costs	X				
Production Flexibility	X				
Production Plan Adherence			X		
Return on Assets	X				
Sales Floor Error Rates on Shelf Locations				X	
Shelf SKU Accuracy				X	
Supplier Fill Rate		X			
Supplier On-Time Delivery Performance		X			
Supply Chain Finance Costs	X				
Supply Chain Response Time	X				
Total Supply Chain Cost	X				
WIP Inventory Days of Supply		X			
Value-Added Productivity	X				

FIGURE C–4

SCOR metrics—*Source* level 2.

Source - Level 2	Stocked Product	Make to Order Product	Engineer to Order Product
% Orders/Lines Processed Complete	x	x	x
Inventory Days of Supply	x	x	x
Product Acquisition Costs	x	x	x
Time and Cost Related to Expediting	x	x	x
Total Source Cycle Time	x	x	x
Value of Assets Provided by Service Provider (Cost Avoidance)			x

FIGURE C–5a

SCOR metrics *Source* level 3.

Source - Level 3	Stocked Product	Make to Order Product	Engineer to Order Product
% Invoice Receipts and Payments Generated via EDI	x	x	x
% Invoices Processed Without Issues and/or Errors	x	x	x
% Orders/Lines Received Defect-Free	x	x	x
% Orders/Lines Received Complete	x	x	x
% Orders/Lines Received Damage-Free	x	x	x
% Orders/Lines Received On-Time to Demand Requirement	x	x	x
% Orders/Lines Received with Correct Shipping Documents	x	x	x
% Potential Suppliers Which Become Qualified			x
% Product Transferred Complete	x	x	x
% Product Transferred Damage-Free	x	x	x
% Product Transferred On Time to Demand Requirement	x	x	x
% Product Transferred Without Transaction Errors	x	x	x
% Qualified Suppliers Which Meet Defined Requirements			x
% Receipts Received Without Item and Quantity Verification	x	x	x
% Receipts Received Without Quality Verification	x	x	x
% Schedules Changed Within Supplier's Lead Time	x	x	x
% Schedules Generated Within Supplier's Lead Time	x	x	x
% Single and/or Sole Source Selections			x
% Supplier Contracts Meeting Target Terms and Conditions			x
Average Days per Engineering Change	x	x	x
Average Days per Schedule Change	x	x	x
Average Release Cycle of Changes	x	x	x
Cost per Invoice	x	x	x
Inventory Days of Supply	x	x	x
Payment Cycle Time		x	

FIGURE C–5b

SCOR metrics—*Source* level 3 (continued).

Source - Level 3	Stocked Product	Make to Order Product	Engineer to Order Product
Product Management and Planning Costs as a % of Product Acquisition Costs	x	x	x
Product Process Engineering as a % of Product Acquisition Costs			x
Receiving Costs as a % of Product Acquisition Costs	x	x	x
Receiving Cycle Time	x	x	x
Source Identification Cycle Time			x
Source Qualification Cycle Time			x
Source Selection Cycle Time			x
Sourcing Costs as a % of Product Acquisition Costs			x
Time and/or Cost Reduction Related to Expediting the Transfer Process	x	x	x
Time and/or Cost Reduction Related to Source Identification			x
Transfer & Product Storage Costs as a % of Product Acquisition Costs	x	x	x
Transfer Cycle Time	x	x	x
Value of Assets Provided by Service Provider (Cost Avoidance)			x
Verification Costs as a % of Product Acquisition Costs	x	x	x
Verification Cycle Time	x	x	x

FIGURE C–6a

SCOR metrics—*Source enable.*

Source Enable	
% Agreements Negotiated Without Error/Change Requirement	Cycle Time Required to Move Product to Point of Use
	Data Maintenance Costs
% Obsolete or Inactive Capital Assets	Defective Product Parts per Million
% Orders Placed Without Error	Degree and Frequency that Purchase Orders/Contract Can Be Altered
Actual Asset Life Maintenance Cost as % of Replacement Value	Degree & Frequency of Conformance to Business Rules
Approval Cycle Time	Degree of Demonstrated Flexibility
Assets as a % of Cost to Administer Business Rules	Degree of Flexibility to Access and Analyze Source Data
Assets as a % of Cost to Maintain Data Repository	Dock-to-Dock Times (Lane Specific)
Assets as a % of Nonconformance Costs	Duty Tax Control
Availability & Accuracy of Supplier/Source Data	Empty-to-Loaded Back-Haul Mile Index
Average Length of Contracts	End-to-End Cycle Time for Business Processes
Business Performance Trends or Patterns	Equipment Utilization Rates (Hours)
Capital Asset Carrying Cost	Equipment Utilization Rates (Product Contribution Margin)
Compliance with Multi-Country Government Regulations	Export Shipment Processing Time
Continuous Improvement Trends or Patterns	Fill Rate
Cost of Compliance	Frequency of Parameter Updates
Cost of Damaged Capital Asset	Frequency of Personnel Changes and Related Impacts
Cost of Maintaining Data as a % of Spend/Revenue	Frequency of Supplier/Source Data Update Feeds
Cost of Managing All Contracts as a % of Spend/Revenue	Inventory Carrying Cost
Cost of Managing Long-Term Agreements as a % of Spend/Revenue	Inventory Days of Supply
	Inventory Value
Cost of Noncompliance to Business Rules	Mean Time to Repair Asset (Tooling & Equipment)
Cost of Obsolete Capital Asset	Minimized Delays In-Transit Caused by Customs Intervention
Cost of Process Documentation, Monitoring and Auditing Business Rules	Number of Data Sources for Data Collection
Costs Related to Specific Types of Non-Conformance	On-Time Delivery Performance (Required Quantities, to Dates Required)
Customs Clearance Cycle Time	

FIGURE C–6b

SCOR metrics—*Source enable* (continued).

Source Enable	
Performance to Requirements Stated in Contracts or Service Agreements	Total Cost of Nonconformance as a % of Revenue
Policy Documentation & Approval Cycle Time	Total Cost to Measure Supply Base Performance as a % of Revenue
Productivity Improvement	Total Delivery Costs
PR (Purchase Requistion)-PO Cycle Time	Total Delivery Time
Quality Improvement	Total Handling Costs
Renegotiation Cycle Time	Total Product Costs
Speed at Which Parameters (e.g., Rates) Are Updated	Total Source Lead Time
Supplier Delivery Performance Percent	Unplanned Maintenance Downtime % of Total Production Time
Supplier Performance Rating	Value of Assets Provided by Service Provider (Cost Avoidance)
Supplier Price Performance Percent	
Supplier Quality Performance Percent	Vehicle Maintenance Costs
Terms and Conditions	Volume of Amendment Compared to Total Contracts
Time to Access Supplier/Source Data as Required to Respond to Need	

F I G U R E   C–7

SCOR metrics—*Make* level 2.

Make - Level 2	Make to Stock	Make to Order Product	Engineer to Order Product
Asset Turns	x	x	x
Average Plantwide Salary		x	x
Capacity Utilization	x	x	x
Cost per Unit	x		
ECO Cost			x
ECO Cycle Time			x
Indirect to Direct Headcount Ratio	x	x	
Inventory Aging	x	x	x
Item/Product/Grade Changeover Time	x	x	
Overhead Cost	x	x	x
Performance to Customer Commit Date		x	x
Performance to Customer Request Date	x	x	x
Plant Operating Cost per Hour	x	x	
Product Losses (Sourced/In-Process/Finished)	x	x	x
RePlan Cycle Time	x	x	
Total Item/Product Manufacture Time	x	x	x
Unit Cost		x	x
Value-Added Productivity	x	x	x
Warranty Costs	x	x	x
Yield	x	x	
WIP Days of Supply	x		

FIGURE C–8a

SCOR metrics—*Make* level 3.

Make - Level 3	Make to Stock	Make to Order Product	Engineer to Order Product
% Orders Scheduled to Customer Request Date		x	x
% Parts Received at Point of Use		x	
% Release Errors	x	x	
Asset Turns	x	x	x
Capacity Utilization	x	x	x
Cash-to-Cash Cycle Time	x	x	x
Deliver to Commit Date Variance			x
Downside Production Flexibility	x	x	x
ECO Cost			x
Fill Rates	x		
In-Process Failure Rates	x	x	x
Intra-Manufacturing Replan Cycle		x	x
Inventory Accuracy	x	x	x
Inventory Carrying Cost	x	x	
Inventory Days of Supply	x	x	x
Plant Finished Good Inventory Days of Supply	x	x	
Inventory Obsolescence	x	x	x
Number of ECOs			x
Out-of-Stock Occurrences	x		
Package Cycle Time	x	x	
Packaging Cost	x	x	
Plant Level Order Management Costs			x
Product/Grade Changeover Time		x	
Production Engineering Cycle Time			x
Quarantine or Hold Time	x	x	
Ratio of Actual to Theoretical Cycle Time	x	x	x
Release Cost per Unit	x	x	

F I G U R E   C–8b

SCOR metrics—*Make* level 3 (continued).

Make - Level 3	Make to Stock	Make to Order Product	Engineer to Order Product
Release Process Cycle Time	x	x	
Schedule Achievement	x	x	x
Schedule Interval	x	x	x
Scheduled Resource Costs	x	x	
Scrap Expense	x	x	x
Scrap Packaging Expense	x	x	
Sourced/In-Process Product Requisition Cycle Time	x	x	x
Staging Time	x	x	
Total Build Cycle Time	x	x	x
Total Production Employment			x
Upside Production Flexibility	x	x	x
Value Added Productivity	x		x
Warranty Costs	x	x	x
WIP Inventory Days of Supply	x	x	
Yield Variability			x
Yields			

F I G U R E C–9

SCOR metrics—*Make enable.*

Make Enable	
% Cost of Assets Used for Compliance/Total Make Asset Cost	Cost of Noncompliance
	Cost of Storage Space
% Downtime Due to Non-Availability of WIP	Cost of WIP Damaged from Handling/Storage as a % of
% Downtime Due to Non-Delivery of WIP	Total Material Cost
% Equipment Utilization for Handling/Storage of WIP	Costs Associated with Managing Production Performance
% Equipment Utilization for In-Transit Handling and	Decision Timeframe Ratio
Movement of WIP	Equipment/Facility Maintenance Cost as % of
% of Data Accuracy	Manufacturing Controllable Cost
% of Information Management Assets Used/Production	Mean Time Between Failure
Assets	Mean Time to Repair Asset
% of New or Modified Equipment & Facilities Available	Plant Level Order Management Costs
when and where needed	Production Downtime Due to Compliance Issues
% of Time Data is Available When Needed	Production Process Validation Frequency
% On Time	Production Rules Preparation Cycle Time (PRPCT)
% Rejects	Regulatory Documentation Cycle Time
% Regulations Met by Required Date	Return on Assets
% Space Utilization for WIP Storage	Severity of Instances of Nonconformance per Unit Time
% Standards Completed On Time	Time for Network Redesign
% Utilization of Production Rules Preparation	Time from Occurrence of an Event to Dissemination of the
% Completed PM Work Orders	Information
% of "Right First-Time" Corrective Actions	Time Interval Between a Performance Standard Request
Actual Asset Life Maintenance Cost as % of Replacement	and Availability
Value	Time Required to Move WIP Material
Administrative Costs Associated with Handling/Storage	Time to Comply with Regulatory Changes
of WIP	Total Costs Resulting from Inaccurate Production Rule
Administrative Costs Associated with Movement of	Details
In-Process Product	Total Manufacture Time
Cost of Compliance Including Administrative Costs	Unplanned Maintenance Downtime % of Total Production
Cost of Handling of WIP	Time
Cost of In-Transit Storage space	WIP Inventory Cycle Counting Accuracy

F I G U R E   C–10

SCOR metrics—*Deliver* level 2.

Deliver - Level 2	Stocked Product	Make to Order Product	Engineer to Order Product	Retail Product
Days of Stock in Retail				X
Deliver Cycle Time	X	X	X	
Delivery Performance to Customer Commit Date		X	X	
Delivery Performance to Customer Request Date		X	X	
Downside Delivery Flexibility	X	X	X	
Fill Rate	X	X		
Finished Goods Inventory Days of Supply	X	X	X	
Inventory Obsolescence as a % of Total Inventory		X		
Order Management Costs	X	X	X	
Perfect Order Fulfillment		X	X	
Published Delivery Cycle Time	X	X	X	
Replenishment Accuracy				X
Replenishment Lead Times				X
Replenishment Timeliness				X
Retail Store Cost				X
Service Levels/Accuracy				X
Shelf Space To Market Share Ratio				X
Shelf Stock Out %				X
Upside Delivery Flexibility	X	X	X	

F I G U R E   C–11a

SCOR metrics—*Deliver* level 3.

Deliver - Level 3	Stocked Product	Make to Order Product	Engineer to Order Product	Retail Product
# Callbacks as % of Total Inquiries	x	x		
% Accuracy or Failure Rates				x
% Faultless Installations	x	x	x	
% Faultless Invoices	x	x	x	
% Item Location Accuracy				x
% Shrinkage				x
Accuracy of Stocking				x
Adoption Rates				x
Capacity Utilization		x		
Carrier Quote Response Time	x			
Checkout Labor as a % of Revenue				x
Complete Manufacture to Order Ready for Shipment Time		x		
Cost Efficiency/Elasticity of Shipping Schedules				x
Create Customer Order Costs	x	x	x	
Customer Invoicing/Accounting Costs	x	x	x	
Customer Receipt of Order to Installation Complete		x	x	
Customer Signature/Authorization to Order Receipt Time	x	x	x	
Days Sales Outstanding	x	x	x	
Deliver Cycle Time		x		
Delivery Performance to Customer Commit Date	x	x	x	
Delivery Performance to Customer Request Date	x	x	x	
Distribution Costs	x	x	x	
Dock to Stock Cycle Time	x			x
Documentation		x		
Downside Delivery Flexibility	x	x	x	
Downside Installation Flexibility	x	x	x	

FIGURE C–11b

SCOR metrics—*Deliver* level 3 (continued).

Deliver - Level 3	Stocked Product	Make to Order Product	Engineer to Order Product	Retail Product
Downside Order Flexibility	X	X	X	
Downside Shipment Flexibility	X	X	X	
End-of-Life Inventor				
Field Finished Goods Inventory Days of Supply	X	X	X	
Fill Rates	X			
Finished Goods Inventory Carry Cost	X			
Finished Goods Inventory Days of Supply	X		X	
In Store Inventory Accuracy				X
Incoming Material Costs	X			
Incoming Material Quality	X			
Installation Costs		X	X	
Installation Cycle Time (Measured in Days)	X			
In-Stock %				X
Inventory Inaccuracies During Pick-Process				X
Inventory Obsolescence as a % of Total Inventory	X			
Items Stocked per FTE				X
Labor $ per Direct Product Cost (DPC)				X
Minimum Stock Levels				X
Number of Restocking Events per Day				X
On-Time In Full		X		
Order Consolidation Profile	X			
Order Entry and Maintenance Costs	X	X		
Order Entry Complete Time to Order Ready for Shipment			X	
Order Entry Complete to Order Ready for Shipment Time	X			
Order Entry Complete to Start Manufacture Time		X	X	
Order Fulfillment Costs	X	X	X	

FIGURE C–11c

SCOR metrics—*Deliver* level 3 (continued).

Deliver - Level 3	Stocked Product	Make to Order Product	Engineer to Order Product	Retail Product
Order Management Costs		x	x	
Order Ready for Shipment to Customer Receipt of Order	x	x	x	
Order Receipt to Order Entry Complete Time	x	x	x	
Perfect Order Fulfillment	x	x	x	
Price Checks per Cashier Shift				x
Product Acquisition Costs	x			
Putaway Labor Cost				x
Rain Check %				x
Requirements Fill %				x
Service Levels				x
Stocking Cycle Time				x
Time to Pick				x
Transportation Costs	x	x	x	
Upside Delivery Flexibility	x	x	x	
Upside Installation Flexibility	x	x	x	
Upside Order Flexibility	x	x	x	
Upside Shipment Flexibility	x	x	x	

F I G U R E   C–12

SCOR metrics—*Deliver enable.*

Deliver Enable	
# Orders Requiring Intervention Due to Rule Violation	Fill Rate
Inventory Value	Frequency of Analysis
% Capacity Utilization	Frequency of Parameter Updates
% Damaged Products Receipts and % Damaged Customer	Inventory Accuracy by Location
Shipments	Inventory Carrying Cost
% Obsolete or Inactive Inventory	Inventory Days of Supply
% Perfect Customer Order Delivery	Inventory Turns per Year
Acquisition Cost for Operational Systems	Minimized Delays In-Transit Caused by Customs
Administration Cost	Intervention
Age of Data	Number of Data Sources for Data Collection
Compliance with Multi-Country Government Regulations	Perfect Order Fulfillment for the Provider
Cost of Acquisition % of Distribution Cost	Ratio of Active Customer Data/Inactive Customer Data
Cost of Capital Systems or 3d Party Services	Rule Implementation Time
Cost of Compliance	Rule Management Cost
Cost of Damaged Inventory	Speed at Which Parameters (e.g., Rates) are Updated
Cost of Nonconformance	Time to Update Customer Records and Status
Cost of Obsolete Inventory	Total Distribution Cost as a % of Revenue
Cost to Maintain the Fixed Assets for the Distribution	Transportation Assets
Network	Vehicle Maintenance Costs
Customs Clearance Cycle Time	Warehouse Distribution Cost
Data Maintenance Costs	
Distribution Capital Cost	
Dock-to-Dock Times (lane specific)	
Duty Tax Control	
Empty-to-Loaded Backhaul Mile Index	
Equipment Utilization Rates (hours)	
Equipment Utilization Rates (product contribution margin)	
Export Shipment Processing Time	

FIGURE C–13

SCOR metrics—*Return* level 2.

Return - Level 2	Defective Product	Source Return MRO Product	Deliver Return MRO Product	Excess Product
% of MRO Deliver Returns Processed Correctly		X	X	
Cycle Time and Cost to Implement Return Authorization Criteria		X	X	
Days of Obsolete Supply				X
MRO Inventory Value		X	X	
Return Inventory Days of Supply	X			
Return Costs				X
Total Cost Associated with Deliver Return Activities			X	
Total Deliver Return Cycle Time			X	
Total Source Return Costs		X		
Total Source Return Cycle Time		X		
Value of Unserviceable MRO Inventory as a % of Total				
Warranty Cost	X			

FIGURE C–14a

SCOR metric—*Return* level 3.

Return - Level 2	Defective Product	Source Return MRO Product	Deliver Return MRO Product	Excess Product
% Authorization Requests Transmitted Error-Free/Total Authorizations Requested		X		
% Error-Free Returns Shipped		X		
% Identified MRO Products Returned To Service		X		
% Lost or Damaged During Transfer			X	
MRO Scheduling Cost as a % of Total Source Return Cost		X		
% of Return Schedules that are Generated Within Suppliers' Lead Time			X	
% Orders/Lines Received Complete			X	
% Orders/Lines Received Damage Free			X	
% Orders/Lines Received with Correct Shipping Documents			X	
% Orders/Lines Received with On-Time Scheduled Receipts			X	
% Product Transfer without Transaction Errors			X	
% Receipts Received without Item and Quantity Verification			X	
% Shipping Schedules that Support Customer Required Return by Date		X		
Capacity Utilization	X			
Confirmed MRO Conditions as a % of Total MRO Service Requests Initiated		X		
Cost of Identifying the MRO Condition as a % of Total Source Return Cost		X		
Cost per Request Authorization		X	X	X
Create Return Product Authorization Costs	X			X
Cycle Time for the Transfer Process			X	

3

FIGURE C–14b

SCOR metric—*Return* level 3 (continued).

Return - Level 2	Defective Product	Source Return MRO Product	Deliver Return MRO Product	Excess Product
Cycle Time from Packaging to Receipt at the Service Provider		X		
Cycle Time from Problem Identification to Condition Confirmation		X		
Cycle Time from Return Authorization to Actual Shipment Pickup		X		
Cycle Time from Return Authorization to Scheduled Shipment Pickup		X		
Cycle Time from Customer Identifying Return Authorization Need to Receipt of Authorization		X		
Cycle Time to Change Condition Criteria		X		
Cycle Time to Incorporate Changes in Return Authorization Processing		X		
Cycle Time to Update Changes to Shipment Schedule		X	X	
Cycle Time to Reach Return Authorization, Return to Service or Discard Decision		X		
Disposal Costs	X			
Excess Inventory Days of Supply				X
MRO Deliver Return Costs			X	
MRO Disposition Costs as % Total Source Return Cost		X		
Obsolete DOS				X
Order Management Costs to Return Product into the Supply Chain	X			X
Ratio of Authorization Cost to Total Deliver Return Costs			X	

F I G U R E   C–14c

SCOR metric—*Return* level 3 (continued).

Return - Level 2	Defective Product	Source Return MRO Product	Deliver Return MRO Product	Excess Product
Ratio of Authorization Cost to Total Source Return Cost		x		
Receiving & Product Storage Cost as a % of Product Return Costs	x			
Receiving Costs as a % of MRO Costs			x	
Receiving Costs as a % of Product Return Costs				x
Receiving Cycle Time			x	
Response Cycle Time			x	
Return Authorization Schedule Creation Cycle Time			x	
Return Inventory Days of Supply				x
Return Order Entry and Maintenance Costs			x	
Return Product Days of Supply	x		x	
Return Product Management and Planning Costs as a % of Product Return Costs	x		x	
Return Shipments Shipped On-Time		x		
Return Transportation Costs		x		
Returned Materials Authorization (RMA) Costs			x	
Time and Cost Related to Expediting the Disposition		x		
Time and Cost Related to Responding to an Increase in Disposition Demand		x		
Time and Cost to Exercise the Transfer			x	
Total Production Employment	x			
Transfer and Product Storage Costs			x	
Value Added Productivity	x			
Value of Return Product	x			x

F I G U R E   C–14d

SCOR metric—*Return* level 3 (continued).

Return - Level 2	Defective Product	Source Return MRO Product	Deliver Return MRO Product	Excess Product
Value of Unserviceable MRO Inventory Awaiting Disposition as a % of Total MRO Inventory		x		
Value of Unserviceable MRO Inventory in Physical Return Stage as a % of Total MRO Inventory		x		
Value of Unserviceable MRO Inventory in Receiving Stage as a % of Total MRO Inventory			x	
Value of Unserviceable MRO Inventory in Request Return Authorization Stage as a % of Total MRO Inventory		x		
Value of Unserviceable MRO Inventory in Scheduling Stage as a % of Total MRO Inventory		x	x	
Value of Unserviceable MRO Inventory in Transfer to Storage Stage as a % of Total MRO Inventory			x	
Verification Costs as a % of Product Return Costs	x			x
Warranty Costs	x			

NOTES

CHAPTER 1

1. Bob Pethick and Torsten Becker, "Dell on Wheels," *Supply Chain Management Review* (December 2000).
2. "Green Granite and Smoked Glass at Les Champs-de-Boujean," *Swiss Watch News* (October 22, 2003).
3. David Rogers, "Value-Based Customer Care," *PRTM's Insight* (Spring 1998).
4. Noshua Watson, "What's Wrong with Hewlett-Packard's Deskjet Printers?" *Fortune* (February 5, 2003).
5. Miguel Helft, "Fashion Fast Forward," *Business 2.0* (May 2002).
6. The Performance Measurement Group, LLC, "Better Project Management Practices Drop Time-to-Market 20–30 percent," *Signals of Performance: Product Development* 2 (11).
7. Stephen Todd, "How to Support New Product Introductions," *Supply Chain Management Review* (July-August 2001).
8. Inditex, FY2002 Results Presentation, March 20, 2003.
9. June Avignone, "Pressing for Change," *Fortune Small Business* (July 31, 2002).
10. The Performance Measurement Group, LLC, "Achieving Delivery Performance: Linking Strategy, Capabilities, and Results," *Signals of Performance: Supply Chain Deliver* 3 (4).

11. Kay Burns, "Supplier Managed Inventory Sweeps through Shell Chemical," *APICS* (December 1997); John H. Sheridan, "Managing the Value Chain," *Industryweek.com* (September 6, 1999); "Supply on Demand," *Shell Chemicals Magazine* (third–fourth quarter, 2000); "Adding Value in a New Economy," *Shell Chemicals Magazine* (Summer 2003); "Supplier Inventory Management," *Shell Chemicals, http://www.shellchemicals.com/products.*

12. Christina Hepner Brodie and Gary Burchill, *Voices into Choices: Acting on the Voice of the Customer* (Joiner Editions, 1997).

13. "Going, Boeing . . . ," *The Economist* (April 17, 2003).

14. Martii Haikio, *Nokia: The Inside Story* (Helsinki: Edita, 2001).

15. Paul Kailha, "Inside Cisco's $2 Billion Blunder," *Business 2.0* (March 2002).

16. Jennifer Baljko Shah, "Cisco Faces Pitfalls as It Builds Hub," *EBN* (June 7, 2002).

17. Michael Porter, "What Is Strategy?" *Harvard Business Review* (November–December 1996).

CHAPTER 2

1. Fred Vogelstein, "Mighty Amazon," *Fortune* (May 26, 2003), pp. 22–28.

2. Based on an interview conducted by Shoshanah Cohen, PRTM director, with Mark Mastandrea, director of fulfillment at Amazon.

3. "Amazon Trims Fulfillment and Marketing Expenses and Loss in First Quarter," *Direct Newsline* (PRIMEDIA, April 27, 2003).

4. Laurent Schwartz, "Alcatel Enterprise délègue le pilotage de sa supply chain," *Logistiques Magazine* (January–February 2002), pp. 52–56.

5. "UPS Logistics Group Provides Fourth-Party Logistics Support for Alcatel Enterprise's Supply Chain," United Postal Service of America, Inc., Case Study, 2002.

6. See note 4.

7. Roberta J. Duffy, editor of *Inside Supply Management*, review of a speech by Theresa Metty, senior vice president and general manager of the worldwide supply chain, Motorola's personal communications, at the Institute for Supply Management's 88th Annual International Supply Management Conference and Educational Exhibit, Nashville, TN, May 18, 2003.

8. "Get Started with a Data Quality Initiative," *Supply Chain Advisor* (April 17, 2002).

9. "Supply Chain Technology Briefing," *Supply Chain Technology Review* 1(9): September 18, 2003.

10. Malcolm McDonald, "A Tool for Supply Chain Optimization," *PRTM's Insight* (August 1, 1995).

11. Michael E. McGrath (ed.), *Setting the PACE in Product Development: A Guide to Product and Cycle-Time Excellence*, rev. ed. (Boston: Butterworth Heinemann, 1996).

12. PRTM and AMR press release, "69 Manufacturers Launch First Cross-Industry Framework for Improved Supply Chain Management," November 21, 1996.

13. CPFR.org (*http://www.cpfr.org*), Introduction page, Voluntary Interindustry Commerce Standards (VICS) Association, 1998.

14. RosettaNet press release, "RosettaNet Global e-Business Standard Reaches Critical Mass in High-Technology Sector," May 12, 2003.

CHAPTER 3

1. Based on an interview conducted by Shoshanah Cohen, PRTM director, with Robert Schlaefli, Stratex vice president of global operations.

2. APICS—The Educational Society for Resource Management (*www.apics.org*) —is a not-for-profit international educational organization recognized globally as a source of knowledge and expertise for manufacturing and service industries in such areas as materials management, information services, purchasing, and quality.

3. Based on an interview conducted by Kate Fickle, PRTM director, with Mike Pearce, Smith Bits vice president, and other Smith Bits executives.

4. Based on an interview conducted by Brad Householder, PRTM principal, with Peter Kelly, Agere executive vice president, global operations group.

5. Jennifer S. Kuhel, "Big Blue Supply Chain: Robert Moffat Discusses IBM's Plan to Link Procurement, Distribution, Manufacturing and Logistics," *Supplychaintech.com*, September 13, 2002.

6. David Drickhamer, "Looking for Value: Reducing Internal Costs and Enhancing Customer Value Draw Attention," *Industryweek.com*, December 1, 2002.

7. Flextronics Web site, Corporate Background Information, *http://www.flextronics.com/corporate/backgrounder/asp*.

8. Based on an interview conducted by Bob Moncrieff, PRTM director, with Mike McNamara, Flextronics COO.

9. Christopher Reilly, "Central Sourcing Strategy Saves Dial $100 Million," *Purchasing.com*, January 17, 2002.

10. Based on PMG benchmarks derived from consumer products companies' supply chain performance (submitted 2003).

11. Based on an interview conducted by Shoshanah Cohen, PRTM director, with Angel Mendez, palmOne senior vice president of global operations.

12. W. L. (Skip) Grenoble, "How Will We Staff Our Supply Chains?" *Global Supply Chain* (February–March 2000).

13. Procter & Gamble Web site, *http://www.pg.com*.

14. Based on an interview conducted by Shoshanah Cohen, PRTM director, with Jeff Rosen, AFC vice president of operations and information technology.

CHAPTER 4

1. "A Global Study of Supply Chain Leadership and Its Impact on Business Performance," Accenture/Stanford/INSEAD study, 2003.

2. Mike Uhl and Kevin Keegan, "Choosing the Right Model(s) for Managing Supply Networks," PRTM white paper used as the foundation for a PRTM article in *EBN* (November 2, 2000).

3. David A. Menachof and Byung-Gak Son, "The Truth about Collaboration," *http://www.totalsupplychain.com*, February 2002.

4. Based on interviews conducted by Shoshanah Cohen, PRTM director, with Nolan Perry, Logitech's director of project management services, and Gray Williams, vice president, worldwide supply chain.

5. Allison Bacon, Larry Lapide, and Janet Suleski, "Supply Chain Collaboration Today: It's a Tactic, Not a Strategy," AMR Research Report, September 2002.

6. *http://www.alcatel.com*.

7. Based on an interview conducted by Steve Palagyi, PRTM director, with Burt Rabinowitz, Alcatel vice president of sourcing and procurement.

8. *http://www.dowcorning.com/main.asp*.

9. *http://w1.cabot-corp.com/index.jsp*.

10. *http://www.jambajuice.com/what/jambadifference.html*.

11. *http://www.calstrawberry.com/facts/industry.asp*.

12. Based on an interview conducted by Shoshanah Cohen, PRTM director, with Anne Kimball, Jamba Juice director of supply chain management.

13. George V. Hulme, "In Lockstep on Security," *Information Week* (March 18, 2002).

CHAPTER 5

1. Dennis Callaghan, with additional reporting by John S. McCright and Lisa Vaas, "Sarbanes-Oxley Balancing Act," *eWeek,* June 2, 2003.

2. Robert S. Kaplan and David P. Norton, *The Balanced Scorecard: Translating Strategy into Action* (Cambridge, MA: Harvard Business School Press, 1996).

3. Based on interviews conducted by Robert Chwalik, PRTM manager, with Dave McGregor, BASF's senior vice president of logistics, and Mary Schneibner, BASF's NAFTA director of supply chain consulting.

4. Bob Moncrieff, Hannah McClellan, and Julie Cesati, "Performance Measurement: Less Pain, More Gain," in *PMG Scorecard Users' Guide* (The Performance Measurement Group, 2003).

5. The Supply-Chain Operations Reference-model (SCOR), version 6.0. Copyrighted © 2003, by the Supply-Chain Council, Inc., Pittsburgh, PA.

6. Based on interviews conducted by Gary Galensky, PRTM principal, with Ari Bose, 3Com's CIO, and Jim Ticknor, 3Com's vice president in charge of supply chain operations.

7. Lee Geishecker and Brian Zrimsek, "Use CPM to Integrate the Enterprise View," Gartner.com, letter from the editor, July 18, 2002 (LE-17-4266).

CHAPTER 6

1. For an overview of the maturity of supply chain information systems, see Gartner's annual "Hype Cycle for Supply Chain Management" analysis.

2. Jakub Wawszczak, Mark Hermans, and Julie Cesati, "Supply Chain Planning: How to Achieve a Competitive Advantage," Webcast conducted by PRTM, PMG, and SAP, June 19, 2003.

3. For a more detailed discussion of the need for architects, see Marco Iansiti, "Integration the RIGHT way, the WRONG way," *CIO* (May 15, 2003).

INDEX